STREETCAR SANDWICHES
PO-BOYS
OUR SPECIALTY

SAUSA E PO-BOY

HAL'S ROAST BEEF INN
NOW OPEN
HOT PO-BOY

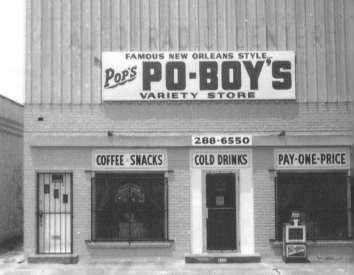

FAMOUS NEW ORLEANS STYLE...
Pop's PO-BOY'S
VARIETY STORE
288·6550
COFFEE · SNACKS   COLD DRINKS   PAY-ONE-PRICE

CHINESE FOOD & PO BOYS
COLD BEER · SOFT DRINKS · SNACKS

HOT ROAST BEEF   DI NER   Cajun JAMBALAYA
TODAYS SPECIALS
POBOYS   GUMBO

EMERIL'S
N·E·W

NEW ORLEANS

COOKING

EMERIL'S N·E·W NEW ORLEANS COOKING

Emeril Lagasse and Jessie Tirsch

Photographs by Brian Smale

WILLIAM MORROW AND COMPANY, INC.

New York

For Tari, Jessica, and Jillian

Library of Congress Cataloging-in-Publication Data

Lagasse, Emeril.
  Emeril's new New Orleans cooking / Emeril Lagasse and Jessie Tirsch ; photographs by Brian Smale.
    p. cm.
  Includes index.
  ISBN 0-688-11284-6
  1. Cookery, American—Louisiana style. 2. Cookery—Louisiana—New Orleans. I. Tirsch, Jessie. II. Title.
TX715.2.L68L34 1993
641.59763—dc20   92-33497
                                                                           CIP

Printed in the United States of America

First Edition

252423

BOOK DESIGN BY GIORGETTA BELL MCREE

Emeril's: That of, or belonging to, Emeril Lagasse, chef/proprietor of Emeril's Restaurant, New Orleans.
—J.T.

♦

New: Made or become fresh; different from one of the same category that has existed previously.
—Webster

♦

New Orleans: A city with a "beguiling personality, a contagious warmth, an unaffected character" . . . whose people have "a special genius for celebration."
—Mel Leavitt, *A Short History of New Orleans*

♦

Cooking: Cookery, cuisine, culinary art.
—Roget

ACKNOWLEDGMENTS

The management and staff at Emeril's Restaurant

Lenny and Sally Radlauer

Ella Brennan and the Brennan family

Maureen Lasher and Eric Lasher

Bill and Anne Grace

Kathryn Hale

Charlie Trotter

Kate Ross

Harriet Bell

Leon Irwin

Sally and Hansen Koch

True Brew Coffee House

Mr. Lou Lynch

André Begnaud

Brian Smale

The staff at William Morrow

CONTENTS

INTRODUCTION

There's a great mystique about New Orleans food, which may explain how I ended up here: I had to come and figure it out. Its flavor and substance are dominated by two distinctly different cooking styles: Cajun, which is the lusty, robust food of the Acadian farmers and fishermen in southwest Louisiana, and Creole, a more refined, cosmopolitan cuisine brought to this city by the early Europeans who emigrated here and their capable cooks. Both styles can be absolutely delicious, and both have been popular here for more than two hundred years. I call it Old New Orleans (hereafter referred to as ONO) food.

When I first arrived in New Orleans in 1983, everyone was eating ONO food, meaning wonderful but heavy Creole and Cajun delicacies such as baked, smothered oysters, shrimp remoulade, crabmeat ravigote, stuffed artichokes, thickly rouxed gumbos, fried fish meunière, crawfish étouffée, and bananas Foster. I was the chef at Commander's Palace and my customers loved eating ONO. I did, too, but I soon grew bored and started experimenting with both the local palate and with the fresh local food products. Gradually I developed a repertoire of what I call New New Orleans (NNO) dishes: food whose roots are planted in a solid foundation of Creole heritage, but which has grown through exposure to other exotic cultures; Creole reinvented with an Oriental, Portuguese, or New Mexican flourish.

For instance, crawfish and Creole seasonings stuff both rellenos with red bean sauce and crunchy egg rolls with hot sesame dipping sauce; Louisiana andouille sausage dominates Italian gnocchi with spicy tomato sauce; fresh gulf fish goes Indian with curry-infused oil; and that old New Orleans standby, oysters Rockefeller, gets a total face-lift in Oysters in Pernod Cream with Fried Spinach. I've stretched in every direction, seeking new methods, trying unexpected flavor combinations, rejecting gimmicks—always trying to be true to my adopted home, New Orleans. NNO food can be whimsical or serious, but it's always delicious.

When I created my own restaurant in New Orleans, I made a vow. I promised myself I would use only the freshest, top-quality products at all times in every dish served at Emeril's, or close the doors. I've never broken this vow. In addition to fresh, I'm hot for homemade; so many of the condiments and other food products that we use are made at the restaurant, including Worcestershire sauce, goat cheese, sun-dried tomatoes, andouille sausage, tasso, and Creole and Southwest seasonings to name a few.

People come to my restaurant, eat a meal, and say, "If only I could cook like you . . . but what you do is so complicated. I could never do it, and besides, I don't have the time." Well, they're wrong. Anyone can cook the elegant, unique dishes in this book if the recipe instructions are carefully followed. As for time, when we started testing these recipes, both Jessie and my test kitchen assistant, Kathryn Hale, exclaimed over and over at the ease and speed with which the dishes were put together.

One of our favorite home testers, Sally Koch, who had very little experience in the kitchen, began retesting and turning out perfect replicas of my recipes. Sally was amazed at how easily she was able to prepare some of her favorite dishes that she orders at the restaurant. And needless to say, Sally's husband, Hansen, was thrilled.

Our basic knowledge of food—or lack thereof—comes from the person or persons who cooked at home for us when we were young. As we went about testing and tasting recipes for this book, Jessie and I would find ourselves remembering how our moms used techniques similar to the ones we were using. I grew up in Fall River, Massachusetts, a small port city populated mainly with Portuguese and French-Canadian people. My mother, Hilda Lagasse, was the first person to influence my palate and teach me the rudiments of food preparation. Although she was the primary cook of the family, my father, John Lagasse, is a good cook, too. Well, Mom taught him everything he knows.

We had little money, but we were rich in the things that mattered—a warm, loving family, lots of good times, and plenty of good food. Every summer we had a garden and grew many of the vegetables we ate. My mother cooked Portuguese family-style dishes like kale or vegetable soup or roast chicken with chorizo. She was also a superb baker and her biscuits and muffins were the best.

I was active in sports and music, and was the only kid in a Portuguese band of older musicians that toured nearby states. I played drums and later taught myself the trumpet, trombone, and flute, and even became a student conductor. But my first love was cooking and baking, which I had learned in my mother's kitchen. When I was ten years old I landed a job at a local Portuguese bakery, where I was put to work washing pans. By the time I was twelve the bakers allowed me to make simple things, including a cornmeal bread, and I was thrilled by the concept that, using a foolproof formula, I could create perfect cakes, breads, and pastries.

As high school graduation loomed, I turned down a full scholarship from the New England Conservatory of Music so I could go to cooking school, and I worked my way through Johnson and Wales University, a prestigious school specializing in the culinary arts. After my requisite trip through Europe, with an emphasis on France, I cooked in several restaurants in New York, Boston, and Philadelphia. Then came the call from Ella Brennan, who was looking for a chef for her flagship restaurant in New Orleans, Commander's Palace. With Ella and me, it was love at first sight, and I worked for her for seven and a half years before opening my own place in 1990, Emeril's Restaurant. I really feel blessed because I've had the opportunity to create my own restaurant and nurture it into a living, breathing entity. It's been the most exciting time of my life.

And now I want to share my cooking with you in the most personal way I know how, and even if you adore ONO food, I hope you'll enjoy this collection of NNO recipes as much as I enjoyed putting it together for you.

CHAPTER 1

Emeril's Pantry: Basic Recipes and Basic Techniques

Many of the recipes in this book include some basic ingredients that you prepare yourself such as seasoning mixes and stocks. I know you're busy, so I've been careful to make them reasonably simple. The trick is to make them ahead of time so they'll be ready on the pantry shelf or in the refrigerator or freezer when you need them.

Creole Seasoning and Southwest Seasoning can be prepared in 10 minutes. Make a batch of each one; you'll use them often. Mole Sauce and the oils—Piri Piri and cilantro—can be made ahead of time. In fact, the peppers in the Piri Piri need to infuse the oil for about a week before it can be used.

It's a mystery to me why people are intimidated by the idea of making their own stocks. All that's required is throwing a few ingredients into a pot of water and letting it all cook for a few hours. In this book you'll never see the words: "1 cup stock or canned broth or water." I'm sorry, but there is no substitute for the real thing—canned broth is oversalted and water is tasteless. A good stock is the indispensable base for most of my dishes. Stocks require a minimum of preparation, can be made well in advance, and stored in the refrigerator or freezer until needed.

A glaze is a stock that has been cooked until much of the water has evaporated and the volume reduced. You can make a glaze with meat, fish, or fowl because the natural gelatin from the bones gives the stock the glutinous quality it needs for successful reduction. The best way to store glazes is in ice trays in the freezer. When preparing a soup or sauce, add one cube of glaze to the stock already in the recipe, and the flavor and texture will be enhanced dramatically.

Don't be lazy . . . come on, these recipes are easy. Fill your pantry, refrigerator, and freezer with these basics, and you'll be ready to cook anything in this book at anytime. Successfully.

Seasoning Blends

People ask me all the time about the secret to good New Orleans cooking. The secret—ta da!—is in the seasoning. Seasoning doesn't mean hot or spicy. It means seasoning that's perfectly balanced, with just the right blend of spices and herbs in just the right amount to complement the meat or fowl, fish, or pasta dish it's used in. There are lots of commercial seasoning blends on the market, some of which are very good. But I've come up with my own blends that are fast and easy to prepare, and work well with the dishes in this book. Mix up a batch of Creole Seasoning and a batch of the Southwest Seasoning and you'll be set to go, without having to mix it up each time. Store the seasoning blends in airtight containers in the cupboard, and they'll keep for up to 3 months.

Emeril's Creole Seasoning

◆

Makes about ⅔ cup

2½ tablespoons paprika
2 tablespoons salt
2 tablespoons garlic powder
1 tablespoon black pepper

1 tablespoon onion powder
1 tablespoon cayenne pepper
1 tablespoon dried leaf oregano
1 tablespoon dried leaf thyme

Combine all ingredients thoroughly and store in an airtight jar or container.

Emeril's Southwest Seasoning

◆

Makes about ½ cup

2 tablespoons chili powder
2 tablespoons paprika
1 tablespoon ground coriander
1 tablespoon garlic powder
1 tablespoon salt

2 teaspoons ground cumin
1 teaspoon cayenne pepper
1 teaspoon crushed red pepper
1 teaspoon black pepper
1 teaspoon dried leaf oregano

Combine all ingredients thoroughly and store in an airtight jar or container.

Piri Piri

◆

Makes about 3 cups

This fiery sauce from Portugal is generously poured over and into many dishes in the Portuguese repertoire. At first taste, Piri Piri seems harmless, rich with the pungent flavors of the peppers; but the heat builds slowly and catches you by surprise in a very pleasant way, bringing a warm hum all the way up from your toes. While it is used in Piri Piri Shrimp with Pasta Salad (page 178), Piri Piri Chicken with Jícama Orange Salad (page 201), and Portuguese Piri Piri Beef on a Stick (page 231), try it on other dishes.

1½ cups olive oil
4 fresh jalapeño peppers, coarsely chopped, stems, seeds, and all
2 fresh poblano peppers, coarsely chopped, stems, seeds, and all

1 tablespoon crushed red pepper
1 teaspoon salt
8 turns freshly ground black pepper
1 tablespoon minced garlic

1. Combine all of the ingredients except the garlic in a saucepan over high heat. Cook, stirring, for 4 minutes. Stir in the garlic, remove from the heat, and allow to cool to room temperature.

2. When the mixture is cool, pour it into the bowl of a food processor and pulse 16 times. Pour the sauce through a funnel into a clean wine or other bottle and cover with a piece of plastic wrap. Allow to sit for 7 days before using. Keeps up to 2 months at room temperature.

Cilantro Oil

◆

Makes ¾ cup

Rub this fragrant oil on chicken breasts or lamb chops before grilling. It is also used in Arugula with Peppered Goat Cheese (page 109) and Cilantro Shrimp (page 33).

½ cup (packed) cilantro leaves
1 teaspoon minced shallots
1 teaspoon minced garlic

½ teaspoon salt
3 turns freshly ground black pepper
¾ cup olive oil

Combine all of the ingredients in a food processor or blender and purée about 1 minute. Store in the refrigerator in an airtight jar or bottle for up to 1 week.

Roux

◆

Makes about ¾ cup

Every Louisianian worth his or her salt can whip up a roux for gumbo and many other local dishes. There are light, medium, and dark roux, the color of each depending on how long it's cooked. Making a dark roux is tricky, since it takes a bit of skill to get it dark enough without burning it. The roux we're making here is a light roux, or what Cajun cooks call "blond." Its color is light caramel and its flavor is more delicate than a dark roux and therefore less apt to overpower dishes that rely on subtle flavors. Make it for Creole Corn and Crab Bisque (page 59).

8 tablespoons (1 stick) unsalted
   butter

1 cup all-purpose flour

1. Melt the butter in a saucepan over medium heat. Whisk in the flour 1 tablespoon at a time and cook, whisking constantly, until the roux is thick and forms a ball, for about 4 to 5 minutes.

2. Remove from the heat or incorporate some immediately into a dish you're preparing. If you prefer, allow the roux to come to room temperature and refrigerate it, covered, for a week or two.

Basic Chicken Stock

◆

Makes 3 quarts

I can't say it enough: Nothing takes the place of homemade stocks. Tasters and testers have reported back that this stock is good enough to be called chicken soup. Be sure to rinse the chicken bones well to remove any impurities and use a slotted spoon to remove any scum that collects on the stock as it cooks.

1 tablespoon olive oil
1 large onion, peeled, halved, and sliced
1 carrot, peeled and chopped
1 stalk celery, chopped, including the leaves
1 whole head garlic, cut in half horizontally
4 bay leaves
½ teaspoon dried leaf basil
½ teaspoon dried leaf thyme

½ teaspoon dried leaf tarragon
½ teaspoon dried leaf oregano
2 pounds raw chicken bones, including the carcass, necks, and feet (no fat or skin, but bits of meat are okay), rinsed thoroughly in cold water
½ teaspoon whole black peppercorns
1 tablespoon salt
4 quarts water, cold or at room temperature

1. Heat the oil in a large stockpot over high heat. Add the onion, carrot, celery, and garlic, and sauté, stirring occasionally, for about 2 to 3 minutes.

2. Add the remaining ingredients and bring to a boil, skimming off the cloudy scum that rises to the surface. (Be careful not to skim off the herbs and peppercorns when you do this.) Reduce the heat to low and simmer, uncovered, for about 2 hours.

3. Skim the surface of the stock (page 17), strain through a large fine-mesh sieve, and allow to cool thoroughly (see Note). Discard the bones and vegetables. Refrigerate overnight. The next day, use a spoon to remove any congealed fat from the surface. Freeze the stock in 2- or 4-cup containers or ice-cube trays for use in individual dishes. Keeps for 1 month.

Note: A good method of cooling stock quickly to avoid bacterial invasion is to place the hot stockpot in a sink filled with ice-cold water. When the temperatures have equalized, refrigerate the stock.

Brown Chicken Stock

◆

Makes 6 to 7 cups

Some of my recipes call for Basic Chicken Stock and some call for Brown Chicken Stock, which is somewhat richer in taste and deeper in color than Basic Chicken Stock. The bones are roasted before being added to the stockpot, and chopped tomatoes are included as well, making it similar to a beef or veal stock. Duck or quail stock, or a combination, can be made using this same recipe.

2 pounds raw chicken bones, including the carcass, necks, and feet (no fat or skin, but bits of meat are okay), rinsed thoroughly in cold water
1 tablespoon olive oil
1 large onion, peeled, halved, and sliced
1 carrot, peeled and chopped
1 stalk celery, chopped
1 whole head garlic, cut in half horizontally

1 large or 2 small tomatoes, coarsely chopped
4 bay leaves
½ teaspoon dried leaf basil
½ teaspoon dried leaf thyme
½ teaspoon dried leaf tarragon
½ teaspoon dried leaf oregano
2 teaspoons salt
½ teaspoon whole black peppercorns
4 quarts water, cold or at room temperature, in all

1. Preheat the oven to 425°F.

2. Place the bones in a roasting pan and drizzle with the oil. Roast for 15 minutes. Remove the baking sheet from the oven and add the onion, carrot, celery, and garlic to the bones. Return to the oven and roast until the bones are brown and the vegetables can be pierced easily with a fork, for about 8 minutes.

3. Remove from the oven and turn the bones and vegetables into a large stockpot over high heat. Add the tomatoes, bay leaves, basil, thyme, tarragon, oregano, salt and peppercorns.

4. Place the roasting pan over medium heat on top of the stove and add 2 cups of the water. Using a wooden spoon, scrape up the brown bits stuck to the bottom of the pan, and add to the stockpot.

5. Add the remaining water and bring to a boil over high heat. Reduce the heat to medium-high and cook, uncovered, for about 1½ hours. Skim the impurities from the surface of the stock, strain, and allow it to cool thoroughly (see Note, page 6). Discard the bones and vegetables. Refrigerate overnight, and remove any congealed fat from the surface the next day. Freeze in 2- or 4-cup containers or ice-cube trays for use in individual dishes. Keeps for 1 month.

Beef, Lamb, or Veal Stock

◆

Makes about 5 cups

Cultivate a friendship with a good butcher and a fishmonger. A butcher who's fond of you might be persuaded to part with some beef, lamb, or veal marrow bones. Your friendly fishmonger will save the best trimmings for you.

You may notice that the recipes for stocks list varying yields. This is because a beef stock cooks longer (and therefore reduces more) than a chicken stock. All of the stocks can be doubled—or even tripled—if you have a stockpot big enough.

6 to 8 pounds beef, lamb, or veal bones, including knuckles and leg bones with marrow, sawed into 2- to 3-inch pieces
2 tablespoons olive oil
1 cup tomato paste
8 tomatoes, coarsely chopped
2 large onions, peeled, halved, and sliced
2 carrots, peeled and chopped
2 stalks celery, chopped
2 whole heads garlic, cut in half horizontally

8 quarts water, cold or at room temperature
12 bay leaves
2 teaspoons dried leaf basil
2 teaspoons dried leaf thyme
2 teaspoons dried leaf tarragon
2 teaspoons dried leaf oregano
½ cup chopped fresh parsley, stems and leaves
1½ teaspoons whole black peppercorns
1 tablespoon plus 1 teaspoon salt
2 cups dry red wine

1. Preheat the oven to 425°F.

2. Place the bones in a roasting pan, drizzle the oil over the bones, and roast until brown, for about 15 minutes. Turn the bones over, and using a pastry brush, spread the tomato paste over them; roast for an additional 10 minutes. Add the tomatoes, onions, carrots, celery, and garlic, and roast until the bones are a deep brown and the vegetables are tender, for about 25 minutes.

3. Remove the roasting pan from the oven, lift out the bones and vegetables from the pan with tongs, and place them in a large stockpot. Do not discard the juices in the pan. Add the water to the stockpot, then the bay leaves, basil, thyme, tarragon, oregano, parsley, peppercorns, and salt and bring to a boil.

4. Meanwhile, place the roasting pan on top of the stove over medium heat. Pour the wine into the pan and deglaze it by using a wooden spoon to scrape up the sticky brown bits clinging to the bottom. When the pan is deglazed, add its contents to the pot. When the mixture comes to a boil, reduce the heat to low and simmer, uncovered, for about 3½ hours.

5. Strain the stock through a fine-mesh strainer, skim the surface, and allow it to cool thoroughly (see Note, page 6). Discard the bones and vegetables. Refrigerate overnight. Remove any congealed fat from the surface the next day, and freeze in 2-cup containers or ice-cube trays for use in individual dishes. Keeps for 1 month.

Fish Stock

◆

Makes 3 quarts

We eat a great deal of seafood in New Orleans, so having a good fish stock in the freezer is a necessity. Fish, shrimp, and crab stock are interchangeable in many recipes.

8 cups *very fresh* raw fish bones, including heads and carcasses, from fish such as cod, pollock, grouper, snapper, or flounder (do *not* use bones from oily fish, such as pompano, redfish, mackerel, or bluefish)

4 quarts water, cold or at room temperature

2 onions, peeled, halved, and sliced

2 carrots, peeled and chopped

2 stalks celery, chopped

2 lemons, halved

8 bay leaves

½ cup chopped fresh parsley, including the stems, not packed

1 teaspoon dried leaf basil

1 teaspoon dried leaf thyme

1 teaspoon dried leaf tarragon

1 teaspoon dried leaf oregano

¾ teaspoon whole black peppercorns

2 teaspoons salt

1. Place the fish bones in water to cover in a large stockpot over high heat and bring just to a boil. Remove from the heat and drain off the water through a colander. Rinse the bones thoroughly under cold water, place them back in the pot with the remaining ingredients and 4 quarts of fresh water. Bring to a boil over high heat.

2. Reduce the heat to low and simmer for 10 minutes. Turn the heat up to medium and continue cooking for 30 minutes. Allow to cool thoroughly (see Note, page 6), strain, and refrigerate or freeze in 2- to 4-cup containers or ice-cube trays for use in individual dishes. Keeps for 1 month.

Shrimp Stock

◆

Makes 3 quarts

Shrimp stock is fairly pungent, so you have to be careful not to use it in a very delicate dish or one in which too much shrimp flavor might be overkill. For instance, in Cucumber Shrimp Soup (page 68) I use chicken, not shrimp, stock so the subtler cucumber flavor is not overpowered. But the sausage and clams in Portuguese Chorizo Clam Stew (page 72) are more than a match for the Shrimp Stock.

8 cups uncooked shrimp heads and
    shells (from about 1 pound large
    shrimp)
2 onions, peeled, halved, and sliced
2 stalks celery, chopped
2 lemons, halved
8 bay leaves
½ cup chopped fresh parsley,
    including stems, not packed

1 teaspoon dried leaf basil
1 teaspoon dried leaf thyme
1 teaspoon dried leaf tarragon
1 teaspoon dried leaf oregano
¾ teaspoon whole black peppercorns
2 teaspoons salt
4 quarts water, cold or at room
    temperature

1. Rinse the shrimp heads and shells quickly under cold water, and place them in a stockpot with the remaining ingredients. Bring to a boil over high heat.

2. Reduce the heat to low and simmer for 10 minutes. Turn the heat up to medium and cook for 30 minutes. Allow to cool thoroughly (see Note, page 6), strain, and refrigerate or freeze in 2- to 4-cup containers or ice-cube trays for use in individual dishes. Keeps for 1 month.

Crab Stock

◆

Makes about 7 cups

Chefs all over New Orleans cook with Crab Stock—first because crabs are so plentiful here, but more importantly, a good Crab Stock gives just the right nuance to a special dish like a hearty seafood gumbo. I use quite a bit of Crab Stock myself. You'll find it in my recipes for Creole Corn and Crab Bisque (page 59) and Creole Callaloo (page 65).

1½ pounds raw gumbo, soup, or any hardshell crabs (about 15 or 16 small crabs), each broken in half
4 quarts water, cold or at room temperature
1 cup chopped onions

½ cup coarsely chopped celery
1 whole head garlic, halved horizontally
4 bay leaves
1½ teaspoons salt
6 turns freshly ground black pepper

1. Combine all of the ingredients in a large soup or stock pot over high heat, and bring to a boil. Reduce heat, simmer for about 1 hour, and remove from the heat.

2. Strain through a fine strainer or sieve. Discard solids. Refrigerate or freeze in 2-cup containers. Keeps for 1 month.

Vegetable Stock

◆

Makes about 2 quarts

This stock is delicious right out of the pot, but is especially meant as a base for other soups, stews, and for vegetarian gumbos. Always use fresh vegetables; remember, a stock is not a garbage pail, and it is only as good as what you put in it.

1 tablespoon olive oil
1 medium-large onion, peeled, halved, and sliced
1 carrot, peeled and chopped
1 stalk celery, chopped
3 whole heads garlic, halved horizontally
4 quarts water, cold or at room temperature
1 green bell pepper, seeded and chopped
2 tomatoes, coarsely chopped

2 ears corn, kernels scraped off, kernels and cobs
½ pound mushroom stems, rinsed and trimmed
6 bay leaves
1 teaspoon chopped fresh basil
1 teaspoon chopped fresh thyme
1 teaspoon chopped fresh tarragon
1 teaspoon chopped fresh oregano
1 teaspoon chopped fresh parsley
1 teaspoon chopped fresh chives
⅓ teaspoon whole peppercorns

1. Heat the oil in a large stockpot over high heat. Add the onions, carrots, celery, and garlic, and sauté, stirring occasionally, until the onions are translucent, for about 3 to 4 minutes.

2. Add the remaining ingredients and bring to a boil. Reduce the heat to low and simmer, uncovered, for about 1¾ hours. Remove from the heat, strain the stock, and allow it to cool thoroughly. Refrigerate or freeze in 2- to 4-cup containers or ice-cube trays for use in individual dishes. Keeps for 2 months.

Glazes

A glaze is a small quantity of stock that has been reduced until it's thick and gelatinous. A little glaze adds an enormous amount of flavor to many dishes; stir a spoonful or an ice-cube-size amount of glaze into a sauce, continue to reduce the sauce until thick, and get ready for rich, heavenly flavor. Glazes are also wonderful in soups and stews.

VEAL, BEEF, QUAIL, OR DUCK GLAZE
◆

Makes ¾ cup

1 quart Veal or Beef Stock (page 8),   ¼ teaspoon salt
  or quail or duck Stock (page 7)

Bring the stock and salt to a boil in a saucepan over high heat. Reduce the heat to medium-high and cook until thickened to a jelly, for about 30 minutes. Can be refrigerated for 3 days or frozen in an ice-cube tray for 1 month.

LAMB GLAZE
◆

Makes 1 cup

1 quart Lamb Stock (page 8)   ¼ teaspoon salt

Bring the stock and salt to a boil in a saucepan over high heat. Reduce the heat to medium-high and cook until it becomes a thick, sticky syrup, for about 30 minutes. Refrigerate for 3 days or freeze in an ice-cube tray for 1 month.

CHICKEN, FISH, OR SHRIMP GLAZE
◆

Makes about ¾ cup

1 quart Basic Chicken Stock   ¼ teaspoon salt
  (page 6), Fish Stock (page 9), or
  Shrimp Stock (page 10)

Bring the stock and salt to a boil in a saucepan over high heat. Reduce the heat to medium-high and cook for about 50 minutes. Freeze in ice-cube trays, empty the cubes into plastic freezer bags, and use 1 cube at a time. Keeps for 1 month.

Basic Techniques

The following techniques can make the difference between a successful dish and a less than successful one. They're geared specifically for the recipes in this book, and they're easy to do, so don't try to slide by.

There's a big difference in the flavors of fire-roasted corn and corn that's simply boiled, or not cooked at all. Roasted nuts have a far superior flavor and texture to nuts that are used as is. And Sun-Dried Tomato Flatbread (page 299) made with regular tomatoes is a no-go. It would be, in fact, flat.

SCRAPING VANILLA BEANS: Vanilla beans are long and thin, like skinny, black string beans. To get the essence of the bean, you must split it and scrape out the resinous, pasty insides. Lay the bean on a flat surface with its seam facing up. Using a sharp paring knife, place the point in the seam at the center and split it to one end. Place the point back in the center and split it to the other end. Use the blade of the knife to scrape the pasty seeds out. When preparing a sauce, throw the empty pod into the pot as well as the seeds for a really intense flavor. Remove the pod from the sauce before serving, rinse it well, and dry it thoroughly. Bury the pod in a jar filled with granulated sugar, close tightly, and you'll have vanilla-flavored sugar on hand for your favorite dessert.

ROASTED PEPPERCORNS: For fullest flavor and aroma, place peppercorns in a dry skillet over medium heat and roast them, shaking almost constantly, until their oils emerge, causing them to crack, for about 4 to 5 minutes.

ROASTED PECANS AND OTHER NUTS: Preheat the oven to 375°F. Place the pecans or other nuts on a baking sheet in the oven and roast until golden and fragrant, for about 5 to 6 minutes. Watch carefully to be sure they don't burn. Store in an airtight container at room temperature for 2 weeks.

TOASTED SESAME SEEDS: Place the sesame seeds in a dry skillet over medium heat and toast, shaking the pan almost constantly, until the seeds are golden, for about 1 minute. Store in an airtight container at room temperature for 2 weeks.

SPICY ROASTED PUMPKIN SEEDS: Preheat the oven to 350°F. Rinse the seeds clean of any pumpkin flesh. Combine the seeds with 1 teaspoon olive oil and 1 teaspoon Emeril's Creole Seasoning (page 3) per ½ cup of pumpkin seeds, using your hands to coat the seeds evenly. Place on a baking sheet and bake until brown and crisp, for about 15 minutes. Store in an airtight container at room temperature for 2 weeks.

COOKED ARTICHOKES: Bring 2 quarts of water to a boil in a nonreactive pan. Add 2 large, trimmed artichokes; 2 lemons, cut in half, squeezed in and the peels added; 4 bay leaves; and 1 tablespoon salt. Cover, reduce the heat to low, and simmer until tender, or until the artichoke base can be easily pierced with the tip of a knife, for about 25 minutes. Remove the artichokes and allow them to cool. If you want to prepare these up to 2 days ahead, toss them with a little olive oil or submerge them in the chilled cooking liquid. Refrigerate in an airtight container.

ARTICHOKE HEARTS: Remove all of the outer leaves of a cooked, cooled artichoke; until only the heart remains. With a spoon or melon baller, carefully scrape out and discard the fuzzy choke from the center.

ARTICHOKE CUPS: Lay a whole cooked, cooled artichoke on its side on a cutting board, trim the base (to make it flat), and cut off about 1 inch from the top. Sit the artichoke on its base, spread apart the outer leaves, and carefully remove and discard the center section (leaving the outer leaves intact), especially the fuzzy choke.

BLANCHING ASPARAGUS: Trim the stem base from baby asparagus; peel and trim larger spears. Use either an asparagus rack or tie the asparagus together in small bundles with butcher's twine. Place the bundles, stem side down, in boiling salted

SPECIAL ORDERS

Always use homemade stock.

Always use fresh garlic and corn.

Always use fresh herbs, unless dried are indicated.

Always use fresh Parmesan cheese, and grate it just before using it.

Unless otherwise indicated, ''chopped'' vegetables means ½-inch pieces.

I use Italian plum—or Roma—tomatoes almost exclusively. If they're unavailable, use the best-smelling, ripest tomatoes you can find, adjusting the number you use for the difference in the size. If you can't find good fresh tomatoes for cooking, use good-quality canned plum tomatoes. For salads, though, use only fresh tomatoes.

water. Bring the water back to a boil and cook for 3 to 4 minutes for baby asparagus, 4 to 5 minutes for medium size, and 6 to 8 minutes for jumbo asparagus. The asparagus is done if the stem snaps crisply when broken.

BLANCHING CORN: Plunge whole husked ears of corn into boiling water and cook until crisp-tender, for about 3 to 4 minutes. Remove the corn from the water and let it cool. Hold an ear vertically and scrape the kernels off, using a small sharp knife, slicing from the top of the ear to the bottom.

FIRE~ROASTED CORN: Husk the corn and place it directly on a gas burner. Turn the flame to medium and roast for about 3 minutes, turning several times with tongs. If you have an electric stove, it should take about 5 minutes.

FIRE~ROASTED ONIONS: Skin small onions and place them, whole, under the broiler of your oven. Roast until tender, turning several times, for about 30 minutes.

ROASTED SHALLOTS AND GARLIC: Preheat the oven to 400°F. Combine 24 peeled shallots and/or garlic cloves with 1 teaspoon olive oil, 2 teaspoons salt, and 5 turns freshly ground black pepper on a sheet of aluminum foil. Fold the edges of the foil together to form a bag and roast until tender, for about 40 minutes. Use immediately, or refrigerate in a little olive oil in an airtight container for 2 or 3 days.

ROASTING PEPPERS: Place the peppers in a 375°F oven and roast, turning several times until the skin is charred, for about 15 minutes. Or impale each pepper on a long-handled fork and hold it over a stove burner on high heat, turning to char the pepper evenly. When the skin is dark and crackly, remove the pepper from the oven or stove top and drop it into a bowl of ice water. Peel off the skins with your fingers. Use immediately, or refrigerate in a little olive oil in an airtight container for 2 or 3 days.

PEELING TOMATOES: Place whole tomatoes in a large pot of boiling water for 30 seconds, until the skins split. Using a slotted spoon, immediately transfer the tomatoes to a bowl of ice water. When they are cool enough to handle, peel off the skins with your fingers. Peaches, plums, and other fruit with skins can be peeled the same way. Use immediately, or refrigerate overnight.

SUN~DRIED TOMATOES: Buy dry sun-dried tomatoes, which are usually sold in cellophane bags in food stores. Place the tomatoes in a strainer and submerge in lightly salted warm water for 2 minutes. Drain the tomatoes. Use immediately, or store, refrigerated, in an airtight container for up to 2 weeks.

SCRUBBING CLAMS AND MUSSELS AND DEBEARDING MUSSELS: Scrub fresh, live clams and mussels with a stiff brush to remove outer dirt. If preparing mussels, use your fingers to pull off any "beards" that remain. Place the clams and mussels in a large pot of ice-cold water and let them soak for at least 2 hours to help rid them of internal sand. If you don't add ice to the water, place the pot in the refrigerator. Discard the water, and cook the clams or mussels immediately as directed.

BOILING SHRIMP: Add shrimp to boiling salted water. When the water returns to a boil, the shrimp are probably done if they're medium to large; remove them immediately. If they're extra-large or jumbo, cook for about 1 minute more. Never let shrimp overcook; they're done the minute they turn pink and are no longer translucent.

BUTTERFLYING SHRIMP: Remove the shell except for the tail and the last ring of shell before the tail. Using a small, sharp knife, slice down the back curve of the shrimp, taking care not to cut all the way through. Remove the vein, and spread the shrimp open.

DEGREASING SOUPS AND STEWS: When the liquid has come to a boil, pull the pot sideways off the burner toward the countertop. The fat will rise to the cooler side of the pot and can be easily skimmed off with a ladle. Or refrigerate the soup or stew overnight and remove the congealed fat from the top the next day.

PERFECT POACHED EGGS: Bring 3 cups of water to a boil with ½ teaspoon white vinegar and ½ teaspoon salt in a small saucepan over high heat. Crack an egg into a cup and slide the egg gently into the water. Crack another egg into the cup and when the water returns to a boil slide this egg into the water as well. When the water returns to a boil, reduce the heat to low and simmer until the eggs are set. Watch carefully and remove the eggs when the yolks are still soft, about 2 to 2½ minutes. (Test by lifting an egg slightly out of the water on a slotted spoon and gently pressing the center with your finger; the yolk should be soft and the white firm.) Drain on paper towels. Poached eggs can be made ahead and kept immersed in a bowl of water in the refrigerator. Reheat by immersing briefly in simmering water.

TOASTED CROUTONS: Preheat the oven to 375°F. Toss cubes of day-old bread with olive oil, and bake until brown, for about 4 minutes. Store in an airtight container at room temperature for 3 days.

CREOLE CROUTONS: Preheat the oven to 375°F. Toss 1 cup of day-old bread cubes with 2 teaspoons olive oil and 1 teaspoon Emeril's Creole Seasoning (page 31) on a baking sheet and bake until golden brown, for about 4 minutes. Store in an airtight container at room temperature for 3 days.

BREAD CRUMBS: Remove the crusts from a dense, homemade-type white bread, and crumb 3 or 4 slices at a time in a food processor or blender. Store in an airtight container at room temperature for up to 3 days.

FRIED PASTA: Heat 8 cups vegetable oil in a large deep pot over medium-high heat until very hot. Fry 1 pound angel hair pasta, cooked and well drained, until golden, for about 1 minute. Use tongs to separate. Remove from the oil, drain on paper towels, and keep warm on a baking sheet in a 200°F oven.

FRIED TORTILLA STRIPS: Heat 2 cups vegetable oil in a large saucepan over medium-high heat until very hot. Fry ⅛-inch tortilla strips (from 6- to 8-inch tortillas) until crisp and golden, turning once, for about 1 minute. Remove from the oil, drain on paper towels, and sprinkle with Emeril's Southwest Seasoning (page 3). Serve immediately.

CLARIFIED BUTTER: To make 1 cup of clarified butter, melt 3 sticks (¾ pound) unsalted butter slowly over a pot of hot water or a tiny flame. Skim off the top foam and use only the clear liquid, discarding the milky residue.

A WORD ABOUT RAW EGGS: Some of the sauces in this book are prepared with raw eggs. Although neither I, nor anyone who has eaten in my restaurant, has had a problem with them, raw eggs are said to be a possible source of harmful bacteria.

To avoid risking illness, use only eggs that are very fresh, and don't leave them standing at room temperature, where bacteria can multiply. If you make the sauces that call for raw eggs, prepare them quickly and serve them immediately. If you make the sauce ahead, refrigerate it, and reheat before serving, if necessary.

MAIL ORDER

Homesick Louisianans know that crawfish tails, tasso, liquid crab boil, or other Louisiana specialties and Gulf seafood are just a phone call away. If you can't buy any of these products where you live, write or call Fisherman's Cove, 3201 Williams Boulevard, Kenner, Louisiana 70065. Telephone (504)-443-3474. They accept Visa, MasterCard, and American Express.

Perishables are shipped with dry ice or a gel pack. Tasso comes in one-pound packages. Liquid crab boil is available in four- or eight-ounce bottles.

CHAPTER 2

New New Beginnings:
Appetizers and
Tantalizers

Appetizers tempt and seduce the palate, preparing it for the next course. Unfortunately, many home cooks ignore appetizers completely and go right to the main course, or they serve too many and their guests are stuffed by the time they sit down to dinner. A good appetizer should complement, not compete with, the rest of the meal, so plan carefully. Appetizers are versatile. Many of them can be doubled to serve as a main course for lunch, dinner, or brunch, and some work as party finger foods.

Cilantro Shrimp can be passed on a tray with toothpicks, and the accompanying Cilantro Oil presented in a small bowl for dipping. Turn Crawfish Cakes with Crawfish Cream into a brunch dish for two, allowing two cakes per serving. Double or triple the recipes for Crawfish Egg Rolls and Corn Flaps with Chive Cream and Caviar to serve a crowd. And if money is no object, buy four 6-ounce pieces of duck liver and double the ingredients in Bill and Lenny's Excellent Foie Gras for a rich main course.

This chapter begins with five recipes that use crawfish. Don't pass them by because you can't buy crawfish in your fish market; you can order already peeled tails or boiled crawfish by mail or phone.

HOW TO EAT CRAWFISH

Hot boiled crawfish are served in restaurants and homes all over New Orleans. You can always spot first-time crawfish eaters because they haven't a clue as to how to eat these freshwater crustaceans that look like mini-lobsters. Here's how to eat boiled crawfish like a native.

1. Twist the tail off the body and immediately suck the juices out of the body shell. (It's what we mean by ''sucking the heads.'')

2. Hold the tail by the bottom and peel off the top ring of the shell.

3. Place the meat between your teeth, pinch the bottom of the tail with your thumb and forefinger, and pull out the meat with your teeth.

Crawfish Pies

◆

Makes 12 first-course servings

I hadn't been living in New Orleans for long when I attended a crawfish festival in Eunice, Louisiana. I knew crawfish were eaten boiled, bisqued, and étoufféed; but when I saw visitors to the festival eating little pies wrapped in paper, my first thought was that they were "frito" pies, or little turnovers filled with corn chips and other Southwestern goodies. They turned out to be crawfish pies, and when I took my first bite, I was hooked. Unfortunately, it's not always easy to find crawfish pies in New Orleans. They appear at some festivals—principally, the Jazz and Heritage Festival that begins at the end of April. But that's just once a year, and I need a crawfish pie fix far more often. So I decided to create my own and serve them at the restaurant to satisfy everyone's craving.

1 recipe Basic Pie Dough (page 313), divided into 12 balls, and chilled
2 tablespoons unsalted butter
¼ cup minced onions
¼ cup minced green bell peppers
¼ cup minced red bell peppers
¼ cup minced celery
1½ tablespoons Emeril's Creole Seasoning (page 3)
½ teaspoon salt
1 tablespoon minced garlic
1 pound (2 cups) peeled crawfish tails (page 241)
½ teaspoon hot pepper sauce
1 teaspoon Worcestershire sauce
¼ cup chopped green onions
½ cup heavy cream
2 large eggs, lightly beaten in separate cups, in all
2 tablespoons bread crumbs (page 17)
2 tablespoons olive oil

1. Prepare the Basic Pie Dough and refrigerate.

2. Melt the butter in a medium skillet over high heat. When the butter sizzles, add the onions, green and red peppers, celery, Creole Seasoning, and salt and sauté, shaking the skillet or stirring occasionally, for 3 minutes. Add the garlic and crawfish tails and cook, stirring occasionally and shaking the skillet, for 2 minutes. Stir in the hot pepper sauce, Worcestershire, and green onions, and cook for 2 minutes. Whisk in the cream. Stir in 1 of the beaten eggs—*slowly*—just a little at a time (if you add it too quickly, you'll have scrambled eggs). Remove the skillet from the heat and stir in the bread crumbs. Makes 3 cups.

3. Preheat the oven to 375°F. Line a baking sheet with parchment or wax paper.

4. Remove the dough from the refrigerator. On a floured surface, roll out each ball into a thin circle of dough, about ⅛ inch thick. Trim the edges of each circle to form a square of dough about 5 by 5 inches.

5. Brush a ¼-inch border around the edges of each dough square with the remaining egg. Place about ¼ cup of the crawfish filling toward the corner of each square and fold the dough over to form a triangle. Crimp the edges with a floured fork and place the pies on the baking sheet. Brush the top of each pie with olive oil. Bake until lightly browned, for about 25 minutes.

6. To serve, wrap the hot pies in paper towels or paper napkins. Serve with mugs of cold beer (Dixie or Abita are New Orleans favorites) and you've got your own crawfish festival.

Crawfish Cakes with Crawfish Cream

◆

Makes 4 first-course servings

One of the best things about living in Louisiana is that you get to go to crawfish boils. These are usually raucous parties where the centerpiece is a huge vat of boiling crawfish and spices. Corn on the cob and little new potatoes are often cooked along with the crawfish. When they're ready, the crawfish are dumped on a newspaper-covered table, and consumed with a lot of noisy sucking and chomping. You can't have a crawfish boil if you can't get live crawfish where you live; but you can have a mighty fine dish of crawfish cakes, made with packaged, peeled crawfish tails. These are available now in fish markets and supermarkets in many parts of the country, or you can order them (page 19). A 1-pound bag will be enough for these crawfish cakes and the wonderfully spicy crawfish cream that accompanies them.

¼ cup plus 1 tablespoon olive oil, in all
2 tablespoons chopped onions
1 tablespoon chopped green bell peppers
1 tablespoon chopped red bell peppers
2 teaspoons minced garlic
½ pound (1 cup) peeled crawfish tails
3 tablespoons plus 1 teaspoon Emeril's Creole Seasoning (page 3), in all

¼ teaspoon salt
2 dashes Worcestershire sauce
2 dashes hot pepper sauce
¼ cup freshly grated Parmesan cheese
2 large eggs, in all
1 cup bread crumbs (page 17), in all
½ cup all-purpose flour
½ cup milk
2 cups Crawfish Cream (recipe follows)
4 tablespoons chopped green onions

1. Heat 1 tablespoon of the oil in a large skillet over high heat. When the oil is hot, add the onions, green and red peppers, and garlic and sauté for 30 seconds. Add the crawfish tails, 2 teaspoons Creole Seasoning, salt, Worcestershire, and hot pepper sauce, and sauté for 1½ minutes, occasionally shaking the skillet. Remove from the heat and pour the contents of the skillet into a bowl.

2. To the crawfish mixture add the Parmesan, 1 teaspoon Creole Seasoning, 1 egg, and ½ cup of the bread crumbs. Using your hands, divide the mixture into 4 equal parts, and shape into cakes approximately 3 inches across by ½ inch high.

3. In a small bowl combine the flour with 2 teaspoons Creole Seasoning. In another bowl whisk together the remaining egg with the milk. In a shallow bowl combine the remaining ½ cup bread crumbs with the remaining 1 teaspoon Creole Seasoning.

4. Prepare the Crawfish Cream.

5. Heat the remaining ¼ cup oil in a large clean skillet over high heat. Dip each crawfish cake into the flour mixture, then the egg mixture, then the bread crumbs. When the oil is hot, add the cakes and fry them until brown, for about 2 minutes on each side. Drain on paper towels.

6. To serve, place 1 crawfish cake on each of 4 plates and nap with ½ cup of the Crawfish Cream. Garnish with chopped green onions and Creole Seasoning.

CRAWFISH CREAM

◆

Makes about 2 cups

½ pound (1 cup) peeled crawfish
   tails
2 teaspoons Emeril's Creole
   Seasoning (page 3)
⅓ cup chopped green onions

½ teaspoon Worcestershire sauce
½ teaspoon hot pepper sauce
1 cup heavy cream
1 tablespoon unsalted butter

1. Sprinkle the crawfish with the Creole Seasoning, and use your hands to coat thoroughly.

2. In a medium skillet over high heat, combine the seasoned crawfish, green onions, Worcestershire, and hot pepper sauce and cook for 1 minute. Stir in the cream, bring to a boil, and cook for 4 minutes, still over high heat. Add the butter and whisk gently until thoroughly incorporated, for about another minute. Remove from the heat. Serve immediately or store, refrigerated, in an airtight container for up to 1 day. Reheat over lowest heat.

Crawfish Egg Rolls with Hot Sesame Drizzle

◆

Makes 8 first-course servings

Chinese food in New Orleans? Absolutely. Light and crispy on the outside, moist and spicy on the inside, these egg rolls are a snap to make, using egg roll skins available in supermarkets. The twist is the Creole-seasoned crawfish, but if you like, you can substitute either lobster meat or shrimp.

1 cup Hot Sesame Drizzle (recipe follows)
2 teaspoons olive oil
½ cup finely diced onions
½ cup finely diced celery
1 cup finely shredded napa or white cabbage
2 teaspoons minced garlic
½ cup finely grated carrots
½ pound (1 cup) peeled crawfish tails (page 24)
2 tablespoons sesame oil

2 teaspoons untoasted sesame seeds
1 teaspoon salt
6 turns freshly ground black pepper
1 teaspoon Emeril's Creole Seasoning (page 3)
4 large eggs, lightly beaten in 2 separate bowls (2 eggs per bowl)
8 egg roll skins
6 cups vegetable oil
¼ cup dry mustard, combined with ¼ cup water

1. Prepare the Hot Sesame Drizzle, and set aside.

2. Heat the olive oil in a medium skillet over high heat. When the oil is hot, add the onions, celery, and cabbage and sauté for 2 minutes. Add the garlic and carrots and sauté, stirring and shaking the skillet, for 1 minute. Add the crawfish tails and sauté, shaking the skillet, for 1 minute. Remove from the heat and pour the mixture into a bowl.

3. To the crawfish mixture, add the sesame oil, sesame seeds, salt, pepper, Creole Seasoning, and 2 of the eggs.

4. Lay the egg roll skins on a flat surface and brush them with some of the remaining egg. Place one-eighth of the filling on one end of each skin, leaving a ¼-inch border at the top and sides, and roll up, tucking in the ends after the first roll.

5. Heat the vegetable oil in a large saucepan or wok over high heat. When the oil is very hot, about 375°F, fry the egg rolls until they're crisp and golden brown, for about 2 minutes. Drain thoroughly on paper towels.

6. While the egg rolls are frying, reheat the Hot Sesame Drizzle over low heat, stirring once or twice.

7. To serve, paint (see The Last Word) each of 8 dishes with a zigzag of mustard. Sprinkle 2 tablespoons of the Hot Sesame Drizzle over the mustard, and top with an egg roll.

HOT SESAME DRIZZLE

◆

Makes 1 cup

2 tablespoons sesame seeds
1 teaspoon salt
1 cup Basic Chicken Stock
   (page 7)
¼ cup sesame oil

¼ cup honey
1 tablespoon plus 1 teaspoon soy
   sauce
8 turns freshly ground black pepper

1. Toast the sesame seeds in a small saucepan over high heat, shaking often to prevent burning, for about 1½ minutes. Add the salt, stock, oil, honey, and soy sauce and whisk over high heat until the mixture comes to a full boil.

2. Turn the heat down to medium, add the black pepper, and cook, whisking, for 3 minutes. Remove from the heat. Serve immediately or store, refrigerated, in an airtight container for 1 day. Reheat over lowest heat.

THE LAST WORD

Food that's beautiful to look at seems to taste better than food that isn't. One of the most eye-catching ways to decorate plates is to "paint" them with dabs of sauces and oils. One effect can be achieved by dipping a clean pastry brush in the sauce and applying the design of your choice. Another look is produced by using plastic squeeze bottles for painting. Before your big dinner party, fill a squeeze bottle with ketchup or mustard, and practice different patterns on a dinner plate.

Crawfish Rellenos with Red Bean Sauce

◆

Makes 4 first-course servings

Rellenos are stuffed chile peppers. I prefer poblanos for stuffing because they are the right size and have the right heat level and flavor. This recipe and the one that follows are my rather unorthodox variations on the usual corn and cheese rellenos. They puff into crisp golden-brown treats, bursting with creamy fillings: one with a Louisiana twist—crawfish—and the other filled with a saucy spiced chicken. And the sauces are the perfect complements: the Red Bean just right for the crawfish, and the Tequila Lime a wonderfully tart foil for the chicken. Mucho gusto!

1½ cups Red Bean Sauce
   (recipe follows)
1 tablespoon olive oil
½ pound (1 cup) peeled and
   chopped crawfish tails (page 24)
⅓ cup chopped green onions
2 teaspoons minced garlic
1 teaspoon Emeril's Creole
   Seasoning (page 3)
½ teaspoon salt
⅓ cup heavy cream
¼ cup grated jalapeño-flavored Jack
   cheese
2 tablespoons bread crumbs
   (page 17)

1 cup masa harina (see Note)
1 cup all-purpose flour, in all
1½ tablespoons Emeril's Southwest
   Seasoning (page 3), in all
2 large egg whites, beaten until
   foamy
1½ cups milk
4 medium-large poblano peppers
   with their stems, roasted and
   peeled (page 16), slit up one side,
   and seeded (see Note)
6 cups vegetable oil
½ cup sour cream
4 cilantro sprigs

1. Prepare the Red Bean Sauce, and keep warm.

2. Heat the olive oil in a large skillet over high heat. When the oil is hot, add the crawfish, green onions, garlic, Creole Seasoning, and salt, and sauté for 2 minutes.

3. Add the cream and the cheese, turn off the heat and stir well. Fold in the bread crumbs, turn the mixture into a bowl, and allow to cool for about 15 minutes. Makes about 1¼ cups.

4. Combine the masa harina with ½ cup of the all-purpose flour and 1 tablespoon of the Southwest Seasoning in a bowl. Fold in the egg whites and add the milk ¼ cup at a time, mixing thoroughly between additions until all the milk is incorporated and the mixture is smooth. In another bowl combine the remaining ½ cup flour with the remaining ½ tablespoon Southwest Seasoning.

5. Spoon a generous ¼ cup of the filling into each pepper through the slit in its side. Dip each filled pepper in the batter, then dredge it in the seasoned flour.

6. In a large saucepan or wok heat the oil to 375°F. When the oil is hot (a bit of batter dropped in the oil should fry quickly), fry the rellenos until golden brown, for about 3 to 4 minutes. Drain on paper towels. Reheat the sauce, if necessary.

7. To serve, pour a generous ⅓ cup of the sauce onto each of 4 dinner plates. Place a relleno on top of the sauce, and garnish with a dollop of sour cream and a sprig of fresh cilantro.

Note: Masa harina is flour made from corn that has been cooked and soaked in lime water. Traditionally used for corn tortillas, it is available in Spanish markets and supermarkets. If you can't get fresh poblanos, substitute New Mexican Green, Cubanelles, or Anaheim chile peppers.

RED BEAN SAUCE

◆

Makes about 1½ cups

1 tablespoon olive oil
⅓ cup chopped onions
2 teaspoons minced seeded jalapeño
   peppers
2 bay leaves
1 cup dried red kidney beans,
   soaked overnight and drained

¼ cup chopped fresh cilantro
4 cups Basic Chicken Stock
   (page 6)
1 teaspoon salt
3 turns freshly ground black pepper

1. Heat the oil in a saucepan over high heat. When the oil is hot, add the onions and jalapeños and sauté for 1 minute. Add the bay leaves, beans, and cilantro and cook for 1 minute.

2. Stir in the stock and bring to a boil. Reduce the heat and simmer until the beans are tender, for about 2 hours. Stir in the salt and pepper and simmer for 5 minutes. Serve immediately or store, refrigerated, in an airtight container for 2 days. Reheat in a saucepan over a low flame.

Spicy Chicken Rellenos with Tequila Lime Sauce

◆

Makes 4 first-course servings

1 cup (½ pound) boned, skinned, and diced chicken breast
2½ tablespoons Emeril's Southwest Seasoning (page 3), in all
1 tablespoon olive oil
1 tablespoon minced shallots
1 tablespoon minced garlic
2 tablespoons chopped fresh cilantro
½ cup heavy cream
½ cup grated jalapeño-flavored Jack cheese
3 tablespoons bread crumbs (page 17)

1 cup masa harina (page 29)
1 cup all-purpose flour, in all
2 large egg whites, lightly beaten
1½ cups milk
¾ cup Tequila Lime Sauce (recipe follows)
4 medium-large poblano peppers with their stems, roasted and peeled (page 16), slit up one side, and seeded (see Note, page 29)
6 cups vegetable oil
4 cilantro sprigs

1. Season the chicken with 1 tablespoon Southwest Seasoning.

2. Heat the olive oil in a large skillet over high heat. When the oil is hot, add the seasoned chicken and stir-fry for about 1 minute. Add the shallots, garlic, and cilantro and sauté for 1 minute. Stir in the cream and the cheese, stir well, and turn off the heat. Stir in the bread crumbs, turn the mixture into a bowl, and allow to cool for 15 minutes. Makes about 1½ cups.

3. Combine the masa harina, ½ cup of the all-purpose flour, and 1 tablespoon Southwest Seasoning in a bowl. Fold in the egg whites and add the milk ¼ cup at a time, mixing thoroughly between additions, until all of the milk is incorporated and the mixture is smooth. In another bowl combine the remaining ½ cup flour with the remaining ½ tablespoon Southwest Seasoning.

4. Prepare the Tequila Lime Sauce and keep warm.

5. Start heating the vegetable oil in a large pot. Spoon a generous ¼ cup of the filling into each pepper through the slit in its side. Dip each filled pepper in the batter, then dredge in the seasoned flour. When the oil is very hot (about 375°F)—a bit of batter dropped in the oil should fry quickly—fry the rellenos until golden brown, for about 3 to 4 minutes. Drain on paper towels.

6. To serve, spoon 3 tablespoons of Tequila Lime Sauce onto each of 4 dinner plates. Top each pool of sauce with a relleno and garnish with a cilantro sprig.

TEQUILA LIME SAUCE

◆

Makes about ¾ cup

½ cup white tequila
2 tablespoons freshly squeezed lime juice
1 tablespoon minced onions
1 teaspoon minced garlic
1 tablespoon chopped fresh cilantro

½ teaspoon salt
3 turns freshly ground black pepper
¼ cup heavy cream
8 tablespoons (1 stick) unsalted butter, cut up, at room temperature

1. Combine the tequila, lime juice, onions, garlic, cilantro, salt, and pepper in a skillet over high heat and bring to a boil. Stir in the cream and simmer for 3 minutes.

2. Whisk in the butter and remove from the heat. Continue whisking until all of the butter is incorporated. Serve immediately, or prepare without the butter and refrigerate overnight in an airtight container. Reheat in a saucepan over a low flame. When the sauce is at a simmer, whisk in the butter and continue from there.

Cilantro Shrimp

◆

Makes 4 first-course servings

So simple. So delicious. So make them once—and you'll make them again and again.

24 large shrimp, peeled and
   deveined (1½ pounds)
1 tablespoon Emeril's Southwest
   Seasoning (page 3)

¾ cup Cilantro Oil (page 5)
¼ cup chopped green onions
¼ cup chopped red bell peppers

1. Sprinkle the shrimp with the Southwest Seasoning and use your hands to coat thoroughly.

2. Heat a large heavy dry skillet over high heat. When the skillet is very hot, add the shrimp and sear them for 3 minutes on each side. Remove from the heat.

3. To serve, spoon 2 tablespoons of the cilantro oil onto each of 4 plates. Arrange 6 shrimp on top and drizzle with another tablespoon of the oil. Sprinkle each serving with 1 tablespoon of the green onions and 1 tablespoon of the red bell peppers.

Poached Oysters in Pernod Cream and Fried Spinach

♦

Makes 4 first-course servings

When in New Orleans, eat Oysters Rockefeller, right? Well, I tried, but they were too heavy for me. So I pulled the recipe apart and reworked it to suit myself. The result is lighter, keeping the traditional flavors while adding a new wrinkle with a touch of Pernod, an anise-flavored liqueur. By the way, did you know that originally Oysters Rockefeller were made with watercress, not spinach?

1 cup vegetable oil
8 ounces fresh spinach, rinsed,
   stemmed, and patted dry
1½ teaspoons salt, in all
2 teaspoons unsalted butter, in all
¼ cup minced shallots
2 teaspoons minced garlic
⅓ cup (packed) chopped fennel,
   leaves and bulb

1 teaspoon white pepper, in all
½ cup Pernod
1 cup heavy cream
24 large freshly shucked oysters,
   with their liquor
2 teaspoons Emeril's Creole
   Seasoning (page 3)
4 fresh fennel sprigs

1. Preheat the oven to 250°F.

2. Heat the oil in a large skillet over high heat. When the oil is hot, add about one-third of the spinach and lightly stir-fry until crisp, for about 1 minute. Drain the spinach on paper towels. Repeat in 2 more batches. Sprinkle with ½ teaspoon of the salt. Keep warm on a baking sheet in the oven.

3. Melt 1 teaspoon of the butter in another large skillet over high heat. When the butter sizzles, add the shallots, garlic, fennel, ½ teaspoon of the salt, and ½ teaspoon of the pepper. Sauté, stirring occasionally, until the vegetables are translucent, for about 2 minutes.

4. Remove the skillet from the stove. Holding it at a distance from the burner, add the Pernod. Carefully set the skillet back on the burner, keeping your face away; the Pernod should flame. If it doesn't, don't worry, just continue to cook it in the same way: Simmer for 1 minute, whisk in the cream, and cook for 2 minutes.

5. Reduce the heat to medium. Fold in the oysters, with their liquor, and the remaining ½ teaspoon each salt and pepper. Cook just until the edges of the oysters begin to curl, for about 2 or 3 minutes, depending on their size. Remove immediately from the heat.

6. Using a slotted spoon, remove the oysters from the skillet, and set the skillet back on the burner over high heat. Cook the sauce, reducing it until it's thick enough to coat a spoon. Swirl in the remaining 1 teaspoon butter, remove from the heat, and whisk just until the butter has melted. Makes about 1 cup of sauce.

7. To serve, spoon about ¼ cup of the sauce onto each of 4 dinner plates. Arrange the oysters like the spokes of a wheel on top of the sauce, leaving a well in the center. Place a mound of the spinach in the center of the plate. Garnish the rim of the plate with Creole Seasoning and add a sprig of fresh fennel.

Fried Oysters with Horseradish Cream and Tomato Corn Salsa

◆

Makes 4 first-course servings

Oysters and horseradish are great together. Sometimes I just open fresh, briny oysters and dot them with freshly grated horseradish. In this recipe the horseradish is mixed with cream and teamed up with a Tomato Corn Salsa, my version of cocktail sauce, a perfect accompaniment to these spicy, corn-crunchy fried oysters.

24 large freshly shucked oysters, liquor drained and reserved for the Horseradish Cream
2 cups Horseradish Cream (recipe follows)
2 cups Tomato Corn Salsa (recipe follows)
1 cup all-purpose flour

2 tablespoons plus ⅛ teaspoon Emeril's Creole Seasoning (page 3), in all
1 cup masa harina (see Note, page 29)
2 large eggs
1 cup milk
½ cup olive oil, in all
½ teaspoon salt

1. Prepare the Horseradish Cream, and keep warm. Prepare the Tomato Corn Salsa, if not already done, and set aside.

2. In a small bowl combine the flour with 1 tablespoon Creole Seasoning. In another bowl combine the masa harina with 1 tablespoon Creole Seasoning. In a third bowl beat the eggs with the milk. Dredge the oysters in the seasoned flour, then the egg, then the seasoned masa harina.

3. Heat ¼ cup of the oil in each of 2 skillets over high heat. When the oil is hot, fry the oysters until they're golden brown, for about 1½ minutes on each side. Drain on paper towels and sprinkle with the salt.

4. To serve, use a spoon to spread about ½ cup of the Horseradish Cream on each of 4 dinner plates. Arrange 6 oysters on each plate like the spokes of a wheel, and mound about ½ cup of the salsa in the center. Garnish the rim of each plate with a sprinkling of Creole Seasoning.

HORSERADISH CREAM

◆

Makes about 2 cups

¾ cup freshly grated horseradish, or
    bottled, if not prepared with cream
3 tablespoons minced shallots
2 teaspoons minced garlic
2 teaspoons Dijon mustard

1½ teaspoons salt
½ teaspoon white pepper
1½ cups heavy cream
¾ cup oyster liquor reserved from
    24 large shucked oysters

Combine all of the ingredients in a saucepan over high heat and bring to a boil, whisking gently. Reduce the heat and simmer, stirring occasionally, until the sauce is thick enough to coat the back of a spoon, for about 12 minutes. Remove from the heat. Serve immediately or store, refrigerated, in an airtight container overnight. Reheat in a saucepan over low heat.

TOMATO CORN SALSA

◆

Makes ¾ cup

¼ cup blanched corn (page 16)
4 ripe Italian plum tomatoes, peeled,
    seeded, and diced
¼ cup minced onions
1 teaspoon minced jalapeño peppers
2 tablespoons chopped fresh cilantro

1 tablespoon freshly squeezed lime
    juice
1 teaspoon freshly squeezed lemon
    juice
½ teaspoon salt
4 turns freshly ground black pepper

Combine all of the ingredients in a bowl and stir until thoroughly blended. This salsa improves in flavor after it sits awhile. For best results, prepare a day ahead and store, refrigerated, in an airtight container. Bring to room temperature before serving.

Mussels with Saffron Wine Sauce

◆

Makes 4 first-course servings

Mussels have such a distinctive flavor, all you have to do is kiss them with a little wine, some seasonings, and saffron, and you've got something indescribably delicious.

½ cup plus 1 tablespoon olive oil, in all
2 tablespoons minced shallots
2 tablespoons chopped fresh parsley
1 tablespoon minced garlic
½ teaspoon salt

¼ teaspoon saffron threads
6 turns freshly ground black pepper
½ cup dry white wine
24 cleaned, bearded, and soaked mussels (page 16)
1 large egg

1. Heat 1 tablespoon of the oil in a large skillet over high heat. Add the shallots, parsley, garlic, salt, saffron, pepper, and wine, and bring to a boil, stirring. Add the mussels, reduce the heat to low, cover, and steam until the shells are open, for about 3 minutes. Discard any unopened mussels. Strain and reserve the liquid (makes about ⅔ cup liquid). Keep the mussels covered and warm.

2. Place the egg in a food processor, turn on the machine, and slowly drizzle in the ⅔ cup mussel cooking liquid. Slowly drizzle in the remaining ½ cup oil. Process until the mixture has the texture of a thin mayonnaise. Makes 1⅓ cups.

3. To serve, arrange 6 mussels in each of 4 shallow soup bowls and drizzle each serving with ⅓ cup of the sauce, making sure to get some of the sauce into all of the mussel shells. Serve immediately.

Scallops Seviche in Herbed Profiteroles

◆

Makes 4 first-course servings

Seviche, which is raw seafood marinated in citrus juices, is often served in tropical climates. The acid from the citrus juices "cooks" and preserves the fish. I decided to use seviche as a stuffing for profiteroles, which are usually sweet and filled with ice cream and topped with hot fudge sauce. These savory profiteroles are laced with fresh herbs and can be used with a filling of your own invention. The recipe can be easily doubled for a light summer lunch or brunch for 4.

½ recipe Herbed Profiteroles
(page 305)
6 ounces sea scallops (about 5 large scallops), quartered
3 tablespoons finely chopped red onions
2 tablespoons finely chopped green bell peppers
2 tablespoons finely chopped red bell peppers
1 teaspoon minced garlic
2 tablespoons chopped fresh cilantro

2 tablespoons chopped fresh parsley
½ teaspoon salt
3 turns freshly ground black pepper
2 tablespoons canned cream of coconut (see Note)
2 tablespoons freshly squeezed lime juice
1 tablespoon freshly squeezed lemon juice
1 tablespoon tequila
1 cup shredded Bibb lettuce

1. Prepare the profiteroles.

2. In a small bowl combine all of the ingredients except the profiteroles and the lettuce. Toss well and allow the seviche to marinate for 1 hour. Makes 1½ cups.

3. Slice about ¼ inch off the top of each profiterole, fill with 3 tablespoons of the seviche, and replace the lid lightly on top.

4. To serve, arrange ¼ cup of the shredded lettuce on each of 4 dinner plates and place 2 profiteroles on top.

Note: Many people use cream of coconut to make piña coladas. It can be found either on the cocktails accessories shelf or with the ethnic foods in your supermarket or grocery.

Gulf Fish Beignets with Tomato Corn Tartar Sauce

◆

Makes 20 to 24 beignets, 4 first-course servings

If you've visited New Orleans, chances are you've been to Café du Monde, where the café au lait is dark and rich, the beignets are puffy and sweet, and you can get both 24 hours a day. I've been fascinated by beignets ever since I arrived here, and I've certainly eaten my fill. From my first bite into one of these wonderful doughnuts—always warm from the fryer with clouds of powdered sugar—I wondered how they'd taste with fruit and other fillings. I began experimenting and came up with many savory versions. My favorite beignet is made with fish—preferably from the Gulf—or crawfish, for an unmistakable Louisiana flavor.

3 cups Tomato Corn Tartar Sauce
   (recipe follows)
2 large eggs
6 ounces (⅔ cup) fish, such as
   drum, catfish, wahoo, scrod, bass,
   or crawfish tails, cut into ½-inch
   dice
1 tablespoon plus 1⅛ teaspoons
   Emeril's Creole Seasoning
   (page 3), in all

¼ cup finely chopped green bell
   peppers
¼ cup finely chopped green onions
1 tablespoon minced garlic
1 teaspoon salt
1½ cups all-purpose flour
1 teaspoon baking powder
½ cup milk
8 cups vegetable oil

1. Prepare the Tomato Corn Tartar Sauce, and set aside.

2. In a large bowl whisk the eggs until frothy. Sprinkle the fish with 1 tablespoon Creole Seasoning, and add to the eggs. Stir in the bell peppers, green onions, garlic, salt, flour, baking powder, and milk, and stir until the consistency of wet dough. Makes about 2 cups.

3. Heat the oil in a large deep saucepan. When the oil is very hot (375°F), drop in about half the beignet mixture by large spoonfuls and fry until golden brown and crispy, for about 3 minutes. (Do this in 2 batches to avoid overcrowding.) Drain the beignets on paper towels, and sprinkle them with 1 teaspoon Creole Seasoning.

4. To serve, place ¾ cup of the sauce on each of 4 dinner plates, and place 5 or 6 beignets on top. Using your fingers, sprinkle the beignets and the rims of the plates with the remaining ⅛ teaspoon Creole Seasoning.

TOMATO CORN TARTAR SAUCE

◆

Makes about 3 cups

1 large egg
1¾ cups olive oil
2 Italian plum tomatoes, peeled and
   diced
1 ear blanched corn (page 16)
1 green onion, finely chopped

1 teaspoon Emeril's Creole
   Seasoning (page 3)
1 teaspoon salt
10 turns freshly ground black
   pepper

Combine the egg with the oil in a blender or food processor and process until it has the consistency of a light mayonnaise, for about 3 minutes. Turn the mixture into a bowl. Fold in the remaining ingredients and stir until thoroughly blended. Store in the refrigerator until ready to use, up to 2 days.

Smoked Duck Mousse Profiteroles with Chile Pepper Glaze

◆

Makes 8 first-course servings

You could serve two of these as a first course to each of 4 people; but they're so rich, just one will do—so you can have more people over. If you want to fill 16 profiteroles and serve them at a party, double the mousse and glaze recipes. Double the recipe for a dynamite party finger food. Smoked duck breast is easily found in specialty food shops and many meat markets.

½ recipe Herbed Profiteroles
    (page 305)
½ pound boneless smoked duck
    breast, cut into 1~inch pieces
    (about 1½ cups)
1 tablespoon minced shallots
2 tablespoons unsalted butter, cut up
¼ cup heavy cream

1½ teaspoons Emeril's Creole
    Seasoning (page 3)
½ teaspoon salt
2 turns freshly ground black pepper
¼ cup Chile Pepper Glaze (recipe
    follows)
1 cup shredded Bibb lettuce

1. Prepare the profiteroles and set aside.

2. Place the duck breast, shallots, butter, cream, Creole Seasoning, salt, and pepper in a food processor and purée, stopping once to scrape the sides, until the mixture is smooth. Makes 1½ cups.

3. Prepare the Chile Pepper Glaze.

4. To serve, slice ¼ inch off the top of each profiterole. Place 1 profiterole on each of 4 plates and, using the tines of a fork, drizzle the inside of each pastry cup with about 1 teaspoon of the Chile Pepper Glaze. Sprinkle the plate with 2 tablespoons lettuce, mound 3 tablespoons mousse into each profiterole, and replace the lids. Dip the tines of the fork into the glaze again, and let the glaze drizzle through onto the lid of each profiterole, using about ½ teaspoon for each.

CHILE PEPPER GLAZE

◆

Makes ¼ cup

1 tablespoon olive oil
1 tablespoon minced seeded jalapeño
   pepper (1 small pepper)
1 tablespoon minced shallots
1½ teaspoons crushed red pepper
   flakes
½ teaspoon salt

2 turns freshly ground black pepper
¼ cup water
1 tablespoon light corn syrup
1 tablespoon honey
2 teaspoons sugar
1½ teaspoons chili powder

1. Heat the oil in a small saucepan over high heat. Add the jalapeño and shallots and sauté for 30 seconds. Add the crushed red pepper, salt, black pepper, and water and cook for 30 seconds. Reduce the heat to medium.

2. Stir in the syrup and honey, bring to a boil, and cook for about 2 minutes. Stir in the sugar and chili powder and simmer for 2 minutes. Remove from the heat. Serve immediately or store, refrigerated, in an airtight container for up to 2 days. Reheat in a small saucepan over low heat.

Bill and Lenny's Excellent Foie Gras

◆

Makes 4 first-course servings

Bill Grace and Lenny Radlauer are good friends of mine and two of my best customers. They have well-developed palates and a taste for the good life, which make them a chef's dream; I love cooking for Bill and Lenny. One day they decided they were in the mood for foie gras, which is fattened duck or goose liver, but they wanted it prepared in a new way. Knowing it's de rigueur to dredge foie gras in flour before sautéing, I decided to toss out all the rules and go my own way. I've given the dish a NNO treatment, adding a light touch of balsamic vinegar, green onions, and garlic. The foie gras is barely seared and is served with a wine and truffle reduction sauce and wilted greens. Bill and Lenny love this dish and order it often.

Since this dish depends for its success on the highest-quality ingredients and is costly, save it for a very special occasion. If you want to cut the cost a bit, the truffles are optional. Foie gras cooks quickly, so have all of the ingredients ready and be on your toes.

4 round Toasted Croutons, about 3 to 4 inches in diameter (page 17)
¼ cup minced shallots
2 tablespoons minced garlic
1 cup port wine
¼ cup peeled and chopped Italian plum tomatoes
2 teaspoons salt, in all
12 turns freshly ground black pepper, in all
2 cups Veal Stock (page 8) or Brown Chicken Stock (page 7)

12 ounces foie gras (duck or goose liver), cut into 4 slices about ½ inch thick
2 tablespoons chopped green onions
2 teaspoons balsamic vinegar
¼ cup thinly sliced black truffles (optional)
2 teaspoons olive oil
4 cups assorted greens (include Belgian endive, frisée, arugula)

1. Prepare the croutons and set aside.

2. Combine the shallots, garlic, port, and tomatoes in a saucepan and bring to a boil. Lower the heat and simmer for 2 minutes. Add 1 teaspoon of the salt, 6 turns of the pepper, and the stock, and bring to a boil. Cook over high heat for 6 minutes.

3. Meanwhile, sprinkle the foie gras with ½ teaspoon of the salt, spreading evenly on both sides of each slice. Heat a large heavy skillet over high heat until very hot. Add the slices of foie gras and sear until brown, for 30 to 45 seconds on each side; don't overcook! Remove the foie gras to paper towels and reserve the fat left in the skillet.

4. When the sauce has cooked for 6 minutes, stir in the green onions, vinegar, and truffles. Stir in the reserved fat from the skillet and cook for 3 minutes. Turn off the heat. Makes 1 cup.

5. Heat the oil in the same skillet over high heat. Add the greens and the remaining ½ teaspoon salt and the remaining 6 turns pepper and wilt the greens, tossing, for about 60 seconds. Remove from the heat.

6. To serve, place 1 crouton on each of 4 plates and top with 1 slice of foie gras. Divide the greens into 4 servings and arrange around the foie gras. Spoon ¼ cup of the sauce over each slice of foie gras.

Corn Flaps with Chive Cream and Caviar

◆

Makes about 20 flaps, 4 first-course or brunch servings

These little flapjacks are brimming with fresh corn and spices that sing of the Southwest. I team them with fresh Louisiana caviar—which is the delicious roe of an unfortunate-looking fish called the choupique, which dates back to prehistoric times. I've also added a cool chive cream for an unusual union of flavors and textures. If you can't find Louisiana caviar, you can use any kind you like; beluga would be my second choice.

¾ cup Chive Cream (recipe follows)
½ cup blanched corn (page 16)
1 large egg
1½ teaspoons salt
½ teaspoon baking powder
1 teaspoon Emeril's Southwest Seasoning (page 3)
1 teaspoon ground cumin
1 teaspoon ground turmeric
½ teaspoon chili powder
⅛ teaspoon cayenne pepper

3 turns freshly ground black pepper
½ cup masa harina (see Note, page 29)
¼ cup all-purpose flour
½ cup milk
2 tablespoons plus 1 teaspoon olive oil, in all
4 teaspoons Louisiana choupique caviar, or other caviar of your choice
8 whole chives

1. Prepare the Chive Cream and set aside.

2. Combine the corn, egg, salt, baking powder, Southwest Seasoning, cumin, turmeric, chili powder, cayenne, black pepper, masa harina, and flour. Whisk in the milk until thoroughly incorporated. Mash the corn with the whisk to break the kernels and release their flavor. Stir in 1 teaspoon of the oil.

3. Heat the 1 tablespoon of the oil in a large skillet over high heat. To make the flapjacks, spoon 10 tablespoons of the batter (about 2 inches across, or the size of a silver dollar) into the hot skillet. As soon as bubbles appear at the edges (about 1½ minutes), lift 1 side of a flap with a spatula. If the bottom is golden brown, flip all of them over and brown the other side, for about 1 minute. Remove the corn flaps to paper towels and add the remaining 1 tablespoon oil to the skillet. When it's hot, repeat the process for the second batch.

4. To serve, spread 3 tablespoons of the Chive Cream on each of 4 dinner plates, and arrange 5 flaps on top, overlapping. Add 1 teaspoon of caviar to the top, and cross 2 chives over the caviar.

CHIVE CREAM

◆

Makes ¾ cup

¾ cup sour cream
2 tablespoons finely chopped chives
2 tablespoons dry white wine

½ teaspoon salt
½ teaspoon white pepper

Combine all of the ingredients in a small bowl and whisk until thoroughly blended. Serve immediately or store, refrigerated, in an airtight container for 2 days.

Wild Mushroom Boxes

◆

Makes 9 boxes

When I was the chef at Commander's Palace, Ashton Phelps, the publisher of the *Times-Picayune,* New Orleans's daily newspaper, was planning a party at the restaurant and asked me to come up with something new and exciting as a first course. I created this wild mushroom tart, which made Mr. Phelps—and his guests—very happy. But for some reason, I never put the dish on the menu. When I opened my restaurant and Ashton Phelps came in for his first dinner there, he reminded me about the boxlike tarts and wondered where they were. I dug into my brain for the original recipe and made it for him. It was so successful, it's become a regular item on our menu. It's easy to make your own boxes using store-bought frozen puff pastry.

2 10-inch-square sheets frozen puff pastry (one 17-ounce box), thawed
1 large egg, lightly beaten
2 tablespoons olive oil
4 cups sliced assorted fresh wild mushrooms, such as shiitakes, oysters, chanterelles, morels, portobellos, or porcini

1½ teaspoons salt
8 turns freshly ground black pepper
⅓ cup chopped green onions
1 tablespoon minced shallots
1 tablespoon minced garlic
1½ cups Veal Glaze (page 13)
2 teaspoons unsalted butter, at room temperature
8 fresh whole chives

1. Preheat the oven to 375°F. Line a baking sheet with parchment or wax paper.

2. On a lightly floured work surface, lay 1 sheet of puff pastry, brush with the beaten egg, and cut into nine 3⅓-inch squares.

3. Place the squares of puff pastry on the baking sheet. Lightly perforate the second sheet of pastry with the tines of a fork and cut it into 9 squares also. Place each of these, perforated side up, on top of an egg-brushed square.

4. Using just the tip of a small sharp knife, outline a 2⅓-inch square cutout within the top square of pastry *only,* taking care not to cut all the way through. This will leave a ½-inch frame in the perforated piece. Do not remove the square you outlined.

5. Bake until puffy and golden brown and the cut section is bursting out, for about 15 to 20 minutes. The pastry will resemble boxes. Remove from the oven, allow the pastry to cool on racks, and carefully remove the cutouts, or lids, with the tip of a sharp knife.

6. While the pastry is baking, heat the oil in a large skillet over high heat. When the oil is hot, add the mushrooms, salt, and pepper and sauté for about 45 seconds. Add the green onions, shallots, and garlic and sauté for 1 minute. Stir in the Veal Glaze and simmer for 3 minutes. Fold in the butter, and cook just until the butter is incorporated, for about 1 minute. Remove from the heat. Makes 3 cups.

7. To serve, place a pastry box on each plate. Spoon some of the mushroom filling into each box, place 2 chives on top of each and replace the lids, letting the chives stick out.

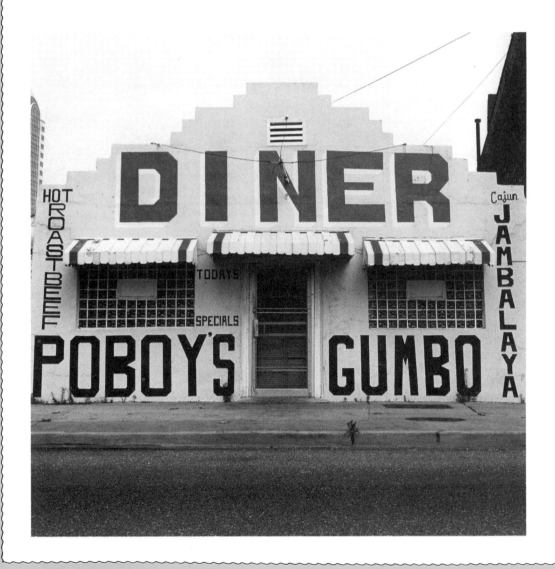

NNO Spanakopita Phyllo Packages

◆

Makes 4 first-course servings

This is my quick and easy knock-off of *spanakopita*, a Greek cheese and spinach pie. My version has no spinach, but the combination of paper-thin phyllo dough, olive oil, and goat cheese is irresistible. Add lean ground lamb, and you've got a fabulous first course. These also make great party finger food, especially since they can be made ahead, refrigerated, then baked at the last minute. Phyllo dough can be purchased in specialty food shops, Middle Eastern markets, and even some supermarkets.

4 tablespoons olive oil, in all
½ pound lean ground lamb
¼ cup minced onions
1 tablespoon minced garlic
1 tablespoon chopped fresh oregano
1½ teaspoons salt
5 turns freshly ground black pepper
8½ ounces (½ cup) goat cheese, such as Montrachet

½ teaspoon Emeril's Creole Seasoning (page 3)
¼ teaspoon Worcestershire sauce
4 12- × 17-inch sheets frozen phyllo dough, thawed
8 sprigs fresh oregano

1. Preheat the oven to 375°F. Line a baking sheet with parchment or wax paper.

2. Heat 2 tablespoons olive oil in a medium skillet over high heat. When the oil is hot, add the lamb and sauté, breaking up the meat with a wooden spoon, for about 2 minutes. Stir in the onions and garlic and sauté for 3 minutes. Stir in the oregano, salt, and pepper and sauté for 1½ minutes, stirring occasionally. Remove the skillet from the heat and turn the mixture into a bowl.

3. Stir in the goat cheese, Creole Seasoning, and Worcestershire. Makes about 1 cup.

4. Lay the sheets of phyllo in a pile on a flat surface. Brush the top sheet with the remaining 2 tablespoons olive oil. Using a knife, cut the sheets in half and then the halves in half, leaving 4 piles of phyllo strips, each about 3 inches wide.

5. Place about ¼ cup of the lamb mixture on the bottom half of 1 pile. Keep the remaining piles covered with a damp cloth as you work. Fold the phyllo by bringing the bottom up over the filling, then folding catty-corner (like folding a flag) twice to form a package that looks like a three-cornered hat. Press the edges together to seal.

6. Place the phyllo packages on the baking sheet. If you're preparing them ahead of time, refrigerate the packages, covered with a damp cloth, until 30 minutes before serving; remove them from the refrigerator and allow to sit for 15 minutes at room temperature before baking. Bake until golden brown, for about 15 minutes. Remove from the oven.

7. To serve, place 1 lamb package on each plate and garnish with oregano sprigs.

THE LAST WORD

To be successful with phyllo dough, allow it to defrost in the refrigerator overnight if frozen, then remove it from the refrigerator about 30 minutes before using it. Don't unwrap or remove the dough from the package until all of your other ingredients are prepped and ready to go. Keep unwrapped phyllo sheets moist and pliable under a clean, damp dish towel. If you leave phyllo open to the air, it will dry up and crack, making it impossible to work with.

Andouille Gnocchi with Spicy Tomato Sauce

◆

Makes 4 first-course servings

One of my favorite Italian foods is gnocchi (pronounced NYOH-kee), puffy little dumplings that make terrific belly-warmers on a cold, rainy day. Lace them with spicy andouille sausage and Creole Seasoning, and you've made New New gnocchi.

2 large baking potatoes
2 cups Spicy Tomato Sauce
  (recipe follows)
1 tablespoon plus 1 teaspoon olive
  oil, in all
6 ounces finely chopped andouille
  sausage
1 teaspoon minced garlic
1 tablespoon chopped fresh basil
1 teaspoon chopped fresh oregano
1½ teaspoons salt, in all
5 turns freshly ground black pepper,
  in all

½ teaspoon Emeril's Creole
  Seasoning (page 3)
1 large egg
¾ cup coarsely grated fresh
  Parmesan cheese, in all
½ cup plus 3 tablespoons
  all-purpose flour, in all
2 cups milk
1 cup water
¼ cup chopped fresh basil

1. Bake the potatoes at 400°F until fork-tender, for about 1 hour. Remove from the oven and set aside until cool enough to handle. Prepare the Spicy Tomato Sauce and set aside.

2. Heat 1 tablespoon of the oil in a small skillet over high heat. Add the andouille, garlic, basil, and oregano and sauté for 2 minutes. Remove from the heat and pour into a large bowl.

3. Scrape the potatoes from their skins into the bowl and mash them into the andouille. Stir in 1 teaspoon of the salt, 3 turns of the pepper, the Creole Seasoning, egg, ¼ cup Parmesan, and ¼ cup plus 3 tablespoons (7 tablespoons) of the flour. Makes 2½ cups.

4. Sprinkle the remaining ¼ cup flour on a baking sheet lined with waxed paper. Using 2 teaspoons, form the gnocchi mixture into 28 dumplings and roll them in the flour on the baking sheet.

5. In a large saucepan over high heat, combine the milk, water, the remaining 1 teaspoon oil, ½ teaspoon salt, and 2 turns pepper and bring just to a boil. Add the gnocchi and poach for 5 minutes. Remove the gnocchi with a slotted spoon.

6. While the gnocchi are poaching, reheat the Spicy Tomato Sauce over low heat.

7. To serve, spoon ¼ cup of the sauce into each of 4 shallow bowls. Arrange 7 gnocchi on top and add another ¼ cup sauce. Sprinkle each serving with 2 tablespoons Parmesan, and top with 1 tablespoon chopped basil.

SPICY TOMATO SAUCE

◆

Makes 2 cups

1 tablespoon olive oil
⅓ cup chopped onions
½ teaspoon salt
4 turns freshly ground black pepper
1 tablespoon minced garlic
¼ cup finely chopped carrots
1 cup peeled, seeded, and chopped
   tomatoes

1 tablespoon chopped fresh basil
1 teaspoon chopped fresh oregano
¼ teaspoon cayenne pepper
1½ cups Basic Chicken Stock
   (page 6)

1. Heat the oil in a large saucepan over high heat. Add the onions, salt, and black pepper and sauté until the onions are translucent, for about 2 minutes.

2. Add the garlic, carrots, tomatoes, basil, oregano, and cayenne. Stir in the stock and bring to a boil. Reduce the heat and simmer, stirring occasionally, for 20 minutes.

3. Remove from the heat and purée in a food processor or blender. Serve immediately or store, refrigerated, in an airtight container for up to 2 days. Reheat in a saucepan over low heat.

CHAPTER 3

---◆---

Pot Food:
Soups and Stews

When I went to cooking school, I was told that soups are a measure of a cook's ability, which I already knew from my earlier apprenticeship as a little boy at my mother's side. In fact, the first thing I ever cooked was a simple vegetable soup. It wasn't great on my first try, but I kept making vegetable soup at least once a week and served it to my very patient, indulgent family until I got it right. All that practice finally paid off the night the soup—perfectly textured, exquisitely seasoned (I may be exaggerating somewhat), and brimming with plump fresh vegetables—arrived at the dinner table. Mom was proud, and the rest of the family was relieved that I'd moved on to another challenge.

Mom, and later my culinary instructors, taught me that the key to great soups and stews is great stock. That, and the understanding that you can't clean out your refrigerator, throwing everything into a pot, and expect good results. Each soup or stew requires careful planning and should be created from only the finest, freshest ingredients.

Pot food to a New Orleanian has often meant gumbo, a traditional Louisiana soup or stew usually prepared with okra, seafood, meat, or vegetables, or any combination of these ingredients. The simply stated intention to make a gumbo could easily start a heated debate. What kind of gumbo? With or without a roux? What color roux? Chicken or seafood or both? How many kinds of sausage? Okra or filé? And the most heated question of all: Whose mama made the best gumbo?

Everything old is new again, including oldfangled soups and stews. We just got a little creative with some ONO favorites: made some lighter, as in Big Easy Seafood Okra Gumbo; some more exciting, like Escolar Stew with Saffron Broth and Wild Mushrooms; and some more interesting, such as Garlic Soup with Creole Croutons. Not to worry—NNO soups and stews are as comforting as the old kind, and I'm sure you'll like them even better.

Bisques—thick, creamy soups—are important in the Big Easy as well, especially the labor-intensive crawfish bisque, filled with spicy stuffed crawfish heads. I've included a Creole Corn and Crab Bisque, which is made with a roux and my not-so-secret ingredient—liquid crab boil.

Etouffées—or "smothered" foods—are more of the comfort dishes that people down here love so much. During Mardi Gras, people who live along the parade routes open their homes to friends and almost always leave a big pot of gumbo or stew on the stove for between-parade nibbling. Guests would be happily surprised to see a kettle of Smoked Duck Stew with Smoked Duck Dumplings bubbling away in the kitchen.

Dr. E.'s Get-Well Chicken Vegetable Soup

◆

Makes 16 cups, 12 healthy servings

One of my good friends in New Orleans is Derby Gisclair, one of the last true gentle men in the world. One day Derby's wife, Claire, called to cancel their dinner reservation because Derby wasn't feeling well. What does a friend do at a time like this? I whipped up a batch of double-strength chicken soup and sent it to the Gisclairs, with instructions from "Dr. E." to bring the soup to a boil and eat it as hot as possible. The next day Derby showed up for lunch at the restaurant, fit as a fiddle. Well, word got around, friends and relatives were putting in orders for "The Cure," and soon I realized these people weren't even sick. Good thing; I didn't want to get busted for practicing medicine without a license.

You'll enjoy this soup even if you're not ailing, but when you prepare it, freeze a couple of individual portions, just in case. One more hint: This is better if it's made a day ahead and reheated.

2 tablespoons olive oil

1 chicken (2½ to 3 pounds), boned, skinned, and visible fat removed (save the bones and the carcass, discard the skin), diced

2½ teaspoons salt

10 turns freshly ground black pepper

1 cup chopped onions

½ cup chopped celery

½ cup diced carrots

½ cup chopped green onions

2 tablespoons minced garlic

¼ cup (loosely packed) fresh parsley leaves

1 tablespoon chopped fresh basil

4 bay leaves

1 tablespoon Emeril's Creole Seasoning (page 3)

2 cups assorted chopped fresh vegetables, such as beans, zucchini, yellow squash, cabbage, or whatever is in season

1 cup (firmly packed) rinsed and torn spinach leaves

¼ teaspoon crushed red pepper

3 quarts Basic Chicken Stock (page 6)

2 cups cooked fine or broad noodles

1. Heat the oil in a large heavy pot over high heat. When the oil is hot, add the chicken meat and bones, salt, and pepper and sauté, stirring occasionally, until the meat and bones are brown, for about 5 minutes. Add the onions, celery, carrots, green onions, garlic, parsley, basil, bay leaves, and Creole Seasoning and sauté, stirring once or twice, for about 4 minutes. Add the chopped vegetables, spinach, and crushed red pepper and sauté for 1 minute.

2. Add the stock to the pot and bring it to a boil. Reduce the heat and simmer, uncovered, for about 25 minutes. Add the noodles, bring back to a boil, and simmer for 5 minutes. Remove from the heat. Remove the carcass and loose bones. Unless you're too ill to wait, the soup will taste even better if you refrigerate it overnight. The next day, remove and discard the congealed fat on the top and reheat the soup over medium-low heat.

Tuesday's Red Bean Soup

◆

Makes 7 cups, 6 hearty first-course servings

Red beans and rice is a Monday special on the menu of virtually every restaurant in New Orleans, either for lunch or dinner. I always wondered what happened to the leftover red beans and rice on Tuesday, and I finally answered my own question by creating a red bean soup. The soup has become so popular, a number of regulars show up at the restaurant on Tuesdays for this dish. In this version, you get to have the soup on Tuesday without having to make the red beans for supper on Monday.

1 tablespoon olive oil
½ cup diced bacon
1½ cups chopped onions
¼ cup chopped green bell peppers
1 tablespoon minced garlic
4 bay leaves
6 ounces sliced andouille sausage
1 small smoked ham hock (about 5 to 6 ounces)
2 cups dried red kidney beans, soaked overnight

1 tablespoon Emeril's Creole Seasoning (page 3)
1 teaspoon Worcestershire sauce
2 quarts Basic Chicken Stock (page 6)
1 teaspoon salt
1½ cups cooked long-grain white rice, warm
6 tablespoons chopped green onions

1. Heat the oil in a large heavy pot over high heat. Add the bacon and sauté for 2 minutes. Add the onions, bell peppers, garlic, bay leaves, andouille, and ham hock and cook, stirring, for 2 minutes.

2. Add the beans and cook for 2 minutes. Stir in the Creole Seasoning, Worcestershire sauce, and the stock, and bring to a boil. Reduce the heat to medium and cook for 1 hour, stirring occasionally. Add the salt, cover the pot, and cook for 15 minutes. Turn off the heat and allow the pot to sit, covered, for about 20 minutes. Discard the ham hock.

3. To serve, ladle a generous cup of the soup into each of 6 bowls. Top each serving with ¼ cup of the rice and sprinkle each with 1 tablespoon of the green onions.

Creole Corn and Crab Bisque

◆

Makes 7 cups, 6 first-course servings

In New Orleans we're bullish on bisque, as opposed to New England, where chowder—or chowdah—is chief. Deep in flavor, this bisque is thickened with a roux and spiked with liquid crab boil for a surprising NNO twist.

3 tablespoons Roux (page 5)
1 tablespoon olive oil
½ cup minced onions
1 cup uncooked corn, scraped from
    about 2 ears
1 tablespoon minced garlic
2 tablespoons minced celery
1 cup Crab Stock (page 11) or
    Fish Stock (page 9)
2 teaspoons salt
¼ teaspoon white pepper

3 bay leaves
3 cups milk
1 cup heavy cream
1 teaspoon liquid crab boil
    (see Note)
½ pound (about 1 cup) lump
    crabmeat, picked over for shells
    and cartilage
¼ cup chopped green onions
½ teaspoon Worcestershire sauce

1. Prepare the Roux, set aside 3 tablespoons, and refrigerate the rest for future use.

2. Heat the oil in a large pot over high heat. When the oil is hot, add the onions and corn and sauté for 1 minute. Stir in the garlic and celery and sauté for 30 seconds. Add the stock, salt, pepper, and bay leaves and bring to a boil.

3. Stir in the milk, cream, and crab boil. Bring back to a boil, reduce the heat, and simmer for 5 to 7 minutes, stirring occasionally.

4. Whisk in the Roux 1 tablespoon at a time until thoroughly incorporated into the soup. Reduce the heat to low and continue to cook, whisking until the mixture thickens.

5. Stir in the crabmeat, green onions, and Worcestershire and simmer for 6 to 8 minutes.

6. To serve, ladle 1 generous cup of the bisque into each of 6 soup plates.

Note: Liquid crab boil can be purchased at many specialty food stores, or see page 19 for mail-order information.

Big Easy Seafood Okra Gumbo

◆

Makes 12 cups, 12 first-course servings or 8 main-course servings

Gumbo—hearty and brimming with fresh seafood and vegetables—seems to be everyone's favorite in Louisiana, and it's gaining popularity throughout the country. But some people hesitate to make gumbo, thinking it requires a great deal of time and energy to prepare. It may have something to do with "rouxphobia," or fear of making roux. *This* gumbo doesn't have a roux; it's thickened with okra and filé powder, which is ground sassafras leaves. Look for filé powder on your grocer's spice rack. So keep in mind that although the ingredient list for this dish may seem long, once you have everything measured and ready to go, it's a quick and easy gumbo to make.

2 tablespoons olive oil
½ cup chopped onions
¼ cup chopped celery
¼ cup chopped green bell peppers
¼ cup chopped red bell peppers
1 tablespoon salt
4 turns freshly ground black pepper
½ cup peeled, seeded, and chopped Italian plum tomatoes
2 tablespoons minced garlic
1 tablespoon minced shallots
2 quarts Fish Stock (page 9)
½ pound (about 1 cup) firm-fleshed fish, such as grouper, tilefish, monkfish, or sea bass, diced
1 teaspoon Worcestershire sauce
½ teaspoon hot pepper sauce
6 bay leaves

1 tablespoon minced fresh basil
1 teaspoon minced fresh oregano
1 teaspoon fresh thyme leaves
1 cup sliced fresh okra (about 8 large okra)
2 teaspoons Emeril's Creole Seasoning (page 3)
½ pound peeled medium fresh shrimp
1 cup shucked fresh oysters, with their liquor
½ pound (about 1 cup) fresh lump crabmeat, picked over for shells and cartilage
1 teaspoon filé powder
4 cups cooked long-grain white rice, warm
½ to ¾ cup chopped green onions

1. Heat the oil in a large pot over high heat. When the oil is hot, add the onions, celery, and green and red peppers and sauté for 1 minute. Add the salt and pepper and sauté for 1 minute. Add the tomatoes, garlic, and shallots and sauté, stirring occasionally, for about 4 minutes.

2. Stir in the stock, add the fish, Worcestershire, hot pepper sauce, bay leaves, basil, oregano, and thyme, and bring to a boil. Cook over high heat, stirring occasionally, for about 8 minutes. Reduce the heat to medium.

3. Fold in the okra and Creole Seasoning, lower the heat, and simmer for 15 minutes. Skim the impurities from the top of the gumbo, turn the heat to high, and cook for 5 minutes. Fold in the shrimp, oysters, and crabmeat, reduce the heat, and simmer for 5 minutes. Slowly sprinkle in the filé, stirring to incorporate it thoroughly, and simmer, stirring, for 2 minutes. Remove from the heat.

4. To serve as a first course, ladle 1 cup of the gumbo into each of 12 gumbo bowls or soup plates, and add ⅓ cup of the rice to each; for a main course, allow 1½ cups gumbo and ½ cup of rice. Sprinkle each serving with 1 tablespoon of the green onions.

Fennel Tomato Soup

◆

Makes 8 cups, 8 first-course servings

When I traveled to Italy, I had the pleasure of eating the most delicious, yet simple salad—a combination of fresh tomatoes, fennel, and garlic. I was blown away by the taste sensation, and when I returned to the States I did some experimenting. This recipe is one of many that resulted from that experience, and the combination of the three flavors is still one of my favorites. Serve this soup with Parmesan Fennel Breadsticks (page 301).

1 tablespoon olive oil
2 cups coarsely chopped fennel, bulb only
½ cup chopped onions
6 whole cloves garlic, peeled
1 tablespoon salt
1½ teaspoons white pepper
1½ cups peeled, seeded, and chopped Italian plum tomatoes (about 6 tomatoes)

¼ cup plus 2 teaspoons Pernod
2 quarts Basic Chicken Stock (page 6)
½ cup heavy cream
1 cup coarsely grated fresh Parmesan cheese
8 sprigs fresh fennel leaves

1. Heat the oil in a large soup pot over high heat. Add the fennel and onions and sauté for 1 minute. Stir in the garlic and sauté for 1 minute. Add the salt and pepper and sauté for 1 minute. Stir in the tomatoes and Pernod and cook for 2 minutes.

2. Stir in the stock and bring to a boil. Reduce the heat and simmer for 1 hour. Whisk in the cream, streaming it in slowly, and cook for 2 minutes longer. Remove from the heat and purée the soup in batches in a food processor. Reheat if necessary.

3. Serve hot, allowing 1 cup of soup per portion. Stir 2 tablespoons Parmesan into each serving. Lay a breadstick across each bowl and hang a fennel sprig from each breadstick, so it drapes into the soup.

Kale and Andouille Soup

◆

Makes 14 cups, 8 main-course servings

My memories of my childhood in Fall River, Massachusetts, are a happy blur of Portuguese festivals, wonderful celebrations of music, dance, and food from the old country. The feast was known as *bon fester,* or "good festival," and the dish that I remember most is what we called *suppische kaldene,* or kale soup. This unusual dish was prepared in many ways, often with chorizo, split peas, and mint accompanying the base of kale, potatoes, and stock.

When I became chef at Commander's Palace, I made kale soup for the staff, substituting local andouille sausage for Portuguese chorizo. The response was so enthusiastic, I began to run kale and andouille soup as a special on the menu in the spring and fall when kale is in season in Louisiana. There's even a sweet little Portuguese song about *suppische kaldene,* but I'll spare you.

2 tablespoons olive oil

1½ pounds (3 cups) andouille or chorizo sausage, sliced in ½-inch rounds

¾ cup chopped onions

2 tablespoons minced garlic

¼ cup coarsely chopped fresh parsley

3 cups diced peeled potatoes, about 2 large (¼-inch dice)

3 quarts Basic Chicken Stock (page 6)

4 cups kale, rinsed, stemmed, and leaves torn into pieces

2 bay leaves

¼ teaspoon dried thyme leaves

1½ teaspoons salt

¼ teaspoon crushed red pepper

5 turns fresh ground black pepper

6 tablespoons chopped fresh mint (optional)

1. Heat the oil in a large pot over high heat. When the oil is hot, add the andouille and the onions and sauté, stirring once or twice, for about 2 minutes. Add the garlic, parsley, and potatoes and cook, stirring occasionally, for about 2 minutes.

2. Add the stock and kale and bring to a boil. Stir in the bay leaves, thyme, salt, red pepper, and black pepper. Reduce the heat and simmer until the potatoes are fork-tender, for about 30 minutes. Remove from the heat and skim the fat from the top.

3. Serve hot in deep bowls, allowing about 1¾ cups per portion. Stir ½ teaspoon of the mint into each bowlful, giving it a minute or two to infuse the soup with its flavor. Serve with a crusty Portuguese or French bread.

Garlic Soup with Creole Croutons

◆

Makes 6 cups, 4 first-course servings

My mother-in-law, Ruth Hohn, is a terrific cook, and she and I love to cook together. Every year we prepare Christmas Eve dinner for the whole family. We always pick a theme for the food, such as Italian, Southwestern, or New Orleans Mardi Gras. But whatever the theme, somehow the garlic soup I created for Ruth finds its way to the Christmas Eve table each year. Its velvety richness and spicy croutons set the festive mood for the rest of the meal.

2 tablespoons olive oil
1½ cups sliced onions
⅓ cup peeled garlic cloves
    (about 12 to 14)
3 bay leaves
2½ teaspoons salt
7 turns freshly ground black pepper
2 quarts Basic Chicken Stock
    (page 6)

1 tablespoon minced garlic
1 teaspoon fresh chopped basil
1 teaspoon fresh chopped thyme
2 cups diced day-old French or
    Italian bread
½ cup heavy cream
⅓ cup coarsely grated fresh
    Parmesan cheese
1 cup Creole Croutons (page 17)

1. Heat the oil in a soup pot over high heat. Add the onions, garlic cloves, bay leaves, salt, and pepper. Stir well and sauté until the onions are caramelized, for about 7 minutes. (Don't let the onions get too dark; they should be sweet-tasting and a rich golden-brown color.)

2. Stir in the stock, minced garlic, basil, and thyme, and bring to a boil. Reduce the heat and simmer for about 40 minutes. Turn the heat back up to high and whisk in the bread and the cream, and continue whisking until the bread has disintegrated into the soup, for about 10 minutes. Whisk in the Parmesan and remove from the heat.

3. While the soup is simmering, prepare the croutons.

4. Purée the soup in a food processor or blender.

5. Serve the soup hot, allowing 1¼ cups per portion. Top with the croutons.

Creole Callaloo with Roasted Red Pepper Rouille

◆

Makes 9 cups, 8 first-course servings

Callaloo is a soup of greens, crabs, pork, and coconut milk that's popular throughout the Caribbean, especially in Trinidad and Jamaica. Callaloo is also the name of the greens used in the soup when it's made in the Caribbean. Since it's almost impossible to get callaloo greens here, I've created my own version of the soup using greens that are plentiful in New Orleans and across the United States, like collards and mustard greens. These are tangy and peppery and give the callaloo a lot of flavor. If you want your callaloo to have a richer crab flavor, sauté 4 soft shells and place half a crab in the bottom of each soup bowl before ladling in the callaloo. The rouille, made of roasted red peppers, is a touch I couldn't resist, although a cook from the islands might think I'm nuts.

1 tablespoon olive oil
1 smoked ham hock (about 8 to 10 ounces)
½ cup chopped onions
2 quarts Crab Stock (page 11)
2 quarts water
1 tablespoon Emeril's Creole Seasoning (page 3)
3 bay leaves

6 cups roughly chopped assorted greens, such as collards, mustard, turnip, chard, dandelion, beet greens, or spinach
1 teaspoon salt
3 turns freshly ground black pepper
¼ pound (½ cup) lump crabmeat, picked over for shells and cartilage
1½ cups Roasted Red Pepper Rouille (recipe follows)
½ cup toasted shredded coconut

1. Heat the oil in a large soup pot over high heat. Add the ham hock and the onions and sauté for 2 minutes. Stir in the stock and water and bring to a boil. Add the Creole Seasoning and bay leaves and cook over high heat, for 20 minutes. Reduce the heat and simmer for 60 minutes.

2. Fold in the greens, salt, and pepper and simmer for 30 minutes. Stir in the crabmeat and simmer for 5 minutes. Remove from the heat. Remove the ham hock and shred the meat off the bone back into the soup.

3. While the soup is simmering, prepare the Roasted Red Pepper Rouille.

4. Serve hot in bowls, allowing 1 generous cup of the callaloo per portion. Drizzle each serving with a generous 3 tablespoons of the Rouille and sprinkle with 1 tablespoon of the coconut.

ROASTED RED PEPPER ROUILLE

◆

Makes 1½ cups

1 red bell pepper, roasted, peeled,
  and diced (page 16)
1 tablespoon minced garlic
1 tablespoon chopped fresh cilantro
1 large egg

1 teaspoon salt
½ teaspoon crushed red pepper
¼ teaspoon cayenne pepper
2 turns freshly ground black pepper
1 cup olive oil

Combine the roasted pepper, garlic, cilantro, egg, salt, crushed red pepper, cayenne, and black pepper in a food processor or blender and purée. Slowly stream in the oil and continue to process until the mixture forms a thick emulsion.

Pumpkin Soup with Spicy Roasted Pumpkin Seeds

◆

Makes 4 cups, 4 first-course servings

There's pumpkin in a can and there's fresh pumpkin from a pumpkin. If you've never cooked with fresh pumpkin, here's the recipe to try it with. A small sugar pumpkin is best; a big jack-o'-lantern doesn't have the right flavor, but you can use the seeds from a big pumpkin to make the Spicy Roasted Pumpkin Seeds. You can purée pumpkin, stir-fry it with chicken or pork, bake it in a pie, or pot it in a stew or in this luscious pumpkin soup.

2 tablespoons Spicy Roasted
   Pumpkin Seeds (page 14)
2 tablespoons unsalted butter
2 cups peeled and diced pumpkin,
   seeds reserved (¼-inch dice)
½ cup chopped onions
1 teaspoon minced garlic
2 bay leaves
2 teaspoons salt

4 cups Basic Chicken Stock
   (page 6)
1 teaspoon ground cinnamon
¼ teaspoon ground nutmeg
3 turns freshly ground black pepper
1½ teaspoons sugar
1 cup heavy cream
¼ cup smooth peanut butter
½ cup chopped green onions

1. Prepare the Spicy Roasted Pumpkin Seeds and set aside.

2. Melt the butter in a soup pot over high heat. When the butter sizzles, add the pumpkin and sauté for 3 minutes. Add the onions and garlic and sauté for 2 minutes. Add the bay leaves, salt, and stock. Stir in the cinnamon, nutmeg, black pepper, and sugar and bring to a boil, whisking often to break up the pumpkin. Reduce the heat to medium and simmer until the pumpkin is very tender, for about 25 minutes.

2. Slowly whisk in the cream, and then the peanut butter. Simmer, stirring occasionally, for 15 minutes. Remove from the heat.

3. Serve the soup in shallow bowls and sprinkle with the roasted pumpkin seeds and chopped green onions.

Cucumber Shrimp Soup with Dill Cream

◆

Makes about 8 cups, 8 first-course servings

The touch of tomatoes in this soup gives it an ONO air, but it's definitely a dish for a contemporary palate. Rich in flavor, it's equally delicious served hot or cold. If you're serving it cold, purée the entire mixture and refrigerate it for several hours; it makes a super summertime lunch. This recipe is for serving the soup hot.

2 tablespoons unsalted butter
½ cup chopped onions
1 tablespoon minced garlic
2 tablespoons chopped fresh dill
1½ teaspoons salt
1 teaspoon white pepper
1 pound (about 2 cups) coarsely
   chopped peeled medium shrimp
3 cups peeled, seeded, and thinly
   sliced cucumbers (about 2 large)

4 cups Basic Chicken Stock
   (page 6)
2 cups heavy cream
¼ cup peeled, seeded, and chopped
   Italian plum tomatoes
   (1 or 2 tomatoes)
½ cup Dill Cream (recipe follows)
16 sprigs fresh dill

1. Melt the butter in a large soup pot over high heat and then add the onions, garlic, dill, salt, and pepper and sauté, stirring, for about 2 minutes. Add the shrimp and sauté for 2 minutes. Stir in the cucumbers and sauté for 1 minute.

2. Stir in the stock, cream, and tomatoes and bring to a boil. Reduce the heat and simmer for 25 minutes. Remove from the heat.

3. While the soup is simmering, prepare the Dill Cream.

4. Purée half the soup mixture in a food processor or blender and return it to the unprocessed half to give the soup a variety of textures. Reheat over low heat.

5. To serve, allow about 1 cup of soup per portion. Add a dollop of the Dill Cream to each, and garnish with 2 sprigs of dill.

DILL CREAM

◆

Makes about ½ cup

½ cup sour cream
3 tablespoons chopped fresh dill
2 tablespoons finely minced shallots

½ teaspoon salt
¼ teaspoon white pepper
2 tablespoons dry white wine

Combine the sour cream, dill, shallots, salt, and pepper in a small bowl and mix well. Add the wine and blend until thoroughly incorporated. Serve immediately or store, refrigerated, in an airtight container for 2 days.

Escolar Stew with Saffron Broth and Wild Mushrooms

◆

Makes 4 main-course servings

Escolar, sometimes erroneously called white tuna, has quickly become a favorite at Emeril's—not only with the customers but with the staff as well. It's simply a delicious fish, one of the tastiest to come out of the Gulf. If you have trouble finding it where you live, you can substitute another firm-fleshed whitefish. But don't be shy about asking your fish market to order it for you.

2 cups Fish Stock (page 9) or Shrimp Stock (page 10)
1 teaspoon saffron threads
2 cups diced escolar or other white firm-fleshed fish steak, such as yellowfin tuna, halibut, amberjack, or monkfish
2 teaspoons Emeril's Creole Seasoning (page 3)
2 tablespoons olive oil
1 cup assorted fresh wild mushrooms, such as chanterelles, shiitakes, oyster mushrooms, or black trumpets, stemmed if needed and thinly sliced

2 tablespoons peeled, seeded, and chopped Italian plum tomatoes
2 tablespoons chopped fresh basil
¼ cup chopped green onions
1 teaspoon minced garlic
1 cup rinsed and stemmed fresh spinach leaves
¾ teaspoon salt
3 turns freshly ground black pepper

1. Combine the stock with the saffron in a bowl and let sit to allow the saffron to infuse the stock, for about 15 minutes.

2. Combine the escolar with the Creole Seasoning and use your hands to coat the fish thoroughly.

3. Heat the oil in a large skillet over high heat. When the oil is hot, add the seasoned escolar and sauté, shaking the skillet, for about 1 minute. Add the mushrooms, tomatoes, basil, green onions, garlic, and spinach and sauté for 1 minute. Stir in the infused stock and simmer for 4 to 5 minutes. Stir in the salt and pepper and remove from the heat. Makes about 4 cups.

4. Serve hot in shallow bowls with hot crusty bread.

Phil Harris's Oyster Stew

◆

Makes 6 cups, 4 first-course servings

As a native of New England, I like to think I know something about oyster stew. But it wasn't until the actor, Phil Harris, turned up at Commander's Palace that I got to make some. It all started when he and I were reminiscing about the great oyster stew they serve at the Oyster Bar in New York City's Grand Central Station. Motivated, I hurried to the kitchen where I created the following recipe. Now whenever I see him, Mr. Harris speaks fondly of this oyster stew. The secret to making an outstanding oyster stew is to use freshly shucked oysters.

½ cup diced peeled boiling potatoes
1 tablespoon olive oil
¼ cup chopped onions
2 pints freshly shucked oysters with their liquor, the liquor drained off and reserved
2 tablespoons minced fresh parsley
2 tablespoons minced garlic
1½ teaspoons salt

¼ teaspoon white pepper
28 turns freshly ground black pepper, in all
½ teaspoon hot pepper sauce
½ teaspoon Worcestershire sauce
1 cup heavy cream
2 green onions or scallions, finely minced
2 tablespoons unsalted butter

1. In 3 cups of boiling water, cook the potatoes until firm-tender (al dente).

2. Heat the oil in a large skillet over high heat. Add the onions and sauté for 30 seconds. Add the reserved oyster liquor and cook 30 seconds more.

3. Add the parsley, garlic, potatoes, salt, white pepper, and 20 turns of the black pepper, and bring to a simmer. Stir in the hot sauce and Worcestershire and simmer for 1 minute. Add the cream and cook for 3 minutes.

4. Fold in the green onions and the oysters and cook just until the edges of the oysters start to curl, for about 2 minutes. Stay with it to be sure the oysters don't overcook.

5. To serve, ladle 1½ cups of the stew into each of 4 shallow soup bowls and top each with 2 turns black pepper. Serve, Louisiana style, with hot mini-biscuits (page 302).

Portuguese Chorizo Clam Stew with Garlic Aioli

◆

Makes 4 main-course servings

This partnering of sausage and clams always reminds me of the many carefree days of clamming I spent as a child, wading waist-deep into the ocean for littlenecks, a burlap bag hanging optimistically from my shoulders. This dish, known as *ameijoas na cataplana* to the Portuguese, is one I've loved since I was a kid, when my mother cooked her own version of it. It's a perfect indulgence for the New New Orleans palate, which loves the taste of seafood combined with the local sausage, andouille.

2 cups quartered unpeeled red
   potatoes
¾ cup Garlic Aioli (recipe follows)
1 tablespoon olive oil
1 pound andouille, chorizo, or other
   good smoked sausage (about 4
   links), each link cut into 3 or 4
   pieces
½ cup chopped onions
¼ cup chopped fresh cilantro
2 tablespoons minced garlic

2 teaspoons salt
½ teaspoon crushed red pepper
8 turns freshly ground black pepper
4 cups Shrimp Stock (page 10)
4 dozen littleneck clams, scrubbed
   (page 16)
1 cup peeled, seeded, and chopped
   Italian plum tomatoes (about 4)
½ cup chopped green onions
2 teaspoons Emeril's Creole
   Seasoning (page 3)

1. Cook the potatoes in 6 cups boiling water until tender, for about 8 minutes. Remove from the heat and drain.

2. Prepare the Garlic Aioli and set aside.

3. Combine the oil and andouille in a large skillet over high heat and brown the andouille, stirring occasionally, for about 3 minutes. Stir in the onions, cilantro, garlic, potatoes, salt, crushed red pepper, black pepper, and the Shrimp Stock and bring to a boil.

4. Add the clams, tomatoes, green onions, and Creole seasoning. Cover the skillet and cook over high heat until all the clams are open, for about 5 minutes. Remove from the heat.

5. To serve, divide the stew among 4 shallow bowls, allowing about 12 clams for each serving, and drizzle with 3 tablespoons of the Garlic Aioli.

ROASTED GARLIC AIOLI

◆

Makes ¾ cup

1 head roasted garlic (page 16)
1 large egg
1 tablespoon freshly squeezed lemon
  juice

1 tablespoon chopped fresh parsley
½ teaspoon salt
2 turns freshly ground black pepper
½ cup olive oil

Combine the garlic, egg, lemon juice, parsley, salt, and pepper in a food processor or blender and purée. Stream in the oil and continue to process until the mixture has formed a thick emulsion. Serve immediately or store, refrigerated, overnight in an airtight container.

Portuguese Seafood Stew with Aioli Crostini

◆

Makes 4 main-course servings

Every country seems to have its own version of a seafood stew; the French have bouillabaisse, we have cioppino, and the Portuguese have the mariscada, upon which this dish is loosely based. With its marriage of Creole and Portuguese seasonings, this is a good example of the new wave of melting-pot food. The crostini, or croutons, baked with a topping of roasted garlic aioli, are a luscious lagniappe.

12 Aioli Crostini (page 307)
2 tablespoons olive oil
½ pound chorizo or andouille
    sausage, cut into 8 pieces
1 cup sliced onions, sliced vertically,
    then across
2 tablespoons minced garlic
1 cup peeled, seeded, and chopped
    Italian plum tomatoes (about 4)
¼ cup chopped fresh cilantro
¼ cup chopped fresh basil
1 teaspoon Emeril's Creole
    Seasoning (page 3)

1 teaspoon salt
6 turns freshly ground black pepper
4 cups Shrimp Stock (page 10)
2 (about 1 pound each) live
    lobsters, cut in half from the head
    through the tail, the claws cracked
    with the side of a heavy knife
24 cherrystone or littleneck clams,
    scrubbed (page 16)
16 mussels, scrubbed and debearded
    (page 16)
12 large headless shrimp in the shell

1. Partially prepare the Aioli Crostini by doing Steps 1 and 2. Set the aioli aside.

2. Heat the oil in a large pot or paella pan over high heat. Add the sausage and sauté for 2 minutes. Add the onions, garlic, tomatoes, cilantro, basil, Creole Seasoning, salt, pepper, and stock and simmer for 3 minutes.

3. Add the lobster, cover, and cook for 5 minutes. Add the clams, cover, and cook for 2 minutes.

4. After the clams go into the pot, spread the aioli on the bread slices (see Aioli Crostini).

5. Add the mussels and shrimp to the pot, cover and simmer just until the shrimp turn pink and the mussels open, for about 2 to 3 minutes. Remove from the heat.

6. While the mussels and shrimp are cooking, bake the Aioli Crostini.

7. To serve, arrange ½ lobster, 6 clams, 4 mussels, and 3 shrimp in each of 4 large bowls. Ladle the soup over the shellfish and garnish each serving with 3 Aioli Crostini.

Rosemary Lamb Stew

◆

Makes 4 main-course servings

The fragrance of this stew fills your kitchen in the happiest way, and the combined flavors of lamb and rosemary will make your taste buds happy, too. New New stews are lighter than ever, without losing their feel-goodness. Serve this with Rosemary Biscuits (page 302).

12 to 14 ounces lamb meat from the leg, trimmed and cubed (½-inch cubes)
1 tablespoon Emeril's Creole Seasoning (page 3)
1 tablespoon olive oil
½ cup chopped onions
½ cup diced peeled potatoes
½ cup chopped carrots
¼ cup chopped rutabagas (increase the carrots by ¼ cup if you can't get rutabagas)

¼ cup chopped turnips
¼ cup peeled, seeded, and chopped Italian plum tomatoes (1 or 2 tomatoes)
1 tablespoon chopped fresh rosemary
1 tablespoon minced garlic
½ teaspoon salt
4 turns freshly ground black pepper
2 cups Lamb Stock (page 8) or Brown Chicken Stock (page 7)

1. Season the meat with the Creole Seasoning and use your hands to coat the meat thoroughly.

2. Heat the oil in a large nonreactive pot over high heat. Add the seasoned lamb and sauté, shaking the pan to brown evenly, for about 2 minutes. Add the onions, potatoes, carrots, rutabagas, and turnips and sauté, stirring occasionally, for 1 minute.

3. Stir in the tomatoes, rosemary, garlic, salt, pepper, and stock, and bring to a boil. Reduce the heat and simmer for 25 minutes.

4. To serve, spoon a generous cup of the stew into each of 4 shallow bowls.

Smoked Duck Stew with Smoked Duck Dumplings

◆

Makes 4 main-course servings

Everyone's heard of chicken and dumplings, and many would say it's the ultimate comfort food, but that's because they haven't yet tasted this dish—a tantalizing twist on a midwinter gem. Its velvety texture, laced with a smoky, tangy goodness, is unforgettable.

1 tablespoon olive oil
6 tablespoons finely chopped onions, in all
¼ cup finely chopped celery
¼ cup finely chopped carrots
¼ cups finely chopped parsnips
¼ cup finely chopped turnips
12 ounces (2 cups) finely chopped smoked duck meat, in all (see Note)
2 tablespoons peeled, seeded, and chopped Italian plum tomatoes
2 tablespoons chopped fresh basil

1 tablespoon plus 1 teaspoon minced garlic, in all
3 cups duck stock or Brown Chicken Stock (page 7)
1 cup water
1½ teaspoons salt, in all
5 turns freshly ground black pepper, in all
1 large egg
¼ cup beer
½ cup all-purpose flour
½ teaspoon baking powder

1. Heat the oil in a large pot over high heat. Add 4 tablespoons of the onions, the celery, carrots, parsnips, and turnips and sauté for 2 minutes. Add 1½ cups of the duck meat, the tomatoes, basil, and 1 tablespoon of the garlic. Stir in the stock, water, 1 teaspoon of the salt, and 3 turns of the pepper and bring to a boil. Reduce the heat and simmer for 20 to 25 minutes. Makes 4½ cups.

2. While the stew is simmering, combine the egg, beer, the remaining 1 teaspoon garlic, ½ teaspoon salt, 2 turns pepper, 2 tablespoons onions, the ½ cup duck meat with the flour and baking powder in a bowl and whisk together.

3. Turn the heat up to high under the stew. When it's bubbling, place spoonfuls of dumpling batter on top of the stew, cover, and cook for 2 minutes. Reduce the heat, simmer for 1 minute or until the dumplings are cooked through, and remove from the heat. Makes about 16 dumplings.

4. To serve, ladle 1 generous cup of the stew into each of 4 shallow bowls and top with about 4 dumplings.

Note: Smoked duck meat can be purchased at specialty food stores and some meat counters.

CHAPTER 4

The New Italian Renaissance: Pasta and Risotto

Everybody loves noodles, including New Orleanians. We eat a lot of pasta here, but in the old days, it was far more imitative of spaghetti and meatballs. Today, we infuse pasta and risotto dishes with our own unique flavors and textures and fresh local products.

We come by our love of Italianesque food honestly, since there was a major influx of Italian immigrants into the New Orleans area in the early part of this century. In fact, at one time the French Quarter was known as Little Italy. Now there is a handful of Italian trattorias in town, and several of our distinguished local restaurants, like Mr. B's, have signature pasta dishes, like jambalaya pasta.

Pasta is a blank canvas on which to create a masterpiece. I'm not saying the pasta has no flavor of its own—it just adapts so well to whatever you care to add to it. So it's not surprising that it takes to Creole sauces and seasonings, tasso, and andouille as deliciously as it does to traditional red sauces and, well, meatballs.

About eight years ago I was introduced to risottos, creamy Italian rice dishes prepared with short-grained Arborio rice. When I started experimenting with them, I realized risottos were just as versatile as pasta. They can be simple or complicated, depending on your mood and the occasion. As with pasta, you just have to know the basics, like how much stock to use to how much Arborio rice, and how long it needs to cook. You may find my method of preparing risotto a bit unorthodox, but I'm sure you'll like the results.

No matter how many wonderful pastas and risottos you create, there is one ingredient you must use to finish them, an ingredient as important to Italian pasta and risotto as it is to NNO pasta and risotto. That ingredient is good-quality Parmesan cheese, especially Parmigiano-Reggiano. Grate it coarsely, just before serving. If you don't grate it fresh, don't even bother to use it, because you won't get much flavor out of a pre-grated cheese.

Wild Mushrooms, Tasso, and Angel Hair Pasta

◆

Makes 4 main-course servings

This dish is a favorite of my friend, Joe Cahn, founder and proprietor of the New Orleans School of Cooking, culinarian, and general all-'round character. The secret to this dish is using as many varieties of wild mushrooms as you can. The wilder, the wilder.

4 cups assorted fresh wild
    mushrooms, such as chanterelles,
    shiitakes, or portobellos
1 tablespoon olive oil
3 tablespoons plus 1 teaspoon
    Emeril's Creole Seasoning
    (page 3), in all
½ cup chopped tasso (see Note)

¼ cup chopped green onions
2 tablespoons minced shallots
1 tablespoon minced garlic
2 cups heavy cream
1 pound angel hair pasta
Coarsely grated fresh Parmesan
    cheese

1. Place the mushrooms in a large bowl and toss with the oil and 3 tablespoons of the Creole seasoning.

2. Heat a large heavy dry skillet over high heat until very hot. Add the mushrooms, cover and cook for 2 minutes. Uncover and cook, shaking and tossing the skillet, for 2 minutes. Add the tasso, green onions, shallots, and garlic and toss well. Stir in the cream and simmer for 5 minutes.

3. Cook the pasta in a large pot of boiling salted water according to package directions. Drain. Fold in the pasta and the remaining 1 teaspoon Creole Seasoning and heat for 2 minutes. Makes about 7 cups.

4. To serve, mound 1¾ cups of angel hair, mushrooms, and tasso into each of 4 shallow bowls. Top with Parmesan cheese.

Note: Tasso is a well-seasoned, smoked Cajun ham. It can be ordered by mail (page 19), or substitute another highly spiced, smoked ham.

THE LAST WORD

When working with fresh mushrooms, don't rinse them way in advance, or they'll deteriorate. For the prettiest, best-tasting mushrooms, set aside a moment to rinse them that's as close to their appearance in the recipe as possible.

Chanterelles, Crabmeat, and Fettuccine with Lemon Butter Sauce

◆

Makes 4 main-course servings

In late spring, rains cool the air north of Lake Pontchartrain and New Orleans, coaxing to life an abundance of chanterelles. Looking like a soft yellow flower, the chanterelle is a wild mushroom prized for its delicate flavor and versatility; and Louisiana is second in the world only to Germany in its production. Every spring the cycle repeats itself: The mushroom hunters descend on the fields, local chefs create lovely dishes using chanterelles picked that morning, and the lucky people who get to eat them smile a lot. This dish, with its unexpected lemony butter sauce, is just one of many ways we treat chanterelles at Emeril's.

1½ cups Lemon Butter Sauce (recipe follows)
3 tablespoons olive oil, in all
2 cups fresh chanterelles, rinsed and sliced (see The Last Word)
3 green onions, chopped
1 teaspoon minced garlic
1 teaspoon minced shallots
2 tablespoons chopped fresh basil

1 teaspoon salt
3 turns freshly ground black pepper
1 pound (2 cups) lump crabmeat, picked over for shells and cartilage
1 pound fettuccine
2 teaspoons Emeril's Creole Seasoning (page 3)

1. Prepare the Lemon Butter Sauce; set aside and keep warm.

2. Heat the remaining oil in a large skillet over high heat. When the oil is hot, add the chanterelles and sauté until the mushrooms are just tender, for about 1 minute. Add the green onions, garlic, shallots, basil, salt, and pepper, and cook until the vegetables start turning translucent, for about 2 minutes. Cook the fettuccine in a large pot of boiling salted water according to package directions. Drain the pasta in a colander.

3. Add the crabmeat and pasta and shake the skillet or toss gently to avoid breaking up the lumps of crabmeat. Sauté for 1 minute.

4. Carefully stir in the Lemon Butter Sauce, reduce the heat to medium, and cook just until the sauce is heated through, for about 1 minute. Remove from the heat. Makes about 4 cups.

5. To serve, get down your best pasta bowls and allow 1 cup of pasta per portion, topped with sauce (including plenty of chanterelles and crabmeat). Sprinkle the rim of each bowl with ½ teaspoon Creole seasoning.

LEMON BUTTER SAUCE

◆

Makes about 1½ cups

1 cup dry white wine
3 lemons, peeled and quartered
2 tablespoons minced garlic
1 tablespoon minced shallots
1 teaspoon salt
3 turns freshly ground black pepper
1 dash Worcestershire sauce

1 dash hot pepper sauce
½ cup heavy cream
½ pound (2 sticks) unsalted butter, cut up, at room temperature
1 tablespoon finely chopped fresh parsley

1. Heat a large nonreactive skillet over high heat. When the skillet is hot, add the wine, lemons, garlic, and shallots. Cook for 3 minutes, breaking up and mashing the lemons with a wire whisk. Stir in the salt, pepper, Worcestershire, and hot sauce and cook until the mixture is somewhat syrupy, for about 3 minutes. Stir in the cream and cook for 1 minute.

2. Over low heat, whisk in the butter a few pats at a time. When all of the butter has been added, remove from the heat, but continue whisking until all of the butter is incorporated into the sauce.

3. Strain the sauce, pressing all of the liquid into a bowl. Stir in the parsley. Serve immediately, or keep warm for a few minutes until ready to use.

Portobello Mushrooms, Angel Hair Pasta, and Fresh Tomato Sauce

◆

Makes 4 first-course servings

If you make only one dish from this book, make this one. It's not complicated and doesn't take much time to prepare, but more important, it's a *must* just for the taste of portobello mushrooms. They're tender, rich in flavor, and remind me of a succulent veal steak.

Mushroom hunts in Louisiana are legendary: Every spring, groups of mushroom aficionados, both professional and amateur, comb the woods of Covington and Abita Springs in search of these treasures. One bite and you'll understand just why they're considered so precious.

2 cups Fresh Tomato Sauce
   (recipe follows)
½ pound angel hair pasta
½ cup all-purpose flour
1 tablespoon Emeril's Creole
   Seasoning (page 3)

¼ cup olive oil
4 portobello mushrooms, each about
   4 to 5 inches in diameter, rinsed
   and stemmed
½ cup coarsely grated fresh
   Parmesan cheese

1. Prepare the Fresh Tomato Sauce, and keep warm.

2. Meanwhile, combine the flour with the Creole Seasoning until thoroughly blended. Dredge the mushrooms thoroughly in the seasoned flour, shaking off any excess.

3. Heat the remaining oil in a large skillet over high heat. When the oil is hot and almost smoking, add the mushrooms, top side first, and sauté them until golden brown, for about 1 minute on each side. Remove the mushrooms from the skillet.

4. Cook the pasta in a large pot of boiling salted water according to package directions. Drain the pasta in a colander.

5. To serve, mound ½ cup of angel hair in each of 4 pasta bowls. Place 1 mushroom, top side up, on each portion of pasta. Nap with ½ cup of the sauce, and sprinkle with 2 tablespoons of the Parmesan.

FRESH TOMATO SAUCE

◆

Makes about 2 cups

1 tablespoon olive oil
⅓ cup chopped onions
2 tablespoons minced garlic
2 teaspoons salt
½ teaspoon white pepper
2 cups peeled, seeded, and chopped
  Italian plum tomatoes

¼ cup chopped fresh basil
½ cup Basic Chicken Stock
  (page 6)
18 turns freshly ground black
  pepper
2 tablespoons unsalted butter

1. Heat the oil in a large nonreactive skillet over high heat. Add the onions, garlic, salt, and white pepper and sauté for 3 minutes. Add the tomatoes and basil and cook, stirring occasionally, for 3 minutes.

2. Stir in the stock and the black pepper and simmer for 2 minutes. Fold in the butter and as soon as it begins to melt, remove the skillet from the heat. Continue to stir in the butter until it's thoroughly incorporated. Serve immediately or prepare without the butter. Store, refrigerated, in an airtight container for up to 2 days. Reheat in a saucepan over low heat. When the sauce is at a simmer, fold in the butter and proceed.

Chile Pepper Lobster over Saffron Linguine

◆

Makes 4 main-course servings

This dish is typical of how we might eat lobster in New Orleans. It's a knockout flavor combination, and great for company because it's both elegant and spicy. We never had lobster like this in New England; it would probably be banned in Boston and considered racy in Fall River. To make it even racier, I always drink champagne with my Chile Pepper Lobster.

1 cup olive oil
2 tablespoons peeled, seeded, and chopped Italian plum tomatoes
2 tablespoons chopped onions
2 tablespoons chopped fresh cilantro
2 teaspoons minced garlic
1 tablespoon chili powder
1 teaspoon crushed red pepper
1 teaspoon ground cumin
1 teaspoon salt

4 turns freshly ground black pepper
4 servings Saffron Linguine (recipe follows)
1 pound cooked lobster meat (from 3 live 1-pound lobsters), cut into ½-inch pieces
¼ cup coarsely grated fresh Parmesan cheese
¼ cup chopped green onions

1. Combine the oil, tomatoes, onions, cilantro, garlic, chili powder, red pepper, cumin, salt, and black pepper in a large skillet over medium heat and cook for 6 minutes. Turn off the heat and allow the mixture to steep for 10 or 15 minutes.

2. Prepare the Saffron Linguine, and cover to keep warm.

3. Turn the heat back up to high under the skillet, and when the mixture bubbles, add the lobster. Cook, shaking the skillet, for 3 minutes. Remove from the heat. Makes about 2 cups.

4. To serve, divide the pasta into 4 portions and mound it in 4 shallow bowls. Add ½ cup of the lobster and sauce, and sprinkle each serving with 1 tablespoon of the Parmesan and 1 tablespoon of the green onions.

SAFFRON LINGUINE

◆

Pasta side dish for 4

8 cups water
½ teaspoon saffron threads
½ teaspoon ground turmeric

½ teaspoon salt
1 tablespoon olive oil
½ pound linguine or other thin pasta

1. Combine the water with the saffron, turmeric, salt, and oil in a large pot over high heat and bring to a boil. Continue to boil for 5 minutes.

2. Add the pasta and cook for 4 to 6 minutes. Remove from the heat and drain.

Oysta Pasta with Caviar

◆

Makes 4 main-course servings

If you make this with Beluga caviar, the very pricey roe of the sturgeon, be sure to make it for someone who's important to you. On the other hand, you could substitute a less expensive variety of caviar, such as Louisiana choupiquet or American golden. Either way, it's delicious, and NNO all the way.

2 cups heavy cream
½ cup green onions
1 tablespoon minced garlic
3 tablespoons Emeril's Creole
  Seasoning (page 3)
½ teaspoon salt
2 turns freshly ground black pepper

40 freshly shucked oysters with
  their liquor
½ pound angel hair pasta
1 ounce Beluga caviar, or other
  caviar of your choice
¼ cup chopped green onions

1. Combine the cream, green onions, garlic, and Creole Seasoning in a large skillet over high heat. Bring to a boil, stirring occasionally. Reduce the heat and simmer for 3 minutes.

2. Stir in the salt and pepper, add the oysters and their liquor, and shake the skillet until the liquid begins to simmer, for about 1½ minutes.

3. Cook the pasta in 2 quarts boiling salted water according to package directions. Drain the pasta in a colander. Add the pasta and toss gently, just until the edges of the oysters start to curl, for about 2 minutes. Remove from the heat.

4. Serve on plates or in shallow bowls and top with a dollop of caviar. Sprinkle each serving and the rim of the plate with 1 tablespoon of the chopped green onions.

NNO Pasta

◆

Makes 4 main-course servings

Jambalaya/pasta is a very popular feel-good dish in New Orleans. It's not exactly Italian, and it's not exactly Cajun, but it certainly is New New Orleans. Here's my version.

½ cup boned, skinned and julienned chicken breasts (about 4 ounces)
2½ teaspoons Emeril's Creole Seasoning (page 3), in all
1 tablespoon olive oil
2 ounces chopped andouille or chorizo sausage
½ pound peeled and deveined medium shrimp

¼ cup chopped green onions
1 tablespoon minced garlic
1½ cups heavy cream
¼ teaspoon Worcestershire sauce
¼ teaspoon hot pepper sauce
½ teaspoon salt
½ cup coarsely grated fresh Parmesan cheese, in all
½ pound fettuccine

1. Toss the chicken strips with 1 teaspoon Creole Seasoning.

2. Heat 1 tablespoon oil in a large skillet over high heat. Add the seasoned chicken and sauté, shaking the skillet occasionally, for about 1 minute. Add the andouille and cook, shaking the skillet and stirring, for 1 minute. Add the shrimp and the remaining 1½ teaspoons Creole Seasoning and sauté for 1 minute. Stir in the green onions, garlic, and cream and cook for 2 minutes. Stir in the Worcestershire, hot pepper sauce, salt, and ¼ cup of the Parmesan and simmer for 3 minutes.

3. Cook the pasta in a large pot of boiling salted water according to package directions. Drain in a colander. Add the cooked fettuccine and toss until the pasta is heated through and thoroughly blended with the sauce, for about 1 minute. Remove from the heat. Makes about 5 cups.

4. To serve, allow 1¼ cups per portion in pasta bowls. Sprinkle each portion with the remaining Parmesan, 1 tablespoon per serving.

Hilda's Portuguese Ravioli with Creole Sauce

◆

Makes 4 main-course servings

This recipe evolved from a salt cod dish my mother used to make. She would soak the dried fish and then simmer it for hours with potatoes and herbs in a wonderful tomato sauce, and serve it at Portuguese *festas,* since it was considered very special. If I was a good boy, Mom might make it for me even if it wasn't a holiday. The happy memories of those times made me want to reproduce the flavors, and so I created this dish for the restaurant, which I topped off with a fine Creole sauce as a salute to New Orleans, my adopted home. In Portugal, salt cod is known as *bacalhau,* in Spain it's *bacalao;* and it's an important staple in almost every Mediterranean country. The cod must be soaked in milk for two days to get rid of the salt that preserves the fish. You can purchase salt cod in Italian, Spanish, and Asian food stores. Use wonton skins for the ravioli.

6 ounces salt cod
2 quarts milk, in all
2⅔ cups Creole Sauce
   (recipe follows)
32 wonton wrappers
3 tablespoons olive oil
½ cup chopped onions
¼ cup chopped green onions
¼ cup chopped celery
¼ cup chopped green bell peppers
2 tablespoons minced garlic

1 cup finely diced peeled potatoes,
   boiled until tender, and drained
½ cup peeled, seeded, and chopped
   Italian plum tomatoes (about 2)
1 teaspoon crushed red pepper
3 turns freshly ground black pepper
¼ cup chopped fresh parsley
1 large egg, lightly beaten
6 cups salted water
½ cup coarsely grated fresh
   Parmesan cheese

1. Two days before serving, place the salt cod in a bowl and cover with 1 quart of the milk to soak. Refrigerate for 24 hours, pour off the milk and discard it, and rinse the cod thoroughly under cold water. Soak the cod in the remaining 1 quart milk for another 24 hours, refrigerated. Repeat the rinsing process and dry the cod thoroughly. Cut the fish into a fine julienne. Makes about 1 cup.

2. Prepare the Creole Sauce, and keep warm.

3. While the sauce is simmering, set out the wonton wrappers and cover with a clean, damp cloth.

4. Heat the oil in a large skillet over high heat. Add the onions, green onions, celery, bell peppers, and garlic and sauté for 2 minutes. Stir in the potatoes, tomatoes, red pepper, black pepper, and parsley and stir-fry for 3 minutes. Stir in the salt cod and stir-fry for 5 minutes. Remove from the heat. Makes 2 cups filling.

5. Separate the wonton wrappers until you have the thinnest possible skin, and brush with beaten egg. Mound 2 tablespoons of the filling on each of 16 wrappers and cover with the other 16. Crimp the edges with a fork.

6. Bring the salted water to a boil in a large deep skillet over medium-high heat. Add the ravioli and simmer until the dough is cooked, for about 5 minutes. Remove from the water with a slotted spoon or spatula.

7. To serve, place 4 ravioli on each of 4 dinner plates. Cover with ⅔ cup of the sauce and top with 2 tablespoons Parmesan.

CREOLE SAUCE

◆

Makes 2⅔ cups

2 tablespoons olive oil
½ cup chopped onions
½ cup chopped celery
½ cup chopped green bell peppers
2 tablespoons minced garlic
2 cups peeled and chopped Italian
   plum tomatoes
¼ cup chopped fresh basil
1 tablespoon plus 1 teaspoon
   chopped fresh oregano
2 teaspoons chopped fresh thyme

2 teaspoons Emeril's Creole
   Seasoning (page 3)
1 teaspoon salt
½ teaspoon cayenne pepper
4 turns freshly ground black pepper
2 teaspoons Worcestershire sauce
3 cups Basic Chicken Stock
   (page 6)
½ cup chopped green onions
8 tablespoons (1 stick) unsalted
   butter, at room temperature

1. Heat the oil in a saucepan over high heat. Add the onions, celery, bell peppers, and garlic and sauté for 1 minute. Stir in the tomatoes, basil, oregano, thyme, Creole Seasoning, salt, cayenne, and black pepper and sauté for 1 minute.

2. Add the Worcestershire and the stock and bring to a boil. Stir in the green onions and cook over high heat for 12 minutes. Turn off the heat and swirl in the butter until thoroughly incorporated.

Shrimp and Artichoke Risotto

◆

Makes 4 main-course servings

I love risotto because of its soft, creamy texture and its versatility; the potential variations are almost endless. You must use Arborio rice—don't even think of substituting any other kind—a special short-grain rice grown in the Po valley region of northern Italy. You can find it in supermarkets, specialty, and ethnic food shops. This risotto reflects New Orleans's love for both shrimp and the artichoke, and my own love for the creamiest risotto ever—with the addition of a little cream.

1 tablespoon olive oil
½ cup chopped onions
2 tablespoons minced garlic
¼ cup chopped fresh basil
2 cups Arborio rice
4 cups Shrimp Stock (page 10)
1 tablespoon softened unsalted butter
½ lemon, juice only
2 teaspoons salt
10 turns freshly ground black pepper

½ cup chopped green onions
2 cups quartered fresh artichoke hearts (page 15), cooked until tender
1 teaspoon Emeril's Creole Seasoning (page 3)
½ pound peeled medium shrimp, halved
½ cup heavy cream
¾ cup coarsely grated fresh Parmesan, in all

1. Heat the oil in a large nonreactive skillet over high heat. Add the onions, garlic, and basil, and sauté for 3 minutes. Stir in the rice and sauté for 1 minute.

2. Add the stock, butter, lemon juice, salt, and pepper and cook, stirring, for about 3 minutes. Fold in the green onions. Add the artichoke hearts and Creole Seasoning and bring to a boil. Reduce the heat and simmer, stirring often, for about 10 minutes. Fold in the shrimp and simmer for 2 minutes; stir in the cream and simmer for 3 minutes. Fold in ½ cup of the Parmesan and turn off the heat. Makes 8 cups.

3. Serve in bowls, 2 cups per serving, sprinkled with 1 tablespoon Parmesan.

Duck and Pumpkin Risotto with Spicy Roasted Pumpkin Seeds and Duck Cracklings

◆

Makes 4 main-course or 8 first-course servings

Crackling, or cracklin', a Southern specialty, is rendered pork fat and crispy-fried skin. In this whimsical risotto, crackling gets an upwardly mobile touch as rendered duck skin, echoing the flavor of the duck in the dish.

½ roast duck (page 210), including the skin
1 tablespoon olive oil
2 cups diced cooked pumpkin
¼ cup chopped onions
1 tablespoon minced garlic
¼ cup chopped fresh basil
2 cups Arborio rice
3 cups Duck or Brown Chicken Stock (page 7)
1½ teaspoons salt

8 turns freshly ground black pepper
1 tablespoon softened unsalted butter
½ cup heavy cream
½ cup coarsely grated fresh Parmesan cheese
½ cup Spicy Roasted Pumpkin Seeds (page 14)
4 or 8 tablespoons coarsely grated fresh Parmesan cheese

1. Remove the duck skin and cut it into a julienne; you'll have about 1 cup. Render the skin in a large skillet over high heat, stir-frying until crisp and brown, for about 6 minutes. Remove from the skillet and drain on paper towels.

2. Shred the duck meat from the bones; you'll have about 2 cups.

3. Heat the oil in the same skillet with a bit of duck fat over high heat. Add the pumpkin, onions, garlic, and basil, and sauté for 1 minute. Stir in the rice and sauté, stirring, for 1 minute. Stir in the stock, salt, and pepper and bring to a boil. Reduce the heat to medium and stir in the butter. Simmer until the rice is tender and creamy, for about 18 minutes. Fold in the duck, cream, and Parmesan and simmer for 3 to 4 minutes. Remove from the heat. Makes 8 cups.

4. To serve, allow 2 cups risotto each for 4 main-course servings; 1 cup each for 8 first-course servings. Serve in bowls and sprinkle with cracklings, pumpkin seeds, and Parmesan.

CHAPTER 5

Greens and Other Colors:
Salads and Dressings

A salad should never be just a dish of greens. Every salad should sparkle with flavor, cleanse the palate, and beef up the appetite. All of my salads are different from one another; each has its own distinct personality. There are warm salads, cold salads, salads for first courses, mains, and sides. There is a jicama salad, a fried tortellini salad, and two potato salads. All are definitely New and New Orleans in character, a light palette of flavors and local seasonings.

My early associations with salad were always timid variations on a theme with iceberg lettuce. When I had my first encounter with romaine via a Caesar salad, I was blown away. Here was a salad with character! A lettuce with real flavor! I quickly became obsessed with rooting out and experimenting with different greens, but the variety in those days was limited. It's only been in the last fifteen years or so that unusual and flavorful greens really became fashionable and more readily available to the home cook.

I've used a variety of greens in the salads on these pages, including frisée, which looks like curly endive, mâche, arugula or rocket, radicchio, spinach, watercress, mustard greens, oak leaf, and Bibb, to name just a few. Teamed with Louisiana goodies like fresh oysters or shrimp, andouille sausage, and fresh wild mushrooms, and tossed with dressings such as Vodka Vinaigrette, Lemon Pepper Vinaigrette, Pernod Buttermilk Dressing, Warm Andouille Dressing, and Fire~Roasted Corn and Onion Dressing, they really exemplify a trend toward new, new, exciting salads.

Warm Greens with Emeril's Herb Vinaigrette

◆

Makes 4 salad servings

A simple salad can be pure heaven. Just combine fresh, tasty greens with a good vinaigrette and you'll know this is true. This one works as a side salad, or can be coupled first with Herbed Pan Roast of Salmon (page 175), then drizzled with my Herb Vinaigrette.

1 tablespoon olive oil
5 cups assorted greens (combine
    frisée, spinach, arugula, or other
    salad greens) (see Note)
⅔ cup water

½ teaspoon salt
½ teaspoon white pepper
1 cup Emeril's Herb Vinaigrette
    (recipe follows)

1. Heat the oil in a large skillet over medium-high heat. Add the greens, water, salt, and pepper and heat, stirring gently, just until the greens wilt, for about 2 minutes. Remove from the heat.

2. If you're preparing the Herbed Pan Roast of Salmon, finish according to that recipe's directions. If you're serving this as a side salad for another dish, toss the greens with some of the vinaigrette just before serving.

Note: To remove dirt from greens, place them in a colander or large strainer and rinse them with cool water, preferably with your sink's spray attachments, if you have one. Spread the greens on a dish towel or several paper towels and gently pat them dry. Or use a salad spinner, if you have one.

EMERIL'S HERB VINAIGRETTE

◆

Makes about 1 cup

This dressing is wonderful on almost any green salad; don't feel you have to limit it to just the Warm Greens.

¼ cup tarragon, basil, or assorted
    herb vinegar
2 tablespoons minced shallots
1 tablespoon minced garlic
¼ cup assorted chopped fresh herbs
    (combine basil, tarragon, cilantro,
    parsley, oregano, or whatever
    herbs you prefer)

1 teaspoon salt
15 turns freshly ground black
    pepper
¾ cup olive oil

Combine the vinegar, shallots, garlic, herbs, salt, and pepper in a bowl. Slowly whisk in the oil and continue whisking until thoroughly emulsified. Store, refrigerated, in an airtight container for 3 days. Whisk before serving.

Greens and Fried Oysters with Pernod Buttermilk Dressing

◆

Makes 4 first-course salads

I have lots of great memories that involve the Brennans, the well-known New Orleans restaurateurs and my former employers at Commander's Palace. One of these memories has to do with our out-of-town jaunts to participate in various benefits and functions. Whenever we had some free time on these trips, we would run to the top restaurants in the area to sample their food. Have you ever tried eating a full meal in four different restaurants in three hours? Dick Brennan taught me the secret to quick digestion: Pernod. Consumed either neat or over ice, this anise-flavored liqueur seems to do the trick. Now, straight Pernod is not for everybody. But combined with the right ingredients almost no one would turn it down, and I haven't yet heard anyone complain about the Pernod dressing in this unusual salad.

1 large egg
½ cup olive oil
¼ cup buttermilk
1 tablespoon minced garlic
¼ cup chopped green onions
½ cup coarsely grated fresh
   Parmesan cheese
1 tablespoon freshly squeezed lemon
   juice

1 teaspoon salt
3 turns freshly ground black pepper
1 tablespoon Pernod
24 Fried Oysters (page 36)
4 cups assorted greens (arugula,
   frisée, radicchio, watercress,
   mustard, or other salad greens)
½ cup roasted pecan pieces
   (page 14)

1. Beat the egg in a large bowl. Slowly whisk in the oil, then the buttermilk. Continue whisking as you add the garlic, green onions, ¼ cup of the Parmesan, lemon juice, salt, pepper, and Pernod. Whisk until thoroughly emulsified. Makes about 1 cup.

2. Prepare the Fried Oysters and keep warm.

3. Add the greens to the dressing in the bowl and toss. Add the pecan pieces and toss again.

4. To serve, mound about 1 cup salad on each of 4 plates. Arrange 5 oysters around each mound of greens and place another oyster on top. Sprinkle each with 1 tablespoon of the remaining Parmesan cheese.

Warm Frisée Corn Salad

◆

Makes 3 cups, about 4 salad servings

Serve this salad with almost any main dish in this book, but be sure to try it with Roasted Shrimp with Roasted Red Pepper Sauce (page 183).

1 tablespoon olive oil
1 cup fresh corn kernels, scraped from 1 or 2 cobs
⅓ cup coarsely chopped onions
1 teaspoon salt
6 turns freshly ground black pepper

1 head frisée (or 1 pound fresh spinach), core removed and leaves pulled apart
¼ cup chopped red bell peppers
¼ cup water

1. Heat the oil over high heat. When the oil is hot, add the corn, onions, salt, and pepper and sauté, shaking the skillet occasionally, for 3 minutes.

2. Add the frisée, bell peppers, and water and cook to wilt the frisée, for about 2 minutes. Remove from the heat and serve warm.

Fried Eggplant Salad with Sweet Corn Dressing

◆

Makes 4 salad servings

This salad has a wonderful blend of flavors—the sweet coolness of the corn dressing playing off the spicy fried eggplant—both of which are New Orleans favorites.

2 cups Sweet Corn Dressing
   (recipe follows), in all
½ cup all-purpose flour
2 tablespoons Emeril's Creole
   Seasoning (page 3), in all
1 large egg
½ cup milk
1 cup yellow cornmeal
1 large eggplant, peeled, sliced, and
   cut into ½-inch-thick sticks (about
   64 sticks)

½ cup olive oil
1 teaspoon salt
8 cups assorted greens (endive,
   arugula, radicchio, or other salad
   greens)
½ cup coarsely grated fresh
   Parmesan cheese

1. Prepare the Sweet Corn Dressing, and set aside.

2. Combine the flour with 1 tablespoon Creole Seasoning in a bowl. Beat the egg with the milk in another bowl. Combine the cornmeal with the remaining 1 tablespoon Creole Seasoning in a third bowl.

3. Dredge the eggplant sticks in the seasoned flour, then the egg wash, then the seasoned cornmeal, shaking off any excess.

4. Heat the oil in a large skillet over medium-high heat until very hot. Add the eggplant and fry, turning occasionally, until crisp and golden brown, for about 5 minutes. Remove the eggplant with a slotted spoon and drain on paper towels. Sprinkle evenly with the salt.

5. Toss the greens thoroughly with 1 cup of the dressing.

6. To serve, mound 2 cups of the salad in the center of each plate. Arrange about 16 eggplant sticks on top, and drizzle the eggplant with the remaining ¼ cup dressing per salad.

SWEET CORN DRESSING

◆

Makes 2 cups

2 ears blanched fresh corn (page 16), kernels only (1 cup)
4 teaspoons minced shallots
2 teaspoons minced garlic
2 large eggs

2 teaspoons honey
1 teaspoon white vinegar
1 teaspoon salt
6 turns freshly ground black pepper
1 cup olive oil

Purée the corn, shallots, garlic, eggs, honey, vinegar, salt, and pepper in a food processor or blender. Slowly stream in the oil until thoroughly emulsified. Serve immediately or store, refrigerated, in an airtight container for up to 2 days. Whisk before serving.

Wilted Wild Mushroom Salad

◆

Makes 2 cups, 4 salad servings

It's surprising how a simple mixture of musky wild mushrooms, green onions, and red peppers can please the palate so completely. Its earthy freshness seems to work well with the unusual fusion of flavors in Lobster with Champagne Vanilla Sauce (page 192). And just a little goes a long way.

2 tablespoons olive oil
4 cups assorted fresh wild
  mushrooms, such as shiitakes,
  chanterelles, oysters, black
  trumpets, porcini, morels, or
  whatever fresh wild mushrooms
  are available

½ teaspoon salt
½ teaspoon white pepper
⅓ cup chopped green onions
2 tablespoons finely diced red bell
  peppers

1. Heat the oil in a large skillet over high heat. When the oil is hot, add the mushrooms, salt, and pepper, and sauté until the mushrooms are wilted, for about 2 minutes. Remove from the heat.

2. Turn the mushrooms into a bowl, add the green onions and bell peppers, and toss until thoroughly blended. Serve at room temperature.

Fried Wild Mushroom Salad with Wild Mushroom Dressing

◆

Makes 4 salad servings

A salad should be a celebration of textures as well as flavors, and this one rings in on all levels. The crispness of the fried mushrooms plays against the silky greens; the grainy bite of the Parmesan with the creamy mushroom dressing. Altogether, it's a symphony. If I do say so.

1 cup Wild Mushroom Salad
   Dressing (recipe follows)
1 cup all-purpose flour
2 tablespoons Emeril's Creole
   Seasoning (page 3), in all
1 cup bread crumbs (page 17)
2 large eggs
⅓ cup milk
3 cups assorted fresh wild
   mushrooms, such as chanterelles,
   morels, shiitakes, and porcinis

½ cup olive oil
8 cups assorted greens (combine
   Bibb, mâche, frisée, radicchio,
   watercress, arugula, or other salad
   greens)
½ cup, plus 2 tablespoons coarsely
   grated fresh Parmesan cheese,
   in all
4 turns freshly ground black pepper,
   in all

1. Prepare the Wild Mushroom Salad Dressing, and set aside.

2. In a small bowl, combine the flour and 1 tablespoon Creole Seasoning. In another bowl, combine the bread crumbs with the remaining 1 tablespoon Creole Seasoning. In a third bowl, beat the eggs with the milk.

3. Stem the mushrooms and dredge them in the seasoned flour, dip them in the egg wash, then dredge them in the seasoned bread crumbs, coating each mushroom thoroughly.

4. Heat the oil in a large skillet over high heat. When the oil is hot, fry the mushrooms in two batches until golden, for about 2 to 3 minutes. Remove them and drain on paper towels.

5. Toss the greens in a salad bowl with the dressing, the fried mushrooms, and 2 tablespoons of the Parmesan.

6. To serve, divide the salad into 4 bowls and grind 1 turn of black pepper over each. Sprinkle each salad with 2 tablespoons of the Parmesan.

WILD MUSHROOM SALAD DRESSING

◆

Makes 1 cup

½ cup olive oil, in all
½ cup sliced fresh wild mushrooms,
   such as chanterelles, shiitakes,
   oysters, black trumpets, or other
   fresh wild mushrooms
1 large egg
2 tablespoons dry sherry
1 tablespoon minced shallots

1 tablespoon minced garlic
1 tablespoon coarsely grated fresh
   Parmesan cheese
1 tablespoon freshly squeezed lemon
   juice
1 teaspoon salt
3 turns freshly ground black pepper

1. Heat ¼ cup of the oil in a medium skillet over high heat. When the oil is hot, add the mushrooms and sauté, stirring occasionally, for 3 minutes. Remove from the heat.

2. Turn the mushrooms and oil into a food processor or blender, add the egg and purée for 30 seconds. Add the sherry, shallots, garlic, Parmesan, lemon juice, salt, and pepper and purée for 15 seconds. With the machine running, stream in the remaining ¼ cup oil and process until thoroughly blended. Serve immediately.

Asparagus and Seared Shrimp with Lemon Pepper Vinaigrette

◆

Makes 4 main-course salads

Here's an unusual combination for a salad, one that's hearty enough to be the meal itself. It's easy to put together, but there is one rule you must follow. Use only *fresh* asparagus and shrimp.

1 cup Lemon Pepper Vinaigrette (recipe follows)
16 large shrimp, peeled except for the tails
2 teaspoons Emeril's Creole Seasoning (page 3)

4 cups assorted greens (Bibb, mâche, frisée, arugula, watercress, radicchio, or other salad greens)
16 spears large fresh asparagus, peeled and blanched (page 15)

1. Prepare the Lemon Pepper Vinaigrette, and set aside.

2. Toss the shrimp in a bowl with the Creole Seasoning. Heat a large heavy dry skillet over high heat. When the skillet is hot, add the shrimp and sear them for 3 minutes on each side.

3. To serve, mound 1 cup of the greens on each plate and fan 4 asparagus spears from the center. Spoon ¼ cup of the Lemon Pepper Vinaigrette in 1 tablespoon pools between the asparagus. Using 4 shrimp per plate, place 1 on each pool between the asparagus spokes.

LEMON PEPPER VINAIGRETTE

◆

Makes 1 cup

1 large egg
2 tablespoons freshly squeezed lemon juice
2 tablespoons chopped fresh parsley

1 tablespoon Roasted Peppercorns (page 14)
1 tablespoon Dijon mustard
½ teaspoon salt
¾ cup olive oil

Combine the egg, lemon juice, parsley, peppercorns, mustard, and salt in a food processor and turn on the machine. Slowly stream in the oil and continue to process until the mixture becomes a smooth emulsion. Serve immediately.

Southwest Shrimp with Fire~Roasted Corn and Onion Dressing

◆

Makes 4 main-course salads

The intense flavors of the American Southwest suit the New Orleans palate to a tee, and the ones that make this salad special are no exception. I especially enjoy preparing the dressing that goes with it, because I find the smell of roasting corn irresistible.

1 ear Fire~Roasted Corn (page 16), kernels only (½ cup)
1 small Fire~Roasted Onion (page 16), peeled, cut into quarters, then eighths
½ cup olive oil
2 tablespoons distilled white vinegar
2 tablespoons chopped fresh cilantro
1 tablespoon plus 1 teaspoon Emeril's Southwest Seasoning (page 3), in all

¼ teaspoon salt
2 turns freshly ground black pepper
4 cups assorted greens (combine mâche, arugula, frisée, radicchio, red oak, or other salad greens)
16 peeled and deveined medium shrimp (about 1 pound)

1. Heat a large heavy skillet over high heat until very hot and smoking, for about 3 minutes. Add the corn and onion and sear, shaking the skillet and stirring until the corn and onions are brown, for about 3 minutes. (The corn will pop a little, so don't stick your face in the skillet.) Turn off the heat but leave the skillet on the hot burner.

2. With the heat off, add the oil, vinegar, cilantro, 1 teaspoon Southwest Seasoning, salt, and pepper and stir for 2 minutes. Makes 1¼ cups.

3. Place the greens in a large bowl and pour the dressing over, leaving a residue of the oil in the skillet.

4. Sprinkle the shrimp with the remaining 1 tablespoon Southwest Seasoning. Turn the heat up to high under the same skillet. When the oil residue is hot, add the shrimp and sear them until brown, for about 3 minutes on each side. Remove from the heat. Add the shrimp to the greens and the dressing and toss well.

5. To serve, divide the salad among 4 plates or shallow bowls, allowing 4 shrimp for each portion.

Arugula with Cilantro Oil, Peppered Goat Cheese, and Roasted Walnuts

◆

Makes 4 salad servings

It might surprise you to know that arugula grows well in and around the 'burbs of New Orleans. One day we had some fresh, pungent arugula, cilantro oil, and goat cheese on hand, so I put together this simple but astoundingly wonderful salad.

½ cup Cilantro Oil (page 5)
1 cup roasted walnuts (page 14)
10 ounces goat cheese, such as Montrachet
60 peppercorns, roasted and cracked (about 2 tablespoons) (see The Last Word)

2 tablespoons chopped fresh cilantro
8 cups arugula
½ teaspoon salt
12 turns freshly ground black pepper

1. Prepare the Cilantro Oil and the roasted walnuts; set aside.

2. Form the goat cheese into a log about 2 inches thick. Combine the cracked pepper and cilantro on a flat plate and roll the log in the mixture until it's completely covered. Wrap in plastic and place the log in the freezer until firm, for about 10 to 15 minutes. Remove the plastic and slice into 12 rounds, or coins.

3. In a large bowl, toss the arugula with the Cilantro Oil. Season with the salt and pepper and toss again.

4. To serve, place 2 cups of the arugula salad in the center of each of 4 dinner plates. Sprinkle each with ¼ cup walnuts and arrange 3 rounds of peppered goat cheese around the greens.

THE LAST WORD

To roast the peppercorns, see page 14. Allow them to cool for about 3 minutes, then crack them with a mallet or heavy skillet, or grind them in a pepper mill.

Spinach and Goat Cheese with Warm Andouille Dressing

◆

Makes 4 salad servings

This salad has been on our menu since the day we opened, and I expect it to remain there. Everyone seems to love it. The teaming of spinach and goat cheese is a worldly trend, but the spicy andouille dressing brings it back down home—in a fresh, new way.

4 cups fresh spinach, stemmed	Warm Andouille Dressing (recipe follows)
1 cup thinly sliced red onions	½ cup (4½ ounces) crumbled goat
2 pinches salt	cheese, such as Montrachet

1. In a large bowl, combine the spinach, onions, and salt.

2. Prepare the Warm Andouille Dressing, add it to the spinach, and toss well.

3. Serve immediately. Divide the salad into 4 servings, arrange on dinner plates, and top each with 2 tablespoons of the goat cheese.

WARM ANDOUILLE DRESSING

◆

Makes 1⅓ cups

4 ounces finely chopped andouille sausage	2 tablespoons balsamic vinegar
1 tablespoon minced shallots	1 teaspoon sugar
1 tablespoon minced garlic	½ teaspoon salt
¾ cup olive oil	4 turns freshly ground black pepper

Heat a medium dry skillet over high heat. Add the andouille and sauté for 1½ minutes. Add the shallots and garlic and sauté for 1 minute. Add the oil and vinegar, cook for 1 minute, and remove from the heat. Stir in the sugar, salt, and pepper. Serve immediately. Refrigerate any remaining dressing.

Stuffed Baked Radicchio with Sun-Dried Tomato Vinaigrette

◆

Makes 4 first-course salads

Lovely heads of red radicchio are at their best when picked young, small, and tender; that's when they're perfect for this dish. This unusual, exciting salad explodes with flavor at every mouthful. It's especially wonderful before a meal of meat or pasta.

½ pound goat cheese, such as
   Montrachet
1 teaspoon olive oil
1 teaspoon minced garlic
2 tablespoons minced fresh basil
½ teaspoon salt

3 turns fresh ground black pepper
4 small heads radicchio, cored ½- to
   ¾-inch deep, cores reserved
1⅓ cups Sun-Dried Tomato
   Vinaigrette (recipe follows)

1. Preheat the oven to 375°F.

2. In a bowl, combine the goat cheese, oil, garlic, basil, salt, and pepper, and blend until thoroughly incorporated. Makes ½ cup.

3. Stuff each radicchio with 2 tablespoons of the cheese mixture and place the cores on as caps. Arrange the radicchio in a pie plate, add about ¼ cup water to the bottom of the plate, and bake until tender, for about 15 to 20 minutes. Remove from the oven.

4. While the radicchio are baking, prepare the Sun-Dried Tomato Vinaigrette.

5. To serve, spread ⅓ cup of the vinaigrette on each of 4 dinner plates and top with 1 baked radicchio. Serve immediately.

SUN-DRIED TOMATO VINAIGRETTE

◆

Makes about 1⅓ cups

¼ cup balsamic vinegar
¼ cup sun-dried tomato pieces
  (page 16)
¼ cup chopped green onions
2 teaspoons minced shallots

1 teaspoon minced garlic
½ teaspoon salt
4 turns freshly ground black pepper
¾ cup olive oil

Combine the vinegar, tomatoes, green onions, shallots, garlic, salt, and pepper in a bowl. Slowly whisk in the oil until the dressing is thoroughly emulsified. Serve immediately or store, refrigerated, in an airtight container for up to 3 days. Whisk before serving.

Jícama Orange Salad

◆

Makes about 3 cups, about 4 salad servings

Jícama (pronounced "HEE-ka-ma") is a root vegetable with a fresh, applelike flavor and texture. It usually grows in tropical climates and looks something like a turnip. Crisp slices of jícama are delicious simply sprinkled with a little fresh lime juice and salt, but combined with oranges, red onions, and cilantro, as it is here, it's pure heaven. This salad is as refreshing and light as a sorbet, and it's a treat for dieters since it's fat-free and low in calories. I serve it with Piri Piri Chicken (page 201).

2 cups diced peeled jícama
  (½-inch dice)
3 peeled seedless oranges, cut into
  sections (about 1 cup)
2 tablespoons freshly squeezed
  orange juice

¼ cup finely chopped red onions
3 tablespoons finely chopped red
  bell peppers
3 tablespoons chopped fresh cilantro
½ teaspoon salt
3 turns freshly ground black pepper

Combine all of the ingredients in a bowl and toss until thoroughly blended. This can be made a day ahead and stored in the refrigerator in an airtight container.

Seared Peppered Tuna with Greens and Vodka Vinaigrette

◆

Makes 4 main-course salads

Although I love eating good sushi, I'm cautious when I'm tracking it down. I have to know where the fish is from, how fresh it is, and who's preparing it before I'll indulge. The closest I come to preparing my own sushi is this dish, which is made with fresh, top-quality tuna. The fish gets a peppery crust and is seared until the outside is just cooked. Add the greens and the vodka vinaigrette, and you have a rare combination. So to speak.

¼ cup whole black peppercorns
1 top-quality end loin yellowfin tuna
   (about 1½ to 2 pounds)
1 tablespoon Emeril's Creole
   Seasoning (page 3)
1¼ cups Vodka Vinaigrette
   (recipe follows), in all

8 cups assorted greens (combine
   Bibb, mâche, arugula, frisée,
   radicchio, red oak, or other salad
   greens)
½ teaspoon salt
6 turns freshly ground black pepper

1. Spread the peppercorns on a work surface and drag the bottom of a small saucepan over them, smashing them as you do this. Repeat about a dozen times until the pepper is coarsely cracked.

2. Sprinkle the tuna with the Creole Seasoning and then roll it in the cracked pepper, using your hands to press the pepper into and all over the loin, including the end.

3. Heat a large heavy dry skillet over high heat until very hot and smoking, for about 4 minutes. Add the tuna and sear for 3 minutes on one side, 3 minutes on the opposite side, then 2 minutes each on the remaining two sides. Remove the tuna from the skillet and refrigerate for at least 2 hours.

4. Prepare the Vodka Vinaigrette.

5. Toss the greens with the salt, pepper, and ¾ cup of the vinaigrette.

6. To serve, use a sharp knife or slicer to slice the loin of tuna into ¼- to ½-inch rounds. Heap about 2 cups of the salad in the center of each of 4 dinner plates. Place 4 slices of tuna around each salad, and drizzle the remaining vinaigrette (2 tablespoons per plate) over each.

VODKA VINAIGRETTE

◆

Makes 1¼ cups

2 tablespoons minced shallots
1 teaspoon minced garlic
½ teaspoon salt
3 turns freshly ground black pepper

¼ cup balsamic vinegar
3 tablespoons vodka
⅔ cup olive oil

Combine all of the ingredients in a small bowl and whisk until blended. Serve immediately or store, refrigerated, in an airtight container for up to 2 days. Whisk before serving.

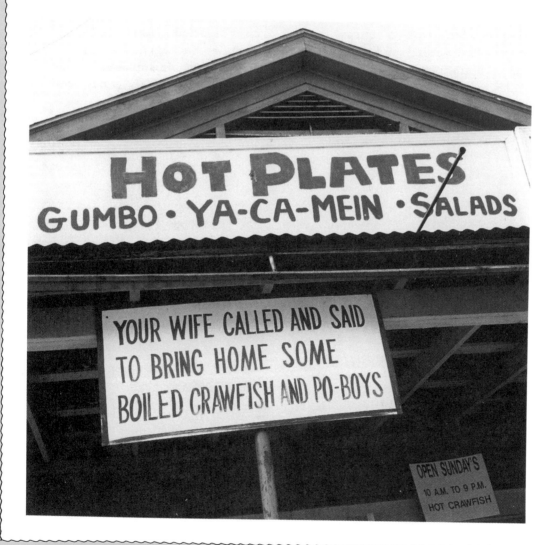

Greens with Fried Tortellini and Prosciutto

◆

Makes 4 main-course salads

If you're adventurous—as I'm sure you are—you'll be excited by the surprising mix of textures in this hearty salad. Fried tortellini, bursting with cheese, are mouthfuls of delight, coupled with herbed prosciutto and peppery greens.

4 tablespoons olive oil, in all
1 onion, halved and sliced
¼ cup julienned prosciutto,
    ⅛-inch-wide strips (2 ounces)
¼ cup peeled, seeded, and chopped
    Italian plum tomatoes
2 tablespoons chopped fresh basil
1 tablespoon chopped fresh oregano
1 teaspoon salt, in all
8 turns freshly ground black pepper,
    in all

2 tablespoons balsamic vinegar
½ pound cooked cheese tortellini
    (preferably fresh)
2 cups assorted greens (frisée,
    arugula, mâche, oak leaf, or
    stemmed whole spinach)
3 tablespoons coarsely grated fresh
    Parmesan cheese

1. Heat 2 tablespoons of the oil in a large skillet over high heat. Add the onion, prosciutto, tomatoes, basil, oregano, ½ teaspoon of the salt, and 4 turns of the pepper, and sauté for 2 minutes. Stir in the vinegar, remove from the heat, and turn into a large bowl.

2. Heat the remaining 2 tablespoons of oil in the same skillet over high heat. When the oil is hot, add the tortellini and the remaining salt and pepper, and fry until golden brown, shaking the skillet and tossing the pasta, for about 4 minutes. Remove from the heat and toss with the prosciutto in the bowl.

3. Add the greens and the Parmesan to the bowl and toss well.

4. To serve, divide the salad among 4 large dinner plates or shallow pasta bowls. Sprinkle with additional Parmesan if you're as self-indulgent as I am.

Cilantro Potato Salad

◆

Makes about 5½ cups, 5 generous salad servings

Bring this tangy, garlicky potato salad along on your picnic and serve it with anything, or just eat it out of the bowl. Or prepare it as I do, to go with Portuguese Piri Piri Beef on a Stick (page 231) and Glazed Baby Back Ribs with Plum Sauce (page 252).

1 large egg
¾ cup whole fresh cilantro leaves
¾ cup olive oil, in all
1 tablespoon minced garlic
1 teaspoon salt, in all

7 turns black pepper, in all
2 pounds cooked unpeeled new potatoes, halved if small or quartered if large
⅓ cup finely minced onions

1. Place the egg and cilantro in a food processor or blender. Start processing and slowly stream in ½ cup of the oil. Add the garlic, ½ teaspoon of the salt, and 4 turns of the pepper, and stream in the remaining ¼ cup of the oil. Process until thoroughly emulsified into a mayonnaise.

2. Pour the mayonnaise into a large bowl and add the potatoes, onions, and the remaining ½ teaspoon salt and 3 turns pepper. Toss to combine thoroughly, cover, and refrigerate for up to 24 hours.

Crabmeat Potato Salad with Warm Saffron Dressing

◆

Makes 4 salad servings

This colorful potato salad—infused with the light, subtle flavor of saffron and brimming with fresh crabmeat—may become everyone's new favorite. Save the left-over saffron stock to use in a soup or stew.

2 cups Basic Chicken Stock (page 6)
1 pound red potatoes, unpeeled and quartered
¼ teaspoon saffron threads
3 tablespoons olive oil, in all
¼ cup chopped green onions
¼ cup minced red bell peppers
1 tablespoon minced garlic

1 tablespoon chopped fresh parsley
1 teaspoon salt
3 turns freshly ground black pepper
4 cups assorted greens (arugula, red oak, frisée, curly endive, or radicchio)
½ pound (1 cup) lump crabmeat, picked over for shells and cartilage

1. Combine the stock, potatoes, and saffron in a medium saucepan over high heat. Bring to a boil and cook the potatoes until they're fork-tender, for about 15 minutes. Remove the pot from the heat, but allow the potatoes to steep in the saffron liquid for about 10 minutes. Drain the potatoes, reserving ½ cup of the saffron cooking liquid.

2. Prepare the dressing by heating 1 tablespoon of the oil in a small saucepan over high heat. Add the green onions, bell peppers, garlic, parsley, salt, and pepper and stir-fry for 30 seconds. Stir in the ½ cup reserved saffron liquid and bring to a simmer. Whisk in the remaining 2 tablespoons of the oil until thoroughly incorporated, and remove from the heat. Makes ¾ cup.

3. To serve, mound 1 cup of the greens on each of 4 dinner plates and top with ¼ cup of the crabmeat. Arrange about 8 quarters of potato around each mound and spoon 3 tablespoons of the dressing over each salad. Serve warm.

Artichoke Seafood Salad

◆

Makes 6 main-course salads

What seafood lover wouldn't enjoy eating fresh shrimp, crabmeat, and crawfish out of artichoke cups? It's a treat in two acts: Eat the seafood salad from the artichoke cup with your fork, then use your fingers to eat the artichoke leaves. Pull the leaves from the cup one at a time, working your way in from the outside. Scrape off the fleshy part of the leaf with your teeth. The artichoke bottom is my favorite part—just cut it up and enjoy it with the vinaigrette.

1 cup Emeril's Herb Vinaigrette (page 3)
½ pound large shrimp (about 16), peeled except for the tails, boiled (page 17), and cooled
½ pound (1 cup) lump crabmeat, picked over for shells and cartilage
½ pound (1 cup) peeled fresh crawfish tails
2 cups shredded Bibb lettuce
2 cups shredded radicchio
1 teaspoon salt
8 turns freshly ground black pepper
6 large Artichoke Cups (page 15)

1. Prepare Emeril's Herb Vinaigrette and set aside.

2. Combine the shrimp, crabmeat, crawfish tails, Bibb, radicchio, salt, pepper, and the vinaigrette in a bowl, and toss well. Makes 6 cups.

3. To serve, use a slotted spoon to fill each artichoke cup with 1 cup of the salad. Place each on a plate, drizzle some of the vinaigrette left in the bowl over each artichoke, and serve immediately.

CHAPTER 6

Midday Sunday: The Brunch Bunch

No other day feels like Sunday. It has a fabric and a texture all its own. Even if I didn't have a calendar, I'd know it from the way it feels. Sunday's my day off, and what do I do on my day off? Cook, of course. My favorite meal on Sunday is brunch, which I prepare for just my wife, Tari, and myself, and maybe a few guests. Even if we're asked to someone else's home for brunch, I almost always wind up cooking. And loving it.

Sunday brunch in New Orleans is very different from brunch elsewhere. In the Big Easy, brunch often includes a gumbo brimming with andouille sausage, *pain perdu* (French toast), *calas* (fried rice balls), crab cakes, and grillades and grits.

Commander's Palace, like many restaurants in New Orleans, features a Jazz Brunch every Sunday. The band always plays the first number in the kitchen for the cooks, and it's a great way to wake up and get moving. When I was chef at Commander's, I always looked forward to Sundays—the festive atmosphere, colorful balloons at the tables, music, and the wonderful New Orleans comfort food I prepared for our customers.

At home, Tari and I don't blow up balloons, but we always put on some good music while I rustle up my version of a Creole brunch that I've planned in my head the day before. We usually start with an appetizer, even if it's just fresh fruit, to prepare our palates for the main event. Then we might proceed to something "breakfasty," like Smoked Duck Hash with Poached Eggs and Woodland Cream, or something slightly less traditional, like Calypso Pork Pie with Plantain Lattice. If I'm cooking for a crowd, Crab and Wild Mushroom Crabmeat Cheesecake with Green Onion Coulis works beautifully, since it can be prepared earlier and it's easy to serve. Many of the recipes in this section can be served as first or main courses at other meals.

Oh, one more thing. Because Sunday's *my* day off, *I* get to say what time brunch begins, and sometimes it might be as late as three in the afternoon, depending on how late the restaurant closed the night before. Starting late takes the pressure off planning another meal that Sunday.

Crab and Corn Pies with Corn Crab Sauce

◆

Makes 8 brunch servings

Puffy and pretty, these savory pies are an elegant version of a bayou special, and set the tone for a lazy Sunday with or without guests. The sauce has a secret snap that makes the dish a Louisiana favorite.

1 tablespoon olive oil
¼ cup chopped onions
½ cup chopped green onions, in all
¼ cup minced red bell peppers
¼ cup minced green bell peppers
1 tablespoon minced garlic
½ cup fresh corn kernels
2 teaspoons Emeril's Creole Seasoning (page 3)

½ pound (1 cup) lump crabmeat, picked over for shells and cartilage
4 10-inch-square sheets frozen puff pastry (two 17-ounce packages), thawed
1 large egg, lightly beaten
2 cups Corn Crab Sauce (recipe follows)

1. Preheat the oven to 375°F. Line a baking sheet with parchment or wax paper.

2. Heat the oil in a large skillet over high heat. Add all of the onions and ¼ cup of the green onions, the red and green peppers, garlic, and corn and sauté for 1 minute. Stir in the Creole Seasoning and cook for 1 minute. Gently stir in the crabmeat and sauté for 2 minutes. Remove from the heat. Makes 2 cups.

3. Cut each puff pastry sheet in half, then in half again, making 4 squares each. Brush each square with the beaten egg. Place ¼ cup of the filling in the center of 1 square and top with another square, egg-washed side down. Crimp the edges with the tines of a fork. Repeat with remaining squares.

4. Place the pies on the baking sheet, brush the tops with more of the beaten egg, and bake the pies until puffy and brown, for about 18 minutes.

5. While the pies are baking, prepare the Corn Crab Sauce.

6. To serve, pour ¼ cup of the Corn Crab Sauce onto each of 8 plates and top each with a pie. Sprinkle each serving with some of the remaining green onions.

CORN CRAB SAUCE

Makes 2 cups

1 tablespoon olive oil
2 tablespoons chopped green onions
¼ cup chopped green bell peppers
¼ cup chopped red bell peppers
1 freshly scraped corncob, broken in half
½ cup freshly scraped corn kernels
1 tablespoon minced garlic

1 teaspoon salt
½ teaspoon white pepper
½ teaspoon liquid crab boil (page 59)
2 cups heavy cream
4 ounces (½ cup) crabmeat, picked over for shells and cartilage

1. Heat the oil in a medium saucepan over high heat. Add the green onions, green and red bell peppers, the broken corncob, corn kernels, garlic, salt, pepper, and crab boil. Cook, stirring occasionally, for 2 minutes.

2. Stir in the cream and bring to a boil. Reduce the heat and simmer until the sauce is thick enough to coat a spoon, for about 9 to 10 minutes.

3. Discard the corncobs, fold in the crabmeat, and remove from the heat. Serve immediately or store, refrigerated, in an airtight container for up to 24 hours. Reheat in a saucepan over low heat.

Crab Cakes with Tomato Mustard Coulis

◆

Makes 8 brunch servings

Crab cakes are as "N'Awlins" as gumbo, but they're also familiar to people all over the country. Each region has its own version, with outstanding entries originating in Maryland and San Francisco. I never met a crab cake I didn't like, but in all my travels I never found a crab cake better than a New Orleans crab cake.

1⅓ cups Tomato Mustard Coulis
   (recipe follows)
6 tablespoons olive oil, in all
⅓ cup chopped onions
¼ cup chopped green bell peppers
½ teaspoon salt
¼ teaspoon white pepper
15 turns freshly ground black
   pepper
¾ cup chopped green onions, in all
1 tablespoon minced garlic
3 tablespoons Emeril's Creole
   Seasoning (page 3), in all

3 large eggs, in all
2 teaspoons Creole or other
   whole-seed mustard
1¼ cups bread crumbs, in all
   (page 17)
6 tablespoons coarsely grated fresh
   Parmesan cheese
1 pound (2 cups) lump crabmeat,
   carefully picked over for shells
   and cartilage
⅔ cup all-purpose flour
¼ cup water

1. Prepare the Tomato Mustard Coulis, and set aside. This can be served at room temperature.

2. Heat 3 tablespoons of the oil in a large skillet over high heat. Add the onions, bell peppers, salt, white pepper, and black pepper and sauté for 1 minute. Stir in ¼ cup of the green onions, garlic, and 1 tablespoon plus 1 teaspoon Creole Seasoning, and cook for 1 minute. Remove the skillet from the heat and turn the vegetables into a bowl.

3. Whisk 2 of the eggs into the vegetables. Stir in the mustard, ¼ cup of the bread crumbs, and the Parmesan. Gently fold in the crabmeat, taking care not to break up the lumps, and continue to fold it through carefully, until the mixture is well blended. Makes 3 cups.

4. Combine the flour with 1 teaspoon Creole Seasoning in a bowl and mix well. Combine the remaining 1 cup bread crumbs with 1 tablespoon Creole Seasoning in another bowl. Whisk the remaining egg with the water in another bowl for an egg wash.

5. Using your hands, gently form 8 cakes from the crab mixture, packing them firmly but not tightly, so they're not dense and heavy. Thoroughly dredge each crab cake in the flour mixture, then the egg wash, then the bread-crumb mixture, shaking off any excess flour or crumbs.

6. Heat the remaining 3 tablespoons oil in a large skillet over high heat. Fry the crab cakes until brown, for about 2 minutes on each side. Drain them on paper towels.

7. To serve, spoon about 2½ tablespoons of the coulis into each of 8 plates and top with 1 crab cake. Garnish each plate with a sprinkle of the remaining Creole Seasoning and chopped green onions.

TOMATO MUSTARD COULIS

Makes 1¼ cups

½ cup peeled, seeded, and chopped Italian plum tomatoes
2 teaspoons minced shallots
2 teaspoons minced garlic
3 tablespoons Creole or other whole-seed mustard
1 teaspoon salt

½ teaspoon white pepper
½ cup Basic Chicken Stock (page 6)
1 large egg
½ cup olive oil
8 turns freshly ground black pepper

1. Combine the tomatoes, shallots, garlic, mustard, salt, white pepper, and stock in a nonreactive saucepan over high heat and bring to a boil, stirring occasionally. Cook for 2 minutes, remove from the heat, and allow to cool for about 15 minutes.

2. Pour the mixture into a food processor or blender, add the egg, and turn on the machine. Stream in the oil and process until fairly smooth, for about 45 seconds. Stir in the black pepper. Serve immediately.

Spicy Salt Cod Cakes with Fondue Piquante and Fava Bean Relish

◆

Makes 4 brunch servings

When I was a kid I ate a lot of *bacalhau,* or salt cod, which is dried, salted codfish. My mother is Portuguese, and the Portuguese are very fond of *bacalhau.* They prepare it in many delicious ways, including soups, stews, and boiled dinners. Many Portuguese settled in New England, and salt cod was actually a prime ingredient in the original New England Boiled Dinner. The cod must be soaked in milk for at least two days with two changes of milk before cooking, or the salt will be overpowering.

6 ounces salt cod (see Note)
2 quarts milk, in all
1⅓ cups Fondue Piquante
   (recipe follows)
1⅔ cups Fava Bean Relish (page 292)
5 tablespoons olive oil, in all
¼ cup chopped onions
¼ cup chopped green bell peppers
¼ cup chopped celery
¼ cup peeled, seeded, and chopped
   Italian plum tomatoes

¼ cup chopped fresh cilantro
¼ cup chopped fresh parsley
1 tablespoon minced garlic
½ teaspoon crushed red pepper
½ teaspoon Emeril's Creole
   Seasoning (page 3)
4 turns freshly ground black pepper
2 large eggs, beaten
¼ cup bread crumbs (page 17)
½ cup all-purpose flour

1. Two days before serving, soak the cod in 1 quart of milk in a covered bowl, refrigerated, for 24 hours. The next day, discard the milk and rinse the cod well under cold water. Replace the cod in a fresh quart of milk and refrigerate for another 24 hours.

2. Prepare the Fondue Piquante, and set aside. Prepare the Fava Bean Relish, and set aside.

3. About 30 minutes before serving, rinse the fish well under cold water and cut into a fine julienne. Makes about 2 cups.

4. Heat 3 tablespoons of the oil in a large skillet over high heat. Add the onions, bell peppers, and celery and sauté for 1 minute. Add the tomatoes, cilantro, parsley, and garlic and stir-fry for 1 minute. Add the crushed red pepper, Creole Seasoning, and pepper, and sauté for 1 minute. Add the cod and stir-fry for 4 minutes. Turn off the heat.

5. Stir the eggs into the mixture, and fold in the bread crumbs. Makes 2 cups. Form 4 cakes using ½ cup of the mixture for each. Roll the cakes in the flour.

6. Heat the remaining 2 tablespoons oil in a large skillet over high heat until very hot. Fry the cakes until golden brown, for about 1½ minutes on each side. Remove from the oil and drain on paper towels.

7. Reheat the Fondue Piquante and the Fava Bean Relish.

8. To serve, spread ⅓ cup of the Fondue Piquante on each of 4 plates. Top with 1 salt cod cake and 4 little mounds of the Fava Bean Relish, using a heaping ⅓ cup for each serving.

Note: Salt cod can be purchased at Spanish, Portuguese, Italian, and Caribbean food markets.

FONDUE PIQUANTE

◆

Makes 1⅓ cups

¼ cup plus 2 tablespoons olive oil, in all
3 tablespoons chopped onions
3 tablespoons chopped green bell peppers
2 tablespoons chopped celery
1 tablespoon seeded and minced jalapeño peppers
1 tablespoon minced garlic
1 tablespoon chopped fresh thyme
1 tablespoon chopped fresh oregano

1 cup peeled, seeded, and chopped Italian plum tomatoes
3 bay leaves
1 teaspoon Emeril's Creole Seasoning (page 3)
½ teaspoon salt
¼ teaspoon cayenne pepper
4 turns freshly ground black pepper
2 cups Basic Chicken Stock (page 6)

1. Heat 2 tablespoons of the oil in a nonreactive saucepan over high heat. Add the onions, bell peppers, celery, jalapeño peppers, garlic, thyme, and oregano and stir-fry for 2 minutes.

2. Stir in the tomatoes, bay leaves, Creole Seasoning, salt, cayenne, black pepper, and stock. Bring to a boil and cook for 4 minutes. Reduce the heat and simmer for 20 minutes. Remove from the heat.

3. Pour the mixture into a food processor or blender and drizzle in the remaining ¼ cup oil while the motor is running. Serve immediately or store, refrigerated, in an airtight container for up to 2 days. Reheat in a saucepan over low heat.

Shrimp Curry with Cilantro Biscuits

◆

Makes 4 brunch servings

In this dish the savory tang of Indian spices blends beautifully with Creole cooking for the newest in culinary fusion. Try to buy a high-quality curry powder from a specialty food store, or make your own: Combine equal parts of ground allspice, cardamom, cinnamon, coriander, cumin, ginger, mustard, red pepper, and turmeric. If you adjust the spices to suit your own taste, this dish will truly bear your signature.

12 cilantro biscuits (page 302)
24 peeled and deveined medium
   shrimp (about 1½ pounds)
1 tablespoon Emeril's Creole
   Seasoning (page 3)
2 tablespoons curry powder, in all
1 tablespoon olive oil
½ cup chopped onions

2 tablespoons minced garlic
2 cups Shrimp Stock (page 10)
1 teaspoon salt
6 turns freshly ground black pepper
½ cup chopped green onions
¼ cup heavy cream
½ cup shredded coconut, toasted

1. Prepare the cilantro biscuits, and keep warm.

2. Sprinkle the shrimp with the Creole Seasoning and 2 teaspoons of the curry powder and use your hands to coat thoroughly.

3. Heat the oil in a large skillet over high heat. Add the shrimp and sear for 1 minute each side. Add the onions and garlic and stir-fry for 30 seconds.

4. Add the stock, the remaining 4 teaspoons curry powder, salt, and pepper and bring to a simmer. Remove the shrimp. Fold the green onions into the sauce and whisk in the cream. Fold in the coconut and simmer for 2 minutes. Makes 1½ cups sauce.

5. To serve, arrange 6 shrimp on each of 4 plates and nap with a generous ⅓ cup of the sauce. Arrange 3 biscuits on each serving.

Smoked Duck Hash with Poached Eggs and Woodland Cream

◆

Makes 4 brunch servings

A feel-good brunch dish that's special enough for company. The earthy flavor of the wild mushrooms—a mixture of fresh and dried—in the Woodland Cream combined with the smoky, duck flavor of the hash is too good to miss.

2 cups Woodland Cream
  (recipe follows)
¼ cup olive oil
2 cups diced (½ inch) cooked
  potatoes
1 pound smoked duck meat,
  chopped in ¼-inch pieces
  (page 77)
6 tablespoons chopped onions
4 tablespoons shredded carrots

2 tablespoons chopped green bell
  peppers
2 teaspoons minced garlic
2 tablespoons chopped fresh parsley
1 teaspoon Emeril's Creole
  Seasoning (page 3)
1 teaspoon salt
6 turns freshly ground black pepper
4 Perfect Poached Eggs (page 17),
  cooked just before serving

1. Prepare the Woodland Cream, and keep warm.

2. Preheat the oven to 200°F.

3. Heat the oil in a large skillet over high heat. When the oil is hot, add the potatoes and sauté, flipping and shaking the skillet, until the potatoes are golden brown, for about 4 minutes.

4. Add the duck meat, onions, carrots, bell peppers, garlic, parsley, Creole Seasoning, salt, and pepper and sauté, shaking the skillet and stirring, for 5 minutes. Makes 4 cups.

5. Keep the hash warm by placing the skillet in the oven. Prepare the Perfect Poached Eggs.

6. To serve, mound 1 cup of the hash on each of 4 plates, place 1 Perfect Poached Egg on top, and nap with ½ cup of the Woodland Cream.

WOODLAND CREAM

◆

Makes 2 cups

½ cup dried wild mushrooms, such
   as porcini or morels
1 tablespoon olive oil
½ cup sliced fresh wild mushrooms,
   such as shiitakes, chanterelles,
   lobsters, or oyster mushrooms
1 tablespoon minced shallots
1 teaspoon minced garlic

¼ cup chopped green onions
1 teaspoon Emeril's Creole
   Seasoning (page 3)
½ teaspoon salt
2 turns freshly ground black pepper
1½ cups Veal Stock (page 8)
½ cup heavy cream

1. In a small bowl, soak the dried mushrooms in ½ cup warm water for 15 minutes. Drain, stem, and slice the mushrooms.

2. Combine the oil, fresh mushrooms, shallots, garlic, green onions, Creole Seasoning, salt, and pepper in a small saucepan over high heat and sauté for 1 minute. Using your hands, squeeze the excess liquid out of the dried mushrooms into a bowl or cup and add the mushrooms to the skillet. Strain the mushroom liquid through a fine sieve and stir the liquid into the skillet. Cook for 2 minutes.

3. Stir in the stock and bring to a boil. Reduce the heat and simmer for 6 minutes. Slowly stir in the cream, bring to a boil, and cook for 2 minutes. Reduce the heat to low and simmer for 5 minutes. Serve immediately or store, refrigerated, in an airtight container for up to 24 hours. Reheat in a saucepan over low heat.

Chicken Andouille Hash with Poached Eggs and Sauce Piquante

◆

Makes 4 brunch servings

This is a knockout brunch dish and a delicious way to use leftover cooked chicken. The savory hash, velvety eggs, and spicy sauce unite to create a taste explosion—a great way to celebrate the "morning after," perhaps accompanied by a Bloody Mary. Or another hair of the dog.

1½ cups Sauce Piquante (recipe follows)
2 tablespoons olive oil
1½ cups diced cooked potato (½-inch dice)
¼ cup chopped onions
2 tablespoons chopped green bell peppers
1 cup (8 ounces) chopped andouille sausage

1 cup (6 ounces) diced cooked chicken breasts (½-inch dice)
1 tablespoon minced garlic
½ teaspoon Emeril's Creole Seasoning (page 3)
¼ teaspoon salt
3 turns freshly ground black pepper
4 Perfect Poached Eggs (page 17), cooked just before serving
¼ cup chopped green onions

1. Prepare the Sauce Piquante, and keep warm.

2. Preheat the oven to 200°F.

3. Heat the oil in a large skillet over high heat. Add the potatoes and sauté, shaking the skillet occasionally, for 2 minutes. Add the onions, bell peppers, and andouille and stir-fry for 1 minute.

4. Add the chicken and sauté for 1 minute. Add the garlic, Creole Seasoning, salt, and pepper and fry, stirring occasionally, for 4 minutes. Remove from the heat. Makes 3 cups.

5. Keep the hash warm by placing the skillet in the oven. Prepare the Perfect Poached Eggs.

6. To serve, mound ¾ cup of the hash on each of 4 dinner plates. Place 1 Perfect Poached Egg on top of each and drizzle with a generous ⅓ cup of the Sauce Piquante. Sprinkle each serving with 1 tablespoon of the green onions.

SAUCE PIQUANTE

◆

Makes 2 cups

1 tablespoon olive oil
2 tablespoons chopped onions
2 tablespoons chopped green onions
2 tablespoons chopped celery
2 tablespoons chopped green bell
   peppers
1 tablespoon minced seeded jalapeño
   peppers
1 tablespoon minced garlic
1 tablespoon chopped fresh basil

1 teaspoon chopped fresh thyme
1 teaspoon chopped fresh oregano
2 bay leaves
1 cup peeled, seeded, and chopped
   Italian plum tomatoes
1 cup Basic Chicken Stock (page 6)
½ teaspoon salt
¼ teaspoon cayenne pepper
2 turns freshly ground black pepper
1 tablespoon unsalted butter

1. Heat the oil with the onions and green onions, celery, bell peppers, jalapeños, and garlic in a medium saucepan over high heat. Add the basil, thyme, oregano, and bay leaves and sauté for 2 minutes.

2. Stir in the tomatoes, stock, salt, cayenne, and black pepper and bring to a boil. Cook over high heat for 2 minutes, then reduce the heat and simmer, stirring occasionally, for about 5 minutes. Stir in the butter and remove from the heat. Serve immediately, or prepare without the butter and store, refrigerated, in an airtight container for up to 2 days. Before serving, reheat over low heat until the sauce is at a simmer, stir in the butter, and proceed.

Smoked Salmon Potato Hash with Poached Eggs and Caviar

◆

Makes 4 brunch servings

I love hash, all different kinds. It has enormous potential for creative variations; if you give it some thought, you can probably come up with a few of your own. This snappy, smoky hash is soft, but you can make it crisp if you prefer. Simply cut the frying oil from 2 tablespoons to 1 and use a nonstick skillet.

1 cup peeled and quartered potatoes, boiled until firm-tender (about 5 to 8 minutes), and drained
1 pound (2 cups) coarsely chopped smoked salmon
2 tablespoons minced shallots
1 teaspoon minced garlic
1 teaspoon capers, drained
1 tablespoon Dijon mustard
1 tablespoon chopped fresh parsley
1 tablespoon Emeril's Creole Seasoning (page 3)

½ teaspoon salt
10 turns freshly ground black pepper
2 teaspoons freshly squeezed lemon juice
1 large egg
2 tablespoons half-and-half
2 tablespoons olive oil
4 Perfect Poached Eggs (page 17), cooked just before serving
2 ounces fresh red salmon caviar

1. Turn the drained potatoes onto a clean surface and mince them.

2. Place the minced potatoes in a large bowl and add the smoked salmon, shallots, garlic, capers, mustard, parsley, Creole Seasoning, salt, pepper, lemon juice, egg, and half-and-half, and blend together with a spoon. Makes 3 cups (packed).

3. Heat the oil in a large skillet over high heat. Turn the salmon mixture into the skillet and sauté, shaking and flipping the skillet, until heated through, for about 6 minutes.

4. To serve, place ¾ cup of the hash on each of 4 dinner plates. Top each with a Perfect Poached Egg, and add 1 teaspoon caviar to the top of each egg.

Smoked Salmon Cakes with Lemon Dill Sauce

◆

Makes 4 brunch servings

When I was a kid, we ate fish on Friday nights; and for a special Friday treat, we sometimes had individual fresh salmon pies, purchased at a store across town in Fall River. When I grew up, I created my own recipe, changing and updating it each time I prepared it. The following is what I consider the ultimate version, using smoked salmon instead of fresh, and teaming it with a velvety sauce. I've also moved it from a Friday dinner dish to a Sunday brunch favorite.

¾ cup Lemon Dill Sauce (recipe follows)
¾ cup peeled and diced potato (about 1 medium), boiled until firm-tender and drained
12 ounces (1½ cups) chopped smoked salmon
2 tablespoons minced shallots
1 teaspoon minced garlic
3 teaspoons capers, drained
1 tablespoon Dijon mustard
1 tablespoon chopped fresh parsley
3½ teaspoons Emeril's Creole Seasoning (page 3), in all

½ teaspoon white pepper
10 turns freshly ground black pepper
2 teaspoons freshly squeezed lemon juice
1 large egg
2 tablespoons half-and-half
¾ cup bread crumbs (page 17), in all
⅓ cup olive oil
¼ cup chopped green onions
¼ cup finely minced red bell peppers

1. Prepare the Lemon Dill Sauce, and set aside.

2. Place the potatoes in a food processor and add the smoked salmon, shallots, garlic, capers, mustard, parsley, 2½ teaspoons Creole Seasoning, white and black peppers, lemon juice, egg, half-and-half, and ¼ cup of the bread crumbs, and process for about 20 seconds. Makes 2 cups.

3. Gently shape the mixture into 4 cakes, using ½ cup of the mixture per cake. Don't pack the cakes too firmly or they'll be heavy.

4. Combine the remaining ½ cup bread crumbs with the remaining 1 teaspoon Creole Seasoning in a bowl. Dredge and redredge each salmon cake in the seasoned crumbs.

5. Heat the oil in a large skillet over high heat. Fry the cakes in the hot oil until golden brown, for about 2 to 3 minutes on each side. Drain on paper towels.

6. While the cakes are frying, reheat the sauce over low heat.

7. To serve, place 1 salmon cake on each of 4 plates and spoon 3 tablespoons of the Lemon Dill Sauce around the cake. Sprinkle with 1 tablespoon each of the green onions and red bell peppers.

LEMON DILL SAUCE

◆

Makes ¾ cup

¼ cup minced shallots
½ cup dry white wine
2 lemons, peeled and separated into sections
½ teaspoon salt
¼ teaspoon white pepper

6 turns freshly ground black pepper
¼ cup chopped fresh dill
1 teaspoon Dijon mustard
½ cup heavy cream
4 tablespoons (½ stick) soft unsalted butter, cut up

1. Combine the shallots, wine, lemons, salt, and white and black peppers in a saucepan over high heat. Bring to a boil, mashing the lemons with the top end of a whisk. Stir in the dill and cook for 3 minutes.

2. Whisk in the mustard and cream and cook, stirring occasionally, for 2 minutes. Whisk in the butter a few pats at a time, turn off the heat, and continue whisking until the butter is thoroughly incorporated. Strain the sauce through a fine sieve, pressing all the liquid through with the back of a spoon. Serve immediately or prepare except for the butter. Store the sauce, refrigerated, in an airtight container for up to 24 hours. Reheat in a saucepan over low heat, and when the sauce comes to a simmer, whisk in the butter and proceed from there.

THE LAST WORD

When finishing a sauce with butter, it's important to track it closely to keep it from separating: Keep whisking in the butter, 1 or 2 pats at a time; but if bubbles begin to form at the edges of the sauce, pull the pan off the heat, continue whisking, and replace over the heat when the bubbles subside. In this way, you keep the temperature high enough to incorporate the butter, but low enough to keep the sauce from breaking.

Smoked Salmon Soufflés with Dilly Egg Sauce and Caviar

◆

Makes 4 brunch servings

Having people in for brunch and tired of the same old omelets and quiches? Here's something really different that satisfies Sunday-noon taste buds and looks wonderfully dramatic when it comes to the table. Make the egg sauce and even the base for the soufflés ahead of time; then you can just finish them and stick them in the oven for about 20 minutes before you're ready to serve.

2 tablespoons plus 2 teaspoons
  unsalted butter, in all
2 tablespoons olive oil
½ cup chopped onions
2 tablespoons minced shallots
2 teaspoons minced garlic
¼ cup chopped fresh dill
½ cup milk
1 teaspoon Emeril's Creole
  Seasoning (page 3)
½ teaspoon salt
½ teaspoon white pepper

4 turns freshly ground black pepper
¼ cup all-purpose flour
1 teaspoon baking powder
½ pound (1 cup) chopped smoked
  salmon
2 large egg yolks
6 large egg whites
1½ cups Dilly Egg Sauce
  (recipe follows)
2 teaspoons fresh red salmon caviar
8 fresh dill sprigs

1. Preheat the oven to 375°F. Butter four ½-cup ramekins, using ½ teaspoon of the butter for each.

2. Heat the oil in a small saucepan over high heat. When the oil is hot, add the onions, shallots, garlic, and dill and sauté for 30 seconds. Reduce the heat to medium.

3. Add the milk, Creole Seasoning, salt, white and black peppers and simmer for 1½ minutes. Whisk in the remaining 2 tablespoons butter, flour, and baking powder and whisk or stir until the mixture forms a thick roux. Remove from the heat.

4. Turn the roux into a bowl, add the salmon, and stir to break it up. Stir in the egg yolks. (If you're preparing these ahead, stop here, refrigerate the mixture, and complete about 20 minutes before serving.) Beat the egg whites in another bowl until stiff. Fold the egg whites gently into the salmon mixture. Divide equally among the ramekins, mounding the mixture in. Place the ramekins on a baking sheet and bake until brown and puffy, for 15 to 20 minutes.

5. While the soufflés are baking, prepare the Dilly Egg Sauce, and keep warm.

6. To serve, break the top of each soufflé and spoon in 4 to 6 tablespoons of the Dilly Egg Sauce. Top with ½ teaspoon caviar and 2 sprigs fresh dill.

DILLY EGG SAUCE

◆

Makes 1½ cups

2 tablespoons minced shallots
2 teaspoons minced garlic
1 cup heavy cream
1 tablespoon Dijon mustard
1 tablespoon chopped dill

½ teaspoon salt
¼ teaspoon white pepper
2 hard-boiled large eggs, peeled and chopped

1. Combine the shallots, garlic, cream, mustard, dill, salt, and pepper in a saucepan over high heat. Stir and cook for 15 seconds.

2. Whisk in the eggs, bring to a boil, and cook for 30 seconds. Remove from the heat. This sauce can be made ahead and refrigerated, then warmed before serving. Serve immediately.

Jazz Brunch Gravlax

◆

Makes about 20 brunch servings

Gravlax, the Swedish word for cured salmon, is a Scandinavian specialty. It's easy to prepare and is an elegant show-stopper at any party. The curing mixture actually "cooks" the salmon, and creates the flavor your guests will keep coming back for. Friends in New Orleans say this was a huge hit when they served it to visitors who were in town for our Jazz and Heritage Festival. It can be prepared a couple of weeks ahead and whipped out of the fridge to be surrounded by its garnishes on the table. Complete the feast with Black Pepper Bread (page 296) or toast points and iced vodka, champagne, or white wine.

1 cup coarse or kosher salt
¼ cup chopped fresh dill
1 tablespoon freshly grated orange zest
1 teaspoon freshly grated lime zest
4 turns freshly ground black pepper
3 tablespoons vodka

1 4-pound side of fresh salmon, filleted, skin on, pin bones removed, and rinsed under cold water
¼ cup sugar
Capers, finely chopped red onions, chopped fresh dill, chopped hard-boiled egg whites, and chopped hard-boiled egg yolks

1. Combine the salt, dill, orange and lime zests, pepper, and vodka in a small bowl and mix thoroughly.

2. Place the salmon, skin side down, on several large sheets of plastic wrap, and pack the salt curing mixture over the entire cut side of the salmon. Press the mixture in firmly. Wrap the salmon completely and tightly in the plastic wrap and place skin side up on a baking sheet. Place something heavy, like a large iron skillet, on top to help infuse the salmon with the mixture. Refrigerate for 24 hours.

3. Remove the salmon from the refrigerator and brush the salt off. Rinse the salmon thoroughly under cold water, removing all of the cure. Sprinkle the salmon with the sugar and pack it in firmly with your hands. Rewrap and refrigerate for at least 1 week before serving. The gravlax will keep up to 2 weeks, well wrapped and refrigerated.

4. To serve, unwrap the gravlax and using a long, very sharp knife, slice it diagonally in paper-thin slices and place on a platter with toast points or thin slices of Pepper Bread. Set out small dishes of capers, chopped red onions, dill, hard-boiled egg whites, and hard-boiled egg yolks.

Smoked Salmon Cheesecake with Green Onion Coulis

◆

Makes 12 to 16 brunch servings

In the early days of Emeril's Restaurant, I worked closely with Mr. Lou, our outstanding baker, to come up with some signature pastries. As a salute to my good friend, the culinarian and cookbook author Lora Brody (who had the idea first), we decided to create a savory cheesecake—as opposed to the standard dessert version. We started by experimenting with crab and wild mushroom, and it was an instant success. At the time, we were smoking our own salmon for an appetizer and decided to use some in the next cheesecake. The resultant Smoked Salmon Cheesecake is a taste of New York—a perfect city brunch without the bagels. What does the future hold? Probably a spicy Creole crawfish cheesecake; look for it in my next cookbook.

1 cup freshly grated Parmesan cheese
1 cup bread crumbs (page 17)
½ cup melted unsalted butter
1 tablespoon olive oil
1 cup chopped onions
½ cup chopped green bell peppers
½ cup chopped red bell peppers
2 teaspoons salt
12 turns freshly ground black pepper

1¾ pounds cream cheese, at room temperature
4 large eggs
½ cup heavy cream
1 cup grated smoked Gouda cheese
1 pound (2 cups) chopped smoked salmon
2¼ cups Green Onion Coulis (recipe follows)

1. Preheat the oven to 350°F.

2. Combine the Parmesan, bread crumbs, and butter until thoroughly blended, and press the mixture into the bottom of a 9-inch springform pan.

3. Heat the oil in a medium skillet over high heat. Add the onions and the green and red bell peppers and sauté, stirring and shaking the skillet, for 2 minutes. Stir in the salt and pepper, sauté for 1 minute, and remove from the heat.

4. Using an electric mixer, beat the cream cheese with the eggs in a large bowl until very thick and frothy, for about 4 minutes. Beat in the cream, Gouda, the sautéed vegetables, and the smoked salmon, and beat until thoroughly incorporated and creamy, for about 2 minutes.

5. Pour the filling over the crust in the springform pan and bake until firm, for about 1 hour 15 minutes. Allow to cool to room temperature; if you refrigerate the cheesecake before serving, remove from the refrigerator and allow to come to room temperature, for about 1 hour.

6. Prepare the Green Onion Coulis.

7. To serve, cut in wedges with a warm knife and serve each wedge with 2 or 3 tablespoons of the Green Onion Coulis.

GREEN ONION COULIS

◆

Makes about 2¼ cups

¾ cup chopped green onions	2 large eggs
½ cup fresh parsley sprigs	1 teaspoon salt
1 tablespoon chopped shallots	6 turns freshly ground black pepper
1 tablespoon chopped garlic	1½ cups olive oil

Place the green onions, parsley, shallots, and garlic in a food processor or blender and purée. Add the eggs, salt, and pepper, and continue to process. With the machine running, stream in the olive oil slowly until it's thoroughly incorporated. Serve immediately.

Crab and Wild Mushroom Cheesecake with Green Onion Coulis

◆

Makes 12 to 16 brunch servings

I don't know why crabmeat tastes so wonderful with wild mushrooms, but it does; and the sweet-earthy combination makes this savory cheesecake a knockout. The sauce that works with both this and the Smoked Salmon Cheesecake (page 140) is a coulis of green onions, which are known in the Northeast as scallions. It's a funny thing about these pungent baby onions—some people use only the green tops, chopping them finely into many dishes. Others use only the white bulb, which is a little sharper and more oniony in flavor than the green tops. I'm a democratic guy, so I use both the green and white parts of the green onion. I've never regretted it.

1 cup freshly grated Parmesan cheese
1 cup bread crumbs (page 17)
½ cup melted unsalted butter
1 tablespoon olive oil
1 cup chopped onions
½ cup chopped green bell peppers
½ cup chopped red bell peppers
4 cups coarsely chopped assorted fresh wild mushrooms, such as shiitakes, chanterelles, porcini, oysters, or lobster mushrooms
2 teaspoons salt

12 turns freshly ground black pepper
1¾ pounds cream cheese, at room temperature
4 large eggs
½ cup heavy cream
1 cup grated smoked Gouda cheese
1 pound (2 cups) lump crabmeat, picked over for shells and cartilage
2¼ cups Green Onion Coulis (page 141)

1. Preheat the oven to 350°F.

2. Combine the Parmesan, bread crumbs, and butter until thoroughly blended, and press the mixture into the bottom of a 9-inch springform pan.

3. Heat the oil in a large skillet over high heat. Add the onions and the green and red bell peppers and sauté, stirring and shaking the skillet, for 2 minutes. Stir in the mushrooms and the salt and pepper, sauté for 1 to 2 minutes, and remove from the heat.

4. Using an electric mixer beat the cream cheese with the eggs in a large bowl until very thick and frothy, for about 5 minutes. Beat in the cream, Gouda, sautéed vegetables, and crabmeat. Mix until thoroughly incorporated and creamy, for about 2 minutes.

5. Pour the filling over the crust in the springform pan and bake until firm, for about 1 hour. Remove from the oven and allow to cool to room temperature. If you refrigerate the cake, allow it to come to room temperature, for about 1 hour before serving.

6. While the cheesecake is cooling, prepare the Green Onion Coulis.

7. To serve, cut the cake in wedges with a warm knife and serve each wedge with about 3 tablespoons of the coulis.

Calypso Pork Pie with Plantain Lattice

♦

Makes 4 to 6 brunch servings

Just one mouthful of this pie and you'll hear the soft echo of steel drums. Two mouthfuls and you're hooked; three, and you're in heaven. The Caribbean breezes blow our way in New Orleans, so it's not surprising to find a dish seasoned with a blend of Creole spices topped with plantains. The plantain is the starchier, more versatile cousin of the banana and must be cooked to be edible. This lovely fruit can be used in various ways depending on its stage of ripeness, but we use only very ripe sweet plantains here to glorify this pork pie. This is especially good accompanied by Red Stripe beer from Jamaica.

½ recipe Basic Pie Dough (page 313)
8 to 10 ounces lean pork from the
   loin, diced (½ inch)
1 tablespoon Emeril's Creole
   Seasoning (page 3)
½ cup diced bacon
½ cup chopped onions
½ cup chopped carrots
¼ cup chopped celery
2 tablespoons minced garlic
½ cup diced cooked sweet potatoes
   (½-inch dice)
2 cups Basic Chicken Stock
   (page 6) or Brown Chicken Stock
   (page 7)

¼ cup ketchup
2 tablespoons corn syrup
2 teaspoons dry mustard
2 teaspoons curry powder
1 teaspoon salt
½ teaspoon cayenne pepper
3 turns freshly ground black pepper
2 tablespoons cornstarch
¼ cup water
1 large ripe peeled plantain
   (see Note)
2 tablespoons light brown sugar

1. Prepare the Basic Pie Dough for a 9-inch pie shell.

2. Preheat the oven to 450°F.

3. Sprinkle the pork with the Creole Seasoning and using your hands, coat the meat thoroughly.

4. In a large skillet over high heat, render the bacon for 2 minutes. Add the pork and stir-fry for 2 minutes. Add the onions, carrots, celery, and garlic and stir-fry for 2 minutes.

5. Add the sweet potatoes and sauté for 1 minute. Stir in the stock, ketchup, corn syrup, mustard, curry powder, salt, cayenne, and black pepper and simmer for 5 minutes.

6. In a small bowl, dissolve the cornstarch in the water. Stir this mixture into the skillet, simmer for 15 to 20 minutes, and remove from the heat. Makes 3 cups filling.

7. Pour the filling from the skillet into the unbaked pie shell. Slice the plantain lengthwise into thin slices. Arrange the plantain slices in a latticework design on top of the filling. Sprinkle the top with the brown sugar and bake the pie until bubbly and brown, for about 30 to 35 minutes. Remove from the oven and allow to cool for about 10 minutes before cutting.

8. Cut the pie in wedges and serve warm.

Note: Plantains can be found in many supermarkets throughout the United States, as well as in Latin American and other specialty food markets. They are green when unripe, and change color slowly to a dark yellow, then black, as they ripen at room temperature.

Southwest Cheese Pie with Pico di Gallo

◆

Makes 6 to 8 brunch servings

There's nothing quite like starting the day with the unique flavors of a Southwestern brunch. This dish could be part of a buffet or served as your main course. The Pico di Gallo, which is a colorful fresh salsa, has a peppery, spicy goodness and is a perfect counterpoint to the creamy cheese pie.

½ recipe Basic Pie Dough (page 313)
1 tablespoon olive oil
3 strips bacon, diced
½ cup chopped onions
¼ cup diced seeded poblano, green New Mexico, or Anaheim chile peppers
1 teaspoon minced garlic
1 teaspoon Emeril's Southwest Seasoning (page 3)

½ teaspoon chili powder
½ teaspoon ground cumin
½ teaspoon salt
4 turns freshly ground black pepper
3 tablespoons chopped fresh cilantro
3 large eggs
2 cups heavy cream
2 cups grated jalapeño-flavored Jack cheese
2 cups Pico di Gallo (recipe follows)

1. Prepare the Basic Pie Dough for a 9-inch pie shell.

2. Preheat the oven to 375°F.

3. Combine the oil and bacon in a large skillet over high heat and sauté, stirring occasionally, for 3 minutes. Stir in the onions, peppers, garlic, Southwest Seasoning, chili powder, cumin, salt, and pepper and sauté for 2 minutes. Remove from the heat and pour into a bowl.

4. Add the cilantro, whisk in the eggs and cream, fold in the cheese, and pour the mixture into the unbaked pie shell. Bake for 15 minutes at 375°, then turn the oven heat down to 350°, and bake until puffy and golden brown, for about 30 minutes longer. Remove the pie from the oven and let it cool for 10 to 15 minutes before cutting and serving.

5. While the pie is baking, prepare the Pico di Gallo.

6. To serve, cut the pie into 6 or 8 wedges and top each with ⅓ or ¼ cup of the Pico di Gallo.

PICO DI GALLO

◆

Makes 2 cups

1⅓ cups peeled, seeded, and
chopped Italian plum tomatoes
¼ cup finely chopped onions
2 tablespoons finely chopped green
bell peppers
1 tablespoon minced seeded jalapeño
peppers
1 tablespoon minced garlic
1 tablespoon freshly squeezed lime
juice

1 tablespoon freshly squeezed lemon
juice
2 tablespoons chopped fresh cilantro
1½ teaspoons sugar
1 teaspoon Emeril's Southwest
Seasoning (page 3)
½ teaspoon salt
4 turns freshly ground black pepper

Combine all of the ingredients in a bowl and allow to sit at room temperature for at least 10 minutes for the flavors to blend. This sauce, or salsa, tastes better if made 1 to 2 days ahead. Store it in an airtight container in the refrigerator.

Goat Cheese Quesadilla with Guacamole and Pico di Gallo

◆

Makes 4 first-course servings

This is an unusual twist on a Tex-Mex favorite; the goat cheese is an unexpected and delightful surprise. Homemade goat cheese would be ideal, and, indeed, we make our own at the restaurant. We were hoping to include a recipe here so you could make your own, too, but found that one ingredient is difficult to come by. That ingredient is rennet, a natural enzyme whose function is to speed the cheese-making process by coagulating the milk. Never mind. Just get yourself some high-quality goat cheese at your local cheese shop.

2 cups Pico di Gallo (page 147)
1 cup Guacamole (page 286)
½ pound soft goat cheese, such as
   Montrachet
2 teaspoons minced shallots
½ teaspoon minced garlic
1 tablespoon chopped fresh cilantro
½ teaspoon ground cumin

½ teaspoon chili powder
½ teaspoon salt
½ teaspoon white pepper
1 tablespoon olive oil
4 teaspoons unsalted butter,
   softened, in all
8 small (6-inch) corn tortillas
   (see The Last Word)

1. Prepare the Pico di Gallo, and set aside.

2. Prepare the Guacamole, cover tightly with plastic wrap, and set aside.

3. Combine the goat cheese, shallots, garlic, cilantro, cumin, chili powder, salt, pepper, and oil in a bowl. Mix with a large spoon until thoroughly blended.

2. Spread ½ teaspoon of the butter on 1 side of each of the 8 tortillas and turn them over.

3. Spread one-quarter of the goat cheese mixture on the unbuttered side of each of 4 of the tortillas. Cover the cheese with another tortilla, buttered side up, sandwich-style. Press together lightly, taking care not to squeeze out any of the goat cheese filling.

4. Heat a medium nonstick skillet over medium-high heat. When the skillet is hot, sauté a quesadilla, turning it 3 times, until golden brown and crisp on both sides, for about 4 minutes in all. Repeat the procedure with the remaining quesadillas, keeping those that are finished warm until they're all ready.

5. To serve, cut each quesadilla into 4 wedges, and arrange on a dinner plate. Place ¼ cup of the Guacamole in the center, and drizzle ½ cup of the Pico di Gallo over the Guacamole and between the quesadilla wedges.

THE LAST WORD

Tortillas dry out very quickly; keep them in their bag or keep them covered with a clean, damp towel until you're ready to butter them.

Duck, Andouille, and Scallion Pancakes with Ginger Orange Sauce

◆

Makes 4 brunch servings

Here's a New New Orleans take on an Oriental favorite. It's like a moo-shu pork pancake with lagniappe—Creole seasonings and andouille sausage. Use leftover duck meat (see Roast Duck, page 210) or cooked chicken. The preparation's easy: Make the batter and sauce ahead of time and put the dish together at the last minute.

1⅓ cups Ginger Orange Sauce (recipe follows)
1 large egg
1 cup milk
1¼ cups all-purpose flour
1 tablespoon chopped onions
¼ cup chopped green onions
1 teaspoon minced garlic

1 cup shredded cooked duck meat
4 ounces (½ cup) chopped andouille sausage
1 teaspoon Emeril's Creole Seasoning (page 3)
1 teaspoon salt
1 tablespoon olive oil

1. Prepare the Ginger Orange Sauce, and keep it warm.

2. In a bowl, whisk together the egg, milk, and flour. Whisk in the onions and green onions, and the garlic. Stir in the duck meat, andouille, Creole Seasoning, and salt. Makes 2¼ cups batter.

3. Heat the oil in a large nonstick skillet over medium-high heat. When the oil is hot, spoon out the batter to form 2½-inch pancakes and cook until golden brown, for about 2 minutes on each side. Makes 8 pancakes.

4. To serve, place 2 pancakes on each of 4 plates and drizzle each serving with ⅓ cup of the Ginger Orange Sauce.

GINGER ORANGE SAUCE

◆

Makes 1⅓ cups

1 large orange, peeled and sectioned
1 tablespoon minced fresh ginger
1½ cups Veal Stock (page 8) or
   Basic Chicken Stock (page 6)
2 tablespoons chopped fresh cilantro

1 tablespoon sesame seeds
1 teaspoon sesame oil
1 tablespoon sugar
¼ teaspoon salt

1. Measure out enough orange sections to make ½ cup. Squeeze the juice from the remainder of the orange into the ½ cup of sections.

2. In a small saucepan, combine the orange sections and juice with the ginger. Stir in the stock, cilantro, sesame seeds, sesame oil, sugar, and salt, and bring to a boil.

3. Cook, whisking to break up the orange, for 10 minutes. Remove from the heat. Serve immediately or store, refrigerated, in an airtight container for up to 2 days. Reheat in a saucepan over low heat.

CHAPTER 7

By the Bayou: New New Seafood

W hen I need to relax, I go fishing. I love fishing. I have, in fact, done so much fishing, I wouldn't dare try scuba diving, because I know the fish would be waiting for me, ready for revenge.

Fish dishes in New Orleans have traditionally been sautéed in butter, as in an old local favorite, trout meunière. In the good old days (ONO), it wasn't unusual for diners to order their fish smothered under a thick sauce like a béchamel or Mornay.

But tastes have changed, and today's NNO fish dishes are lighter and more apt to taste like the fish, rather than the sauce that accompanies it. Today, we reduce sauces instead of thickening them with flour. To bring out the natural flavors of the fish we cook at the restaurant, we use only olive oil when we sauté, rather than cooking the fish in butter. We sear many fish at high temperatures, sometimes with no fat at all, and pan-roast others with herbs.

The most important element, of course, is the fish itself. We go to great lengths to find the freshest and most flavorful varieties available. In the Gulf waters, fish called "by-catch," such as wahoo, mahimahi, escolar, and lemonfish, swim with schools of tuna for protection, be-cause the tuna are generally a lot larger than these fish. In the past, tuna fishermen have thrown back the by-catch fish since there was no market for them. But in recent years the demand for these fish has grown considerably.

I've included recipes in this chapter that represent the fish dishes that are most popular at the restaurant. In addition, there are recipes for New New shellfish dishes, like Emeril's New New Orleans Paellaya and Stir-Fry of Sesame Ginger Crawfish over Fried Pasta, and new twists on ONO standbys, like André's Barbecued Shrimp.

Emeril's New New Orleans Paellaya

◆

Makes 8 main-course servings

This is truly voluptuous food. It's earthy and you can eat some of it with your hands without ruffling Miss Manners's feathers. Paellaya is my own mélange of paella and jambalaya, two closely related dishes—one a traditional Spanish delight, the other a Cajun specialty, sometimes called "poor man's paella."

1 whole chicken (about 3 pounds), cut into 12 pieces, bone in
2 teaspoons salt
18 turns freshly ground black pepper
½ cup olive oil
1½ cups chopped onions
¾ cup chopped green bell peppers
¾ cup chopped celery
6 tablespoons minced garlic
12 ounces (1½ cups) chopped andouille sausage
3 cups uncooked long grain white rice
1½ cups peeled, seeded, and chopped Italian plum tomatoes

1 tablespoon Worcestershire sauce
1 tablespoon hot pepper sauce
9 bay leaves
3 tablespoons Emeril's Creole Seasoning (page 3)
½ teaspoon saffron threads
6 cups Basic Chicken Stock (page 6)
3 small uncooked lobsters (about 1 to 1¼ pounds each), cut into pieces
36 scrubbed littleneck clams
36 scrubbed and debearded mussels (page 16)
18 medium shrimp in their shells (about ¾ pound)

1. Sprinkle the chicken pieces evenly with the salt and pepper and use your hands to coat the meat thoroughly.

2. Heat the oil in a large stockpot over high heat. Add the chicken and brown on all sides, for about 4 minutes. Add the onions, bell peppers, celery, garlic, sausage, and rice and stir-fry for 2 minutes. Stir in the tomatoes, Worcestershire, hot pepper sauce, bay leaves, Creole Seasoning, and saffron and simmer for 1 minute. Add the stock, stir well, and bring to a boil. Lower the heat, cover, and simmer for 5 minutes.

3. Add the lobster, tucking the pieces into the rice, cover, and cook for 5 minutes. Add the clams, cover, and cook for 5 minutes. Add the mussels and shrimp, cover, and cook for 3 minutes. All of the clam and mussel shells should be opened. Discard any that are still closed.

4. To serve, divide the shellfish, chicken, and rice among 8 large serving bowls. Place some empty bowls for shells in strategic spots on the table, and provide nutcrackers, lobster forks, and extra napkins. Now dig in!

Pecan-Crusted Lemonfish with Lemon Butter Sauce and Pecan Crab Relish

◆

Makes 4 main-course servings

Nuts on top of fish? The man who created this incredibly delicious taste sensation in the Louisiana mode is none other than the culinary genius Paul Prudhomme. Who else would have the nerve and skill to try something that at the time seemed outrageous? Although Chef Paul resigned his post as head of the kitchen at Commander's Palace a few years before I joined the staff, he left a legacy that was pure inspiration for me. This dish is my tribute to Chef Paul.

2 cups Pecan Crab Relish (page 289)
1½ cups Lemon Butter Sauce
   (page 83)
3 tablespoons Emeril's Creole
   Seasoning (page 3), in all
4 lemonfish steaks or fillets (5 to 6
   ounces each); you can substitute

mahimahi, snapper, grouper, or
   bass
2 cups all-purpose flour, in all
1 cup ground pecans
2 large eggs
1 cup milk
½ cup olive oil

1. Prepare the Pecan Crab Relish, and set aside. Prepare the Lemon Butter Sauce, and keep warm.

2. Preheat the oven to 375°F.

3. Sprinkle ¾ teaspoon Creole Seasoning over each fish steak or fillet, and pat it on with your hands.

4. In a bowl combine 1 cup of the flour with 1 tablespoon Creole Seasoning. In another bowl combine the pecans with the remaining 1 cup flour and the remaining 1 tablespoon Creole Seasoning. In a third bowl beat the eggs together with the milk.

5. Dredge the seasoned fillets first in the seasoned flour, then in the egg wash, and finally in the pecan/flour mixture. Gently shake off the excess.

6. Heat the oil in a large ovenproof skillet over high heat. When the oil is hot and almost smoking (about 375°F), add the fish and sauté until golden, for about 1½ to 2 minutes on each side. Turn the fish back to the first side and place the skillet in the oven until the fish is brown and crisp, for about 4 minutes.

7. To serve, pour about ⅓ cup of the Lemon Butter Sauce on each of 4 dinner plates, place a fillet on the sauce, and top with ½ cup of the Pecan Crab Relish.

Pompano with Potato Crust and Roasted Red Pepper Sauce

◆

Makes 4 main-course servings

Pompano is one of my favorite fish—both to eat and to catch. They're fun to catch because they swim in schools, and sometimes it's possible to reel in 2 or 3 on the same line. Pompano is a treat to all who live along the Gulf Coast and is very popular in New Orleans. In this dish the oily pompano is a perfect match for the "hash-brownesque" potato crust for a fantastic taste-texture combo. If you can't get fresh pompano where you live (no frozen fish here!), the substitutes listed below will work well.

2 cups Roasted Red Pepper Sauce (recipe follows)
4 fillets (6 to 8 ounces each) pompano, snapper, catfish, sea bass, grouper, or lemonfish
2 teaspoons Emeril's Creole Seasoning (page 3), in all

4 teaspoons Dijon mustard, in all
2 large raw potatoes
1 teaspoon salt, in all
8 turns freshly ground black pepper, in all
½ cup olive oil, in all
4 tablespoons snipped fresh chives

1. Prepare the Roasted Red Pepper Sauce, and set aside. (This doesn't have to be reheated.)

2. Spread the fillets on a clean surface and sprinkle the top of each with ½ teaspoon Creole Seasoning. Spread 1 teaspoon of the mustard on each fillet. Peel and grate the potatoes by hand on the large holes of a grater. Top each fish fillet with ½ cup of the grated potatoes, packing them down with a spatula. Sprinkle the potatoes on each fillet with ¼ teaspoon of the salt and 2 turns of the pepper.

3. Heat the oil in 2 nonstick skillets over high heat, ¼ cup of the oil per skillet. When the oil is hot, gently slide 2 fillets into each skillet with a spatula, crust side up, taking care to keep the crust intact. Fry for 2 minutes, flip the fillets quickly and carefully, and fry crust side down until golden brown, for about 2 to 3 minutes. Remove from the heat.

4. To serve, pour ½ cup of the Roasted Red Pepper Sauce into each of 4 dinner plates. Place 1 fillet, crust side up on each plate, and sprinkle with the chives.

ROASTED RED PEPPER SAUCE

◆

Makes 2 cups

2 tablespoons olive oil
3 medium-large red bell peppers,
   roasted (page 16) and cut up
   coarsely
¼ cup coarsely chopped onions
2 teaspoons minced garlic
1 teaspoon chopped fresh basil

1 teaspoon salt
⅛ teaspoon cayenne pepper
3 turns freshly ground black pepper
2 cups Basic Chicken Stock
   (page 6)
2 tablespoons heavy cream

1. Combine the oil, roasted peppers, onions, garlic, basil, salt, cayenne, and black pepper in a medium saucepan over high heat and cook for 3 minutes. Stir in the stock and the cream and bring to a full boil. Reduce the heat and simmer, stirring occasionally, for about 8 minutes.

2. Remove from the heat and purée in a food processor or blender for about 2 minutes. Serve immediately or store, refrigerated, in an airtight container for up to 24 hours. Reheat in a saucepan over low heat.

Tipsy Snapper with Ginger Sake Sauce and Fried Arugula

◆

Makes 4 main-course servings

This marinated snapper is so juicy and delicious, everyone always sits and picks it clean. Warn your fish-pickers to be careful of bones, though, since there are bound to be more hidden even after you fillet the meat off the carcass. The sauce combines some of the best Oriental flavors, such as soy, ginger, sesame, and sake. To make it even better, serve it with warm sake to drink.

2 whole snapper, catfish, or trout, scaled and gutted (about 1¾ pounds each)
¼ cup chopped onions
3 tablespoons peeled and grated fresh gingerroot
2 tablespoons chopped fresh cilantro
2 teaspoons minced garlic
1 teaspoon salt
3 turns freshly ground black pepper

2 tablespoons freshly squeezed orange juice
¾ cup olive oil, in all
1 tablespoon plus 2 teaspoons Emeril's Creole Seasoning (page 3), in all
1 cup all-purpose flour
1 cup Ginger Sake Sauce (recipe follows)
4 servings Fried Arugula (page 278)

1. Rinse the snapper, pat them dry, and use a small sharp knife to puncture and cut slits in them 1 inch apart on both sides of each fish.

2. To make the marinade, combine the onions, ginger, cilantro, garlic, salt, pepper, orange juice, ½ cup of the oil, and 1 tablespoon Creole Seasoning in a small bowl. Makes about ¾ cup. Place the fish side by side in a dish large enough to hold them flat. Pour the marinade over both sides of each fish and allow them to marinate, refrigerated, for 1 hour, turning once.

3. Preheat the oven to 500°F.

4. Combine the flour with the remaining 2 teaspoons Creole Seasoning in a large bowl. Drain, then submerge each snapper completely in the flour, covering both sides.

5. Heat a large dry skillet over high heat until very hot. Add 2 or 3 tablespoons of the marinade to the skillet and add 1 of the snappers. Drizzle 1 tablespoon of the oil on top and sear for 2 minutes. Turn the snapper, drizzle with 1 tablespoon of the oil, and sear for 2 minutes more. Remove from the skillet and place on a baking sheet. Repeat the process with the second snapper.

6. Prepare the Ginger Sake Sauce, and set aside to sit at room temperature until you're ready to serve.

7. Spread the remaining marinade over the snappers and bake until brown and juicy, for about 20 minutes. Remove from the oven.

8. About 5 minutes before the fish is done, prepare the Fried Arugula.

9. To serve, cut the head from each fish, make a long incision along the top edge and the bottom, and loosen the fish horizontally from the central bone or backbone. Divide the arugula among 4 dinner plates, add half a snapper, removing the central bone as you go, and spoon ¼ cup of the Ginger Sake Sauce over each.

GINGER SAKE SAUCE

◆

Makes 1 cup

2 tablespoons peeled and grated
   fresh gingerroot
¼ cup chopped green onions
2 tablespoons chopped fresh cilantro
1 teaspoon minced garlic
½ teaspoon salt
6 turns freshly ground black pepper

½ cup sake wine
3 tablespoons sesame oil
1 tablespoon rice vinegar
1 tablespoon Tamari or soy sauce
1 tablespoon honey
1 teaspoon Worcestershire sauce

Combine all of the ingredients in a small bowl, stir well, and allow it to sit at room temperature for about 30 minutes. Serve immediately or store, refrigerated, in an airtight container for up to 2 days. Bring to room temperature before serving.

Salt-Shell Snapper with Black Bean Chili

◆

Makes 4 main-course servings

Here's to New Orleans restaurateur Ella Brennan and chef Leon Leonides of the extraordinary Coach House restaurant in New York. I was headed for New York some years ago, and Ella suggested I eat at the famous old restaurant. Ella wanted me to try the bass in a salt crust, hoping it would inspire me to create something similar. It worked.

2 tablespoons olive oil
2 whole red snapper or bass, scaled
    and gutted (about 1½ pounds
    each)
½ cup chopped onions
2 tablespoons minced garlic

2 tablespoons chopped fresh cilantro
2 teaspoons salt
8 turns freshly ground black pepper
2 cups kosher (coarse) salt
1½ cups Black Bean Chili
    (page 263)

1. Preheat the oven to 500°F.

2. Spread the oil on a baking sheet large enough to hold both fish. Place the fish in the oil and turn them to coat both sides of each fish.

3. Sprinkle the onions, garlic, cilantro, salt, and pepper in the cavities and over the outsides of the fish, using half of the seasonings for each fish.

4. Encase each fish with 1 cup of the coarse salt, covering all surfaces and forming a shell, or crust. Bake until the crust is hard, for about 25 minutes. Remove from the oven.

5. While the fish is baking, prepare the Black Bean Chili, and keep warm.

6. Break the crust by tapping gently with a knife. Brush and peel away the coarse salt. Carefully separate the head, then remove the top half of each fish from the center bone, and remove the bone itself and any other bones that are visible.

7. To serve, mound a generous ⅓ cup of the chili on each of 4 plates and place ½ fish on top of the succotash. Be careful of bones.

Roast Smothered Monkfish with Onion Crisps

◆

Makes 4 main-course servings

This dish tastes something like a Provençal stew. Its unusual flavor and texture comes from the monkfish (*lotte* in French), which is reminiscent of lobster and is underutilized in this country. The onion crisps create an exciting counterpoint.

4 monkfish fillets (about 5 ounces each), trimmed and membranes removed
1 tablespoon Emeril's Creole Seasoning (page 3)
1 tablespoon olive oil
3 cups diced peeled eggplant (½-inch dice)
8 Italian plum tomatoes, cut into vertical slices

½ cup chopped onions
1 tablespoon minced garlic
3 tablespoons chopped fresh basil
1 teaspoon salt
5 turns freshly ground black pepper
½ cup peeled, seeded, and puréed Italian plum tomatoes
½ cup Basic Chicken Stock (page 6)
2 cups Onion Crisps (page 277)

1. Preheat the oven to 375°F.

2. Sprinkle the fillets on both sides with Creole Seasoning.

3. Heat the oil in a large nonreactive ovenproof skillet over high heat. When the oil is hot, add the fish fillets and sear the first side, for about 1 minute. Flip the fillets with a spatula, add the remaining ingredients except the Onion Crisps, gently stir them in, and bring to a boil.

4. Remove the skillet from the burner, place in the preheated oven, and roast for 25 minutes.

5. While the fish is cooking, prepare the Onion Crisps, and place them on a baking sheet.

6. Turn off the oven heat. Remove the skillet from the oven, place it on a burner over high heat and cook for 5 minutes longer. Meanwhile, place the baking sheet in the oven (leave the door ajar) for about 2 minutes, to recrisp the Onion Crisps.

7. To serve, place a fish fillet in each of 4 shallow bowls and spoon some of the tomato/eggplant mixture over it. Pile a handful of the Onion Crisps on top.

Swordfish with Portuguese Sauce

◆

Makes 4 main-course servings

A dish similar to this one is a favorite of Portuguese people all over the world, including those in my hometown of Fall River, Massachusetts. The sauce is a good example of the spices and flavors well known to most Portuguese, originally borrowed from India, Africa, and South America and blended into an earthy culinary tradition.

4 swordfish steaks (about 7 or 8
  ounces each), 1½ inches thick
1 tablespoon Emeril's Creole
  Seasoning (page 3)

1⅓ cups Portuguese Sauce
  (recipe follows)
1 tablespoon olive oil
¼ cup chopped green onions

1. Sprinkle both sides of the swordfish steaks with Creole Seasoning and use your hands to coat the fish thoroughly.

2. Prepare the Portuguese Sauce, and keep warm.

3. Heat the oil in a large skillet over high heat. When the oil is hot, add the swordfish steaks and sauté until medium rare, for about 3 to 5 minutes on each side.

4. To serve, place a swordfish steak on each of 4 dinner plates, top with ⅓ cup of the Portuguese Sauce, and sprinkle each serving with 1 tablespoon green onions.

PORTUGUESE SAUCE

◆

Makes 1⅓ cups

2 tablespoons olive oil
¼ cup chopped onions
1 tablespoon minced garlic
3 finely peeled and chopped Italian
   plum tomatoes
⅓ cup pitted and halved Greek or
   Italian black olives
⅓ cup halved pimiento-stuffed green
   olives
2 teaspoons finely minced anchovy
   fillets or anchovy paste

1 tablespoon chopped fresh parsley
1 tablespoon chopped fresh basil
1 teaspoon chopped fresh oregano
1 teaspoon salt
10 turns freshly ground black
   pepper
8 tablespoons (1 stick) unsalted
   butter, in pats

1. Heat the oil in a large nonreactive skillet over high heat. When the oil is hot, add the onions and sauté for 1 minute. Add the garlic, tomatoes, black and green olives, anchovy, parsley, basil, oregano, salt, and pepper. Bring to a boil, lower the heat, and simmer, stirring occasionally, for about 3 minutes.

2. Fold in the butter. When the butter is half melted, remove from the heat and continue to stir until thoroughly incorporated.

Emeril's Fish in a Bag

◆

Makes 4 main-course servings

Here's a dish well known to New Orleanians, usually ordered by its original moniker, "fish en papillote." Veddy fawncy for a hunk of flounder in a paper bag. Actually, it's a lovely dish if the fish isn't drowning in a gloppy sauce. So I set out to make my version light and naturally juicy, afloat in a crackly puff of a parchment bag. The real beauty of this dish is that once you catch on, you can use it to create your own favorite recipe, choosing from a variety of fish and fresh vegetables. It's a wonderful dish for dinner parties because you can prepare the bags of fish and vegetables in the morning, refrigerate them, and bake them just before serving. And they make a sensational presentation.

6 tablespoons plus 2 teaspoons olive oil, in all

4 fillets (about 6 ounces each) flounder, pompano, scrod, snapper, haddock, bass, tile, redfish, drum, sole, grouper, or your favorite flaky fish

4 tablespoons Emeril's Creole Seasoning (page 3), in all

2 large onions, sliced in rings, in all

8 Italian plum tomatoes, cut into ½-inch slices, in all

1 teaspoon salt, in all

32 turns freshly ground black pepper, in all

4 teaspoons minced garlic, in all

¾ cup chopped fresh basil, in all

1. Preheat the oven to 425°F.

2. Fold 4 sheets of parchment paper (16½ by 24½ inches) in half, and clip off the 2 open corners, cutting them round to create an ear shape. Spread the parchment sheets (now oblong shaped) open on a flat surface, and brush each with 1 tablespoon of the oil.

3. Sprinkle each fillet all over with 1 tablespoon Creole Seasoning. Pat the seasoning on with your hands and place each fillet on half of a parchment sheet.

4. Fan one-quarter of the onion rings and 2 of the sliced tomatoes over each fillet; sprinkle each with ¼ teaspoon of the salt, 8 turns of the pepper, 1 teaspoon of the garlic, and 3 tablespoons of the basil. Drizzle 1 teaspoon of the oil over each.

5. To close each bag, fold the second side of the paper over the layered food, fold the bottom edge over the top, and work your way edge over edge, folding and twisting, until the bag is sealed. Turn each bag over and place it on an ovenproof plate, or place all on a baking sheet. (If you bake them on plates, you won't have to transfer them later.) Brush the top of each bag with the remaining oil (1 teaspoon per bag), and bake until the paper is puffed up and golden brown, for about 20 minutes.

6. To serve, place a bag on each plate, slit the bag in an "X," and fold back the paper. Serve steaming hot.

Note: Parchment paper can be bought at most supermarkets or any culinary equipment store. If you absolutely can't find any, use aluminum foil, but the effect won't be as elegant.

THE LAST WORD

Try creating your own "papillote" using any flaky fish and your favorite vegetables: carrots, bell peppers, summer squash, snow peas, baby green beans, or eggplant, to suggest just a few.

Beer-Battered Fish with Twice-Fried Vinegar Chips and Basil Mayonnaise

◆

Makes 4 main-course servings

When I was a kid, Friday was the best day of the week. Not only because there was no school the next day, but because Friday was fish and chips day. Mom would send me over to a little neighborhood store called Shapel's, where I'd wait in a long line for what seemed like hours, drunk on the smells of the frying fat, fish, and potatoes. But the wait was always worth it when I dug into my plate of crisp-fried, juicy fish and crunchy chips sprinkled liberally with tangy vinegar. There are places all over the Massachusetts coast where you can still get great fish and chips. My favorite is a place called Higgins' on Main Street in Fall River, which used to be just a fish market. A few years ago, they added cooking equipment; now they make fish and chips every Friday, using whitefish such as scrod, haddock, or pollock. If you're ever in Fall River, drop into Higgins' for a treat. If not, try my version, and serve it with beer.

1 cup Basil Mayonnaise
  (recipe follows)
1 12-ounce can of beer
2 large eggs
3 cups all-purpose flour, in all
1 teaspoon baking powder
½ teaspoon salt
¼ teaspoon white pepper
1 tablespoon Emeril's Creole
  Seasoning (page 3), in all

4 whitefish fillets (5 ounces each),
  such as scrod, haddock, grouper,
  or catfish
6 cups Twice-Fried Vinegar Chips
  (page 270)
10 cups vegetable oil (omit if you
  make the chips; use the same oil)

1. Prepare the Basil Mayonnaise, and refrigerate.

2. Make a beer batter by combining the beer, eggs, 2½ cups of the flour, the baking powder, salt, and pepper in a bowl. Beat with a whisk until thick, frothy, and thoroughly blended.

3. In a bowl, combine the remaining ½ cup flour with 1 teaspoon Creole Seasoning. Dust each fillet with ½ teaspoon Creole Seasoning, and cut each fillet in half across. Dredge each half in the seasoned flour.

4. Prepare the Twice-Fried Vinegar Chips through Step 1 only. Reheat the oil to 375°F.

5. While the potatoes are cooling, dip each piece of fish into the beer batter, covering it completely. Shake off the excess batter and place the fish in the hot oil. (Make sure the oil is very hot or the fish will sink and stick to the bottom.) Fry in two batches, turning the fish once or twice, until puffed and crispy and golden brown, for about 4 to 5 minutes.

6. Remove the fish with a slotted spoon, drain on paper towels. Place the fish in a slow oven (200°F) and keep warm while preparing Step 2 of the Twice-Fried Vinegar Chips. Remove the Basil Mayonnaise from the refrigerator.

7. To serve, place 2 fish fillet halves on each of 4 dinner plates, add 1½ cups of the Vinegar Chips and ¼ cup of the Basil Mayonnaise.

BASIL MAYONNAISE

◆

Makes 1 cup

1 large egg
1 teaspoon freshly squeezed lemon juice
⅓ cup chopped fresh basil

2 tablespoons chopped green onions
1 teaspoon salt
8 turns freshly ground black pepper
1 cup olive oil

1. Combine the egg, lemon juice, basil, green onions, salt, and pepper in a food processor or blender and purée for 15 seconds. While the processor is running, slowly stream in the oil.

2. When all of the oil has been added, turn off the machine and scrape down the sides and cover. Process again until the mixture becomes a thick mayonnaise. Remove the mayonnaise to an airtight container and refrigerate for at least 30 minutes. Use within 24 hours.

Shrimp-Stuffed Flounder with Sauce Piquante

◆

Makes 4 main-course servings

When I was a small boy, my father took me to the town of Tiverton, Rhode Island, where we fished for flounder off a little bridge. We took the fish home, cleaned and filleted them, and Mom stuffed and baked them for dinner. Here's my version—a New Orleans twist on a great New England tradition.

3 tablespoons olive oil, in all
¼ cup chopped onions
¼ cup chopped green onions
¼ cup chopped celery
¼ cup chopped green bell peppers
1 tablespoon minced garlic
½ pound (1 generous cup) peeled medium shrimp, cut in thirds
2 tablespoons plus 1 teaspoon Emeril's Creole Seasoning (page 3), in all
½ teaspoon salt

3 turns freshly ground black pepper
½ cup Shrimp Stock (page 10)
½ teaspoon Worcestershire sauce
¼ teaspoon hot pepper sauce
½ cup bread crumbs (page 17)
4 whole flounder (1 to 1¼ pounds each), skin on, headless, boned, cleaned, split down the center of the belly, and ready to be stuffed
2 cups Sauce Piquante (page 132)
¼ cup coarsely grated fresh Parmesan cheese

1. Preheat the oven to 400°F.

2. Heat 2 tablespoons of the oil in a large skillet over high heat. Add the onions, green onions, celery, bell peppers, and garlic and stir-fry for 1 minute. Add the shrimp, sprinkle them with 1 tablespoon Creole Seasoning and stir-fry for 1 minute. Sprinkle with salt and pepper, and stir in the stock, Worcestershire, and hot pepper sauce. Bring to a boil and cook for 2 minutes. Remove from the heat. Stir in the bread crumbs until thoroughly incorporated. Makes 2 cups stuffing.

3. Spread the remaining 1 tablespoon oil on a baking sheet, rub the flounder in the oil, and place belly-up on the sheet. Open the flaps to expose the insides of the fish, and using the remaining Creole Seasoning, sprinkle 1 teaspoon all over the inside of each flounder. Stuff each with ½ cup of the stuffing and replace the flaps. Bake until brown and juicy, for about 18 minutes.

4. While the fish are baking, prepare the Sauce Piquante.

5. To serve, place a whole stuffed flounder on each of 4 dinner plates and spoon ½ cup of the Sauce Piquante over each. Sprinkle each fish with 1 tablespoon Parmesan.

Grilled Tuna with Tortilla Sauce, Black Bean Chili, and Salsa

◆

Makes 6 main-course servings

This recipe is dedicated to Rosalie Murphy, a native New Orleanian who took her considerable culinary talents to Santa Fe, New Mexico, where she opened The Pink Adobe restaurant. Her menu marries the very compatible flavors of Louisiana and New Mexico with delicious results. Rosalie grills a mean tuna, and I hope she'll enjoy this one. Don't be intimidated by the four separate steps—once you've prepped, the rest is easy. Serve with Tin-Can Margaritas or Rosalitas (see The Last Word).

2 cups Black Bean Chili (page 263)
2½ cups Tortilla Sauce
  (recipe follows)
¾ cup Tomato Corn Salsa (page 37)
6 skinless and boneless yellowfin
  tuna steaks (about 6 to 7 ounces
  each)

2 tablespoons Emeril's Southwest
  Seasoning (page 3)
2 tablespoons olive oil
6 sprigs fresh cilantro

1. Prepare the Black Bean Chili, and keep warm. Prepare the Tortilla Sauce, and keep warm. Prepare the Tomato Corn Salsa, and set aside.

2. Sprinkle the tuna steaks on both sides with the Southwest Seasoning and use your hands to coat the fish.

3. Heat the oil in a large skillet over high heat. When the oil is hot, add the tuna and sauté for 2 minutes on each side for rare, 3 minutes on each side for medium rare.

4. To serve, pour a generous ⅓ cup of the Tortilla Sauce in each of 6 plates, and top each with a tuna steak. Spoon ⅓ cup Black Bean Chili on each tuna steak and top with 2 tablespoons Tomato Corn Salsa. Garnish with a sprig of cilantro.

TORTILLA SAUCE

◆

Makes about 2½ cups

8 (6-inch) corn tortillas
1 tablespoon olive oil
½ cup chopped onions
1 tablespoon minced garlic
1 teaspoon minced fresh jalapeño
  peppers
1 teaspoon Emeril's Southwest
  Seasoning (page 3)

½ teaspoon salt
4 turns freshly ground black pepper
4 cups Basic Chicken Stock
  (page 6)
¼ cup heavy cream
½ cup grated jalapeño-flavored Jack
  cheese

1. Preheat the oven to 375°F.

2. Place the tortillas on a baking sheet and bake until crisp, dry, and golden, for about 5 minutes. Remove from the oven and set aside.

3. Heat the oil in a saucepan over high heat. When the oil is hot, sauté the onions, garlic, and peppers for about 30 seconds. Add the Southwest Seasoning, salt, pepper, and stock and bring to a boil. Cook for 10 minutes. Stir in the cream, and reduce the heat to medium.

4. Crumble the tortillas and whisk them into the sauce. Whisk in the cheese and simmer for about 15 minutes. Remove from the heat.

5. Pour the sauce into a food processor or blender and purée until smooth and creamy. Serve immediately or store, refrigerated, in an airtight container for up to 24 hours. Reheat in a saucepan over lowest heat.

THE LAST WORD

TIN-CAN MARGARITAS

In the container of a blender place 1 can frozen limeade, 1 limeade can filled with good-quality tequila, and ½ limeade can Triple Sec. Fill the container of the blender to the top with ice cubes. Cover and blend about 20 seconds.

ROSALITAS

Substitute ¼ can Grand Marnier for the Triple Sec.

Sautéed Escolar with Curry Oil and Apple Mint Couscous

◆

Makes 4 main-course servings

There may not be a better tasting, more melt-in-the-mouth fish than escolar. It sautés beautifully, with a creamy moist inside and a crunchy brown crust. It's native to the Gulf of Mexico, but markets and restaurants are beginning to have it flown in fresh to big cities like New York, so I hear. If you can't find it where you live, you can substitute salmon steaks or any firm-fleshed fish, such as pompano. If you use a fish that's thin like pompano, adjust the cooking time, since escolar and salmon are thicker and will take a little longer.

½ cup Curry Oil (recipe follows)
4 escolar fillets, sometimes called
   white tuna (7 ounces each)
2 tablespoons Emeril's Creole
   Seasoning (page 3), in all

2½ cups Apple Mint Couscous
   (page 269)
2 tablespoons olive oil
4 fresh mint sprigs

1. Prepare the Curry Oil, and set aside.

2. Sprinkle each fillet with ½ tablespoon Creole Seasoning.

3. Prepare the Apple Mint Couscous through Step 2.

4. Heat the oil in a large skillet over high heat. Add the fillets and sauté until brown, for about 4 minutes on the first side and 3 minutes on the second. Flip the fillets over again, turn off the heat, and allow to sit for 2 minutes.

5. Meanwhile, unmold the couscous on each of 4 plates. Place an escolar fillet beside it, and drizzle 2 tablespoons of the Curry Oil over each serving. Garnish with fresh mint sprigs.

CURRY OIL

◆

Makes ½ cup

½ cup olive oil
2 tablespoons curry powder
2 teaspoons minced garlic

½ teaspoon salt
3 turns freshly ground black pepper

Place all of the ingredients in a food processor or blender and blend for 15 seconds. Store in an airtight jar or bottle for up to 1 week.

Tuna Niçoise

◆

Makes 4 main-course servings

Close your eyes and you're eating in Nice. Open them and you're eating Niçoise in New Orleans. Either way, you win.

½ cup plus 1 tablespoon olive oil, in all

¼ cup chopped onions

1 tablespoon minced garlic

½ cup peeled, seeded, and chopped Italian plum tomatoes

½ cup pitted and halved Greek or Italian black olives

½ cup pimiento-stuffed green olives, halved

1 tablespoon finely chopped anchovy fillets

1 teaspoon freshly squeezed lemon juice

1 tablespoon chopped fresh parsley

1 tablespoon chopped fresh basil

1 tablespoon chopped fresh oregano

½ teaspoon salt

6 turns freshly ground black pepper

4 (6 to 7 ounces each) yellowfin tuna steaks

2 teaspoons Emeril's Creole Seasoning (page 3)

1. In a bowl combine ½ cup oil, the onions, garlic, tomatoes, black and green olives, anchovy, lemon juice, parsley, basil, oregano, salt, and pepper, and stir until thoroughly blended. Makes about 1½ cups.

2. Sprinkle the tuna steaks evenly on both sides with the Creole Seasoning.

3. Heat the remaining tablespoon of olive oil in a large skillet over high heat. When the oil is hot, add the tuna and sauté until brown, for about 2 minutes on each side.

4. To serve, place a tuna steak on each of 4 plates and spoon a generous ⅓ cup of the sauce over each.

Herbed Pan Roast of Salmon with Warm Greens and Herb Vinaigrette

◆

Makes 4 main-course servings

This dish has been on the menu since the restaurant opened and has become something of a signature dish. Two tips: You can make the vinaigrette a day ahead and refrigerate it, since it gets better as it sits. Also, for maximum flavor, be sure tarragon is one of the fresh herbs you use, on both the salmon and in the vinaigrette. This is an easy dish to make, so it's great for a dinner party. Especially if you like to show off.

1 cup Emeril's Herb Vinaigrette (page 99)
4 salmon steaks, preferably tail end, 1 inch thick (7 to 8 ounces each)
1 teaspoon salt
1 teaspoon white pepper
4 teaspoons Dijon mustard

1½ cups chopped fresh assorted herbs (tarragon, basil, chives, parsley, oregano, cilantro, or any other herb of your choice)
1 cup water
4 servings Warm Greens (page 98)

1. Prepare Emeril's Herb Vinaigrette, and set aside.

2. Preheat the oven to 400°F.

3. Sprinkle the salmon fillets on both sides with the salt and pepper. Spread the mustard on both sides of each fillet, dredge them in the herb mixture, and pack the herbs into the fillets with your hands.

4. Heat a large ovenproof skillet over high heat until very hot. Place the salmon fillets in the skillet and sear them on the first side, for about 1½ minutes. Flip the fillets over and remove the skillet from the heat.

5. Add the water carefully *around* the fillets, place the skillet in the oven, and bake until the fish is medium rare, for about 6 minutes.

6. While the salmon is baking, prepare the Warm Greens.

7. To serve, place 1 serving of the greens on each plate, top with a salmon fillet, and spoon ¼ cup of the vinaigrette over.

Sautéed Scallops with Saffron Corn Sauce

◆

Makes 4 main-course servings

The velvety sauce, brimming with fresh corn, makes an unusual bed for scallops. Sea scallops, large and sweet, are the ones that work best in this recipe. If you can only buy little bay scallops, buy more and cook for less time—about 45 seconds per side.

2 cups Saffron Corn Sauce
  (recipe follows)
20 (about 2 pounds) very large sea
  scallops

4 teaspoons Emeril's Creole
  Seasoning (page 3)
1 tablespoon olive oil
¼ cup chopped green onions

1. Prepare the Saffron Corn Sauce, and set aside.

2. Sprinkle the scallops on both sides with the Creole Seasoning and use your hands to coat them thoroughly.

3. Heat the oil in a large skillet over medium-high heat. When the oil is hot, add the scallops and sauté until golden brown, for about 2 minutes on each side (3 minutes if they're very large).

4. To serve, reheat the Saffron Corn Sauce over low heat (don't bring to a boil; just heat it through). Pour ½ cup of the sauce (be sure to spoon some corn out with the sauce) onto each of 4 dinner plates. Arrange 5 scallops on each. Sprinkle with 1 tablespoon of the green onions.

SAFFRON CORN SAUCE

◆

Makes about 2 cups

1 teaspoon olive oil
1 ear fresh corn, kernels and cob
1 tablespoon minced shallots
2 teaspoons minced garlic
1 teaspoon salt

¾ teaspoon white pepper
½ cup Fish Stock (page 9)
¼ teaspoon saffron threads
1 cup heavy cream
1 tablespoon unsalted butter

1. Heat the oil in a small saucepan over high heat. When the oil is hot, add the corn kernels, the corncob, shallots, garlic, salt, and pepper and sauté for 2 to 3 minutes. Stir in the stock and saffron and cook for 2 minutes.

2. Stir in the cream and simmer until the sauce is thick enough to coat a spoon, for about 6 to 7 minutes. Discard the corncob and whisk in the butter. Remove from the heat and whisk until the butter is thoroughly incorporated. Set aside for at least 15 minutes to allow the saffron to infuse the sauce. Serve immediately, or prepare except for the butter and store, refrigerated, in an airtight container for up to 24 hours. Reheat the sauce over low heat, whisk in the butter, and proceed from there.

THE LAST WORD

Believe it or not, there may be a few rotten fishmongers (or rotten-fish mongers) who might try to sell you rounds stamped out of fish and call them scallops. To be sure you have real scallops instead of just a hunk of fish, look for a slight ridge on one side. This is where the scallop was connected to the shell at its hinge.

Piri Piri Shrimp with Pasta Salad

◆

Makes 4 main-course servings

Here's a dynamite dish you can throw together in minutes. Dynamite is the operative word here, since the shrimp and the pasta salad are tossed in the uniquely flavorful piri piri, creating a delicious glow from your nose to your toes. If you really want to start a fire, marinate the shrimp in the Piri Piri for an hour or so before cooking. Making Piri Piri is easy; prepare a bottle a few weeks before you want to use it. You'll find yourself drizzling it over chicken and fish before you throw it on the barbie.

¼ cup Piri Piri (page 4)
5 cups Pasta Salad (recipe follows)
32 large shrimp (about 2 pounds),
   peeled

1 tablespoon Emeril's Creole
   Seasoning (page 3)

1. Prepare the Piri Piri at least a week ahead.

2. Prepare the Pasta Salad, and set aside while you prepare the shrimp, or make the salad up to 1 day ahead, and refrigerate.

3. Toss the shrimp with the Piri Piri and Creole Seasoning.

4. Heat a large skillet over high heat until hot. Add the shrimp and Piri Piri and sear for 2 minutes. Turn the shrimp and sear for 1 minute. Add the pasta salad on top and cook for 1 minute without stirring. Then toss together and remove from the heat.

5. To serve, use tongs to remove the shrimp from the pasta, and place 8 shrimp on each of 4 plates. Top the shrimp with 1¼ cups Pasta Salad.

PASTA SALAD

◆

Makes about 5 cups

4 cups cooked rigatoni, fusilli, ziti,
  or penne
⅓ cup pitted black olives, halved
⅓ cup pimiento-stuffed green olives,
  halved
¼ cup chopped green onions
¼ cup peeled and chopped tomatoes

¼ cup chopped fresh basil
1 tablespoon minced garlic
¼ teaspoon salt
4 turns freshly ground black pepper
3 tablespoons olive oil
½ cup coarsely grated fresh
  Parmesan cheese

Toss all of the ingredients together in a bowl until thoroughly blended. Serve immediately or store, refrigerated, in an airtight container for up to 24 hours.

André's Barbecued Shrimp and Homemade Biscuits

◆

Makes 4 main-course servings or 6 first-course servings

This is a new twist on an old New Orleans sacred cow, which I had the audacity to tamper with. I decided my version was good enough to be a signature dish for the restaurant; but I was so busy putting the restaurant together, I didn't have time to refine it for customer consumption. So I turned it over to my friend and sous chef, André Begnaud, who edited and retested it until it was just right for Emeril's. Today it's one of the most popular dishes on the menu, served as an appetizer or a main course with perfect bite-size Southern biscuits.

2 pounds medium-large shrimp in their shells, about 42 shrimp
2 tablespoons Emeril's Creole Seasoning (page 3), in all
16 turns freshly ground black pepper, in all
2 tablespoons olive oil, in all
¼ cup chopped onions
2 tablespoons minced garlic
3 bay leaves

3 lemons, peeled and sectioned
2 cups water
½ cup Worcestershire sauce
¼ cup dry white wine
¼ teaspoon salt
12 mini Buttermilk Biscuits (page 302)
2 cups heavy cream
2 tablespoons unsalted butter

1. Peel the shrimp, leaving only their tails attached. Reserve the shells, sprinkle the shrimp with 1 tablespoon Creole Seasoning and 8 turns of the black pepper. Use your hands to coat the shrimp with the seasonings. Refrigerate the shrimp while you make the sauce base and biscuits.

2. Heat 1 tablespoon of the oil in a large pot over high heat. When the oil is hot, add the onions and garlic and sauté for 1 minute. Add the reserved shrimp shells, the remaining 1 tablespoon Creole Seasoning, the bay leaves, lemons, water, Worcestershire, wine, salt, and the remaining 8 turns black pepper. Stir well and bring to a boil. Reduce the heat and simmer for 30 minutes. Remove from the heat, allow to cool for about 15 minutes, and strain into a small saucepan. There should be about 1½ cups. Place over high heat, bring to a boil, and cook until thick, syrupy, and dark brown, for about 15 minutes. Makes about 4 to 5 tablespoons of barbecue sauce base.

3. Prepare the Buttermilk Biscuits, and keep warm.

4. Heat the remaining 1 tablespoon of oil in a large skillet over high heat. When the oil is hot, add the seasoned shrimp and sauté them, occasionally shaking the skillet, for 2 minutes.

5. Add the cream and all of the barbecue base. Stir and simmer for 3 to 5 minutes. Remove the shrimp to a warm platter with tongs and whisk the butter into the sauce. Remove from the heat. Makes about 2 cups.

6. To serve 4, allow ½ cup of sauce, about 10 shrimp, and 3 biscuits each; for 6 servings, ⅓ cup sauce, about 7 shrimp, and 2 biscuits.

Roasted Shrimp with Saffron Potatoes and Tomato Mirliton Relish

◆

Makes 4 main-course servings

The mirliton is a tropical green squash—a staple in many Cajun homes, where it's often stuffed with bread crumbs and seafood. Cajuns might find my relish quirky, but I like its cool, delicate flavor against the spicy roasted shrimp. If you can't find mirlitons, also known as chayote or christophine, you can substitute cucumbers. When you invite your guests for this dinner, alert them not to wear a favorite white linen shirt, since they're going to be peeling their own shrimp. Of course, once they taste this dish they won't mind a bit. Just be sure to provide warm, damp cloths for cleaning up after the main course.

12 Saffron Potatoes (page 273)
1⅓ cups Tomato Mirliton Relish
   (page 288)
24 jumbo shrimp (about 2 pounds)
   in their shells, preferably with
   their heads

2 teaspoons Emeril's Creole
   Seasoning (page 3)
½ cup olive oil
¼ cup chopped green onions

1. Prepare the Saffron Potatoes, and set aside; they don't have to be reheated. Prepare the Tomato Mirliton Relish, and set aside.

2. Preheat the oven to 400°F.

3. In a large ovenproof skillet, combine the shrimp, Creole Seasoning, and oil, and toss to blend well. Remove the skillet from the heat, place it in the oven, and roast the shrimp until they are opaque and pink, for about 3 to 4 minutes on each side. Remove from the oven and reserve the pan juices.

4. To serve, place ⅓ cup of the Tomato Mirliton Relish in the center of each dinner plate. Arrange 3 Saffron Potatoes and 6 shrimp around the relish on each plate. Drizzle with the pan juices and sprinkle with 1 tablespoon of the green onions.

Roasted Shrimp with Roasted Red Pepper Sauce and Warm Frisée Corn Salad

◆

Makes 4 main-course servings

In New Orleans we can get the best fresh shrimp at the lowest prices almost 10 months out of the year. In fact, dollar for dollar, consumers in New Orleans may eat better than those anywhere else in the country. Around town you can buy fresh shrimp from vendors who've pulled their pickups to the side of the road and are selling the shrimp from cooler chests overflowing with the morning's catch. We buy them with their heads on, and sometimes I leave them on when I cook them, as I do in this dish, and the juices keep the shrimp sweet and moist. When you visit New Orleans, don't be surprised if you hear the locals calling this seafood favorite "swimps" or "s'rimps." Makes 'em taste even better.

2 cups Roasted Red Pepper Sauce
  (page 157)
3 cups Warm Frisée Corn Salad
  (page 101)
24 jumbo shrimp in their shells, and
  with their heads, if you can buy
  them that way (about 2 pounds)

1 tablespoon plus 1 teaspoon
  Emeril's Creole Seasoning
  (page 3)
2 tablespoons olive oil
8 long fresh chives

1. Preheat the oven to 350°F.

2. Prepare the Roasted Red Pepper Sauce, and keep warm. While the sauce is simmering, prepare the Warm Frisée Corn Salad, and keep warm.

3. Place the shrimp in a bowl, sprinkle them with the Creole Seasoning, and rub it into the shells with your hands. Bake the shrimp on a baking sheet for 5 minutes; turn them over and bake for another 5 minutes. Remove from the oven.

4. To serve, pour ½ cup of the Roasted Red Pepper Sauce into each of 4 plates. Mound ¾ cup of the Warm Frisée Corn Salad in the center and arrange 6 shrimp on top, like spokes radiating from the center. Top with chives and serve.

Crab-Stuffed Shrimp with Tomato Butter and White Bean Relish

◆

Makes 4 main-course servings

As a native of New England, I can tell you that you can't go out to dinner at any restaurant in that part of the world without seeing baked stuffed shrimp proudly displayed on the menu—often proclaimed the specialty of the establishment. Sadly, the dish rarely lives up to its fanfare. It usually arrives dry and rubbery, the shrimp overbaked, tasteless vehicles for a sticky stuffing of crushed Ritz crackers. Yet I always knew there was potential here; after all, shrimp are delicious when properly prepared and thoughtfully stuffed. So here's my version, paired with a White Bean Relish and finished with a spicy Tomato Butter.

2 cups White Bean Relish
  (page 293)
1 tablespoon unsalted butter
¼ cup finely minced onions
¼ cup finely minced celery
¼ cup finely minced green bell
  peppers
2 tablespoons finely minced red bell
  peppers
1 tablespoon minced garlic
4 teaspoons Emeril's Creole
  Seasoning (page 3), in all
1 teaspoon salt, in all
4 turns freshly ground black pepper

1 pound lump crabmeat, picked over
  for shells and cartilage
1 large egg
¼ cup freshly grated Parmesan
  cheese
1 tablespoon Creole or other
  whole-seed mustard
¼ cup bread crumbs (page 17)
16 large shrimp, peeled except for
  the tails, and butterflied (page 17)
1½ cups Tomato Butter
  (recipe follows)
Chopped green onions

1. Prepare the White Bean Relish, and set aside.

2. Preheat the oven to 375°F. Line a baking sheet with parchment or wax paper.

3. Melt the butter in a medium skillet over high heat. Add the onions, celery, green and red bell peppers, garlic, 2 teaspoons Creole Seasoning, ½ teaspoon salt, and the pepper, and sauté for 2 to 3 minutes. Add the crabmeat and toss gently, taking care not to break up the crabmeat lumps, for about 1 minute. Remove from the heat and allow to cool for 3 to 4 minutes.

4. Whisk the egg in a large bowl, and stir in the mixture from the skillet. Stir in the Parmesan, mustard, and bread crumbs. Makes 2½ cups. Allow to cool a minute, then shape loosely into 16 balls, using about 2½ tablespoons of the mixture for each ball.

5. Sprinkle the shrimp with the remaining 2 teaspoons Creole Seasoning, and use your hands to coat them thoroughly. Press one ball of stuffing into the cavity of each shrimp and arrange the shrimp on the baking sheet. Sprinkle the shrimp with the remaining ½ teaspoon salt. Bake until brown, for about 10 minutes, and remove from the oven.

6. Prepare the Tomato Butter and warm the White Bean Relish.

7. To serve, spread a generous ⅓ cup of the Tomato Butter in each of 4 dinner plates. Mound ½ cup of the White Bean Relish in the center, arrange 4 shrimp around the relish, and sprinkle green onions around the plate.

TOMATO BUTTER

◆

Makes 1½ cups

¾ cup peeled, seeded, and chopped
   Italian plum tomatoes (about 3)
2 teaspoons minced garlic
½ cup Shrimp Stock (page 10)

½ teaspoon salt
1 light pinch cayenne pepper
2 turns freshly ground black pepper
1 stick unsalted butter, cut up

1. Mash the tomatoes with a whisk in a small nonreactive saucepan over high heat for about 1 minute. Add the garlic, Shrimp Stock, salt, cayenne, and black pepper and bring to a boil, whisking. Continue cooking, whisking constantly, for about 1 minute.

2. Add the butter a few pats at a time, and when half incorporated, remove the pot from the heat and continue whisking until all of the butter is incorporated.

3. Serve immediately or prepare only through Step 1; store, refrigerated, in an airtight container. Reheat in a saucepan over low heat. When the sauce comes to a simmer, proceed with Step 2.

Steamed Ginger Shrimp Dumplings with Stir-Fried Sesame Vegetables

◆

Makes 4 main-course servings

Creole? No. Oriental? Yes. Delicious? You betcha. Serve with Tsing-tao beer or warm sake.

1 tablespoon olive oil
½ pound shrimp, peeled and
  coarsely chopped
¼ cup chopped onions
2 teaspoons minced garlic
3 tablespoons peeled and grated
  fresh gingerroot
½ cup chopped green onions, in all
3 tablespoons chopped fresh cilantro
1 tablespoon plus 1 teaspoon sesame
  oil, in all
3 teaspoons toasted sesame seeds
  (page 14)

1 large egg
1 teaspoon soy sauce
1 dash Worcestershire sauce
½ teaspoon grated orange zest
⅛ teaspoon cayenne pepper
½ teaspoon salt
4 turns freshly ground black pepper
20 wonton skins (see Note)
4 cups Shrimp Stock (page 10)
2 cups Stir-Fried Sesame Vegetables
  (page 278)

1. Heat the olive oil in a large skillet over high heat. When the oil is hot, add the shrimp and stir-fry for 1 minute. Add the onions, garlic, and ginger, and stir-fry for 1 minute. Stir in ¼ cup green onions and the cilantro, stir-fry for 1 minute, and remove from the heat.

2. Turn the skillet mixture into a bowl. Add 1 teaspoon of the sesame oil, the sesame seeds, egg, soy sauce, Worcestershire, orange zest, cayenne, salt, and pepper and stir well. Makes 2 cups.

3. Place the wonton skins on a clean counter and brush just the top side with water. Mound 1 tablespoon of the filling in the middle of each skin. Bring up the corners to the center and twist, sealing the edges with water.

4. Combine the stock with the remaining 1 tablespoon sesame oil in a large saucepan or soup pot and bring to a boil over high heat. Slip the dumplings into the boiling stock, reduce to a simmer, and poach the dumplings until they're tender, for about 4 minutes. Remove with a slotted spoon. (You'll probably have to poach the dumplings in 2 batches.)

5. While the dumplings are poaching, prepare the Stir-Fried Sesame Vegetables.

6. To serve, mound ½ cup of the Stir-Fried Sesame Vegetables on each of 4 plates. Arrange 5 dumplings around the vegetables and spoon about ¼ cup of the broth over them. Sprinkle with 1 tablespoon of the remaining chopped green onions.

Note: Wonton skins can be bought in many supermarkets and specialty food stores.

Stuffed Soft-Shell Crabs with Pesto Cream

◆

Makes 4 main-course servings

In New Orleans we're lucky that we can get soft-shell crabs throughout most of the year, depending on the weather. This is a twist on the sameoldsameold way to serve them. It pairs the soft shells with a rich, spicy cream for an unexpected treat.

4 ounces soft goat cheese, such as
  Montrachet
3 tablespoons roasted pine nuts
  (page 14)
1 tablespoon chopped fresh basil
1 tablespoon minced shallots
1 teaspoon minced garlic
½ teaspoon salt
2 turns freshly ground black pepper
¼ cup plus 1 tablespoon olive oil,
  in all

4 huge soft-shell crabs, cleaned
  (have your fish market do this),
  and patted dry
1⅓ cups Pesto Cream
  (recipe follows)
1 cup all-purpose flour
1 tablespoon Emeril's Creole
  Seasoning (page 3), in all

1. In a bowl combine the goat cheese, pine nuts, basil, shallots, garlic, salt, pepper, and 1 tablespoon olive oil, and blend with a wooden spoon until smooth. Makes ½ cup stuffing mixture.

2. Place the crabs belly-up on a flat surface. Lift the side of a crab to expose the underside of the shell (there is a natural pocket under the point of the shell). Spoon 1 tablespoon of the stuffing mixture into each of these pockets, with a total of 2 tablespoons per crab.

3. Prepare the Pesto Cream, and keep warm.

4. Combine the flour with the Creole Seasoning and dredge the crabs in the mixture.

5. Heat the remaining ¼ cup oil in a large skillet over high heat and sauté the crabs (shell side down first) until golden brown, for about 2½ minutes on each side.

6. To serve, spread ⅓ cup of the Pesto Cream on each of 4 plates and top with a crab.

PESTO CREAM

◆

Makes 1⅓ cups

1 large egg
1 cup (packed) fresh basil leaves
⅓ cup roasted pine nuts (page 14)
2 tablespoons minced shallots
1 tablespoon minced garlic
½ teaspoon salt

3 turns freshly ground black pepper
½ cup olive oil
¼ cup coarsely grated fresh
  Parmesan cheese
¼ cup heavy cream

1. Combine the egg, basil, pine nuts, shallots, garlic, salt, and pepper in a food processor or blender and purée. Slowly stream in the oil and continue to process until the mixture becomes thoroughly emulsified. Add the Parmesan and process for 15 seconds.

2. Heat the cream in a small saucepan over high heat, add the mixture from the food processor or blender, and cook, whisking constantly, for 2 minutes. Remove from the heat. Serve immediately.

Stir-Fry of Sesame Ginger Crawfish over Fried Pasta

◆

Makes 4 main-course servings

*E*ast meets bayou in this dazzling dish for the cross-cultural adventurer. It's surprising how well fresh, juicy crawfish work in an Oriental setting. Instead of the traditional Chinese noodles, we've fried up some pasta to complete the world tour.

1 pound peeled fresh crawfish tails	¼ cup nuts (pecans, pistachios, pine nuts, or peanuts)
3 tablespoons Emeril's Creole Seasoning (page 3), in all	3 tablespoons sesame oil
3 cups Fried Pasta (page 17)	1 tablespoon minced garlic
2 tablespoons olive oil	2 tablespoons peeled and minced fresh gingerroot
½ cup bias-cut thinly sliced celery	1 cup Basic Chicken Stock (page 7) or Shrimp Stock (page 10)
¼ cup chopped onions	
¼ cup chopped green onions	½ teaspoon salt
4 cups shredded bok choy	3 turns freshly ground black pepper
1 cup stemmed snow peas	

1. Combine the crawfish tails with 2 tablespoons Creole Seasoning in a small bowl and mix with your hands until the seasoning is thoroughly blended in.

2. Prepare the Fried Pasta, and keep warm on a baking sheet in a 200°F oven.

3. Heat the oil in a large skillet over high heat. Add the celery, onions and green onions, bok choy, and snow peas and stir-fry for 1 minute. Add the nuts and sesame oil and stir-fry for 1 minute. Stir in the garlic and ginger and stir-fry for 1 minute. Stir in the stock and bring to a simmer. Add the crawfish, salt, pepper, and the remaining 1 tablespoon Creole Seasoning and cook, stirring, for 1 minute. Makes 4 cups.

4. To serve, divide the Fried Pasta into 4 equal portions (reserving a few noodles for garnish), and stack them in shallow soup bowls. Spoon 1 cup stir-fried crawfish over the noodles. Sprinkle a few reserved noodles on top.

Steamed Mussels in Fennel Pernod Broth

◆

Makes 4 first-course servings

Mussels in wine may sound familiar, but mussels in a broth flavored with Pernod and fennel is a bit more unusual in New Orleans. This dish is such a snap to make, you won't believe how delicious it tastes. Whatever you do, don't overcook the mussels, or they'll shrivel up to little marbles.

1 tablespoon olive oil
1 cup chopped fennel, bulb only
1 onion, cut in half and sliced
2 teaspoons salt
10 turns freshly ground black pepper
2 tablespoons minced garlic

½ cup Pernod
½ cup peeled and chopped Italian plum tomatoes
2 cups Shrimp Stock (page 10)
40 mussels, cleaned and debearded (page 16)
½ cup chopped green onions

1. Heat the oil in a large nonreactive skillet over high heat. Add the fennel, onions, salt, and pepper and sauté for 2 minutes. Add the garlic and Pernod and stand back in case it flames.

2. Stir in the tomatoes and shrimp stock and bring to a simmer. Add the mussels and green onions, cover, and steam over high heat until all of the mussel shells have opened, for about 4 minutes.

3. Remove the mussels with tongs and let the broth cook for 2 minutes longer. Remove from the heat. Makes 3 cups broth.

4. To serve, arrange 10 mussels in each of 4 shallow bowls, and spoon ¾ cup of the broth over them.

Lobster with Champagne Vanilla Sauce and Wild Mushroom Salad

◆

Makes 4 main-course servings

This medley of flavors may seem unusual to you; actually, it was to me at first, too. I mean, it sure doesn't come from my French-Canadian/Portuguese ancestry, nor is it a traditional specialty of New England, where I was raised. And, certainly, the Cajuns and Creoles from Louisiana will think I've lost my mind. But stay with me here; this works. There's something about fresh vanilla beans—the aroma, the flavor—that inspires a combination with fresh shellfish. And what better complement than champagne? This sauce is exquisite with lobster but is also marvelous with scallops and the beautiful crabmeat we get here in New Orleans. So, now, don't turn up your nose because you've never heard of such a thing, or you'll miss out in a big way. And, for a special occasion, serve this with chilled champagne.

1½ cups **Wilted Wild Mushroom Salad (page 104)**
1 cup **champagne or sparkling wine**
½ teaspoon **freshly squeezed lime juice**
1 **vanilla bean, split and scraped (page 14)**
3 tablespoons **minced shallots**
1 tablespoon **sugar**

1 cup **heavy cream**
2 teaspoons **salt**
1 teaspoon **white pepper**
3 tablespoons **unsalted butter, in all**
1¼ pounds **freshly cooked lobster meat, the tails cut into 1-inch chunks and the claws left whole**
2 tablespoons **finely chopped fresh chives**

1. Prepare the Wilted Wild Mushroom Salad, and set aside.

2. Combine the champagne, lime juice, vanilla bean (including the pasty insides and the pod), shallots, and sugar in a medium skillet over high heat. Bring to a boil, breaking up the vanilla bean paste with a whisk to disperse it into the liquid, and simmer until the liquid is reduced by about half.

3. Stir in the cream, salt, and pepper and cook, stirring occasionally, until the sauce is thick enough to coat a spoon, for about 5 minutes. Whisk in 1 tablespoon of the butter, remove the skillet from the heat, and whisk until the butter is thoroughly incorporated. Strain through a sieve or cheesecloth, and keep warm until ready to serve. Makes 1 cup.

4. Heat the remaining 2 tablespoons butter in a large skillet over high heat. When the butter is half melted, add the lobster and sauté, tossing occasionally until the lobster meat is just warmed through, for about 1 minute. Remove the skillet from the heat, add the chives, and toss to mix well.

5. To serve, pour ¼ cup of the sauce into each of 4 dinner plates. Divide the mushroom salad into 4 equal portions and heap it in the center of each plate. Divide the lobster meat into 4 equal portions and arrange it around the mushroom salad.

CHAPTER 8

Fowl Play: Chicken, Duck, and Quail

A simple roast chicken is one of my favorite dishes. My father was the one who roasted the chickens at home, and the memories of those dinners give me a rosy glow.

I'll bet you could prepare chicken a different way every night for a month and never grow tired of it. I know I could. That's because chicken is so adaptable. That old-fashioned roast chicken is great, but in this chapter you'll find new ways to stuff it, season it, or "borderize" it, as with the Albuquerque Roast Chicken with Black Bean Chili, Guacamole, and Fried Tortilla Strips. You'll find chicken in new packages, as in Stuffed Chicken Legs in Pastry with Andouille Cream, or as the package itself, in Chicken Pockets Stuffed with Goat Cheese, Chorizo, and Pine Nuts.

Duck seems to be something everyone loves, and I've included two of the most popular dishes we serve at the restaurant, Tangerine Duck, which is really very different from the old orange duck, and Duck Roulades with Avocado, Pistachios, and Pistachio Armagnac Sauce. Roulades are cross-section slices cut from a piece of meat rolled up around an avocado-pistachio filling or duxelles. They're pretty, and pretty wonderful.

I've also included a quail dish, since quail is so popular in New Orleans. Elsewhere, some people are turned off by the diminutive proportions of the quail (they're so small, you serve two per person); but quail are tender, have a lovely flavor all their own, and work beautifully with many stuffings and sauces. So don't let their size keep you from trying them. Ask your butcher to order some of these little birds for you, and try the Quail Milton in this chapter.

Roast Rosemary Chicken and Vegetables

◆

Makes 4 main-course servings

Question: What's the best feel-good family dinner for a Sunday afternoon? Answer: Roast Rosemary Chicken and Vegetables—made my way. If you really want to feel good, start off with Dr. E's Get-Well Chicken Vegetable Soup (page 56). If there are only two of you, you can feel very good knowing there will be leftovers.

2 whole chickens (about 2½ pounds each), cleaned and rinsed thoroughly
12 whole peeled garlic cloves, in all
½ cup coarsely chopped onions, in all
½ cup coarsely chopped celery, in all
½ cup coarsely chopped carrots, in all
4 bay leaves, in all
2 sprigs fresh rosemary, in all

2 tablespoons olive oil, in all
2 teaspoons salt, in all
24 turns freshly ground black pepper, in all
4 whole carrots, peeled and halved vertically, in all
4 whole stalks celery, in all
4 onions, quartered, in all
2 large russet potatoes, peeled and quartered, in all
4 parsnips, peeled and halved, in all
2 cups water

1. Preheat the oven to 400°F.

2. Push 6 cloves of the garlic under the skin of each chicken (3 under each breast). Place ¼ cup each of the chopped onions, celery, and carrots into the cavity of each chicken, along with 2 bay leaves for each.

3. Strip the leaves from the rosemary sprigs and chop them. Push the leaves under the skin of each breast and sprinkle some over the skin; place a rosemary stem in each cavity. Rub the skin of each chicken with 1 tablespoon of the oil, and sprinkle each with ½ teaspoon of the salt and 6 turns of the pepper.

4. Place the halved carrots in a large roasting pan. Place the whole celery stalks across the carrots to form a bed for the chickens. Place the quartered onions, potatoes, and parsnips around the pan and add the water. Sprinkle the vegetables with the remaining 1 teaspoon salt and the remaining 12 turns black pepper.

5. Place the chickens on top of the vegetables and roast for 45 minutes. Reduce the oven temperature to 350°F and roast until the meat is falling off the bones, for about 50 to 60 minutes more.

6. To serve, halve the chickens and allow one-half per portion, surrounded by the vegetables.

Albuquerque Roast Chicken with Black Bean Chili, Guacamole, and Fried Tortilla Strips

◆

Makes 4 main-course servings

The irresistible flavors of garlic, onions, and American Southwest seasoning escort this juicy-crisp chicken to the table, my version of a New New Mexican dish, if you will. The presentation—with its colorful accompaniments, including fried tortilla strips piled high on each serving—is a knockout.

2 whole chickens (about 3 pounds each), cleaned and rinsed thoroughly
2 tablespoons olive oil
12 peeled whole cloves garlic
½ cup chopped onions, in all
¼ cup chopped celery, in all

¼ cup peeled chopped carrots, in all
2 teaspoons Emeril's Southwest Seasoning (page 3), in all
2 cups Black Bean Chili (page 263)
1 cup Guacamole (page 286)
4 handfuls Fried Tortilla Strips (page 18)

1. Preheat the oven to 400°F.

2. With your hands, rub the chickens inside and out with the oil, using 1 tablespoon per chicken. Insert the garlic cloves—3 per breast, 6 per chicken—between the breast meat and skin.

3. Sprinkle each chicken inside and out with ¼ cup of the onions, 2 tablespoons of the celery, and 2 tablespoons of the carrots. Sprinkle each chicken inside and out with 1 teaspoon Southwest Seasoning; use your hands to coat the chicken thoroughly.

4. Prepare the Black Bean Chili so it will simmer on the stove while the chicken is roasting. If it's finished first, keep warm.

5. Place the chickens, breast side up, on a rack in a baking pan and roast until crisp but tender, for about 1 hour 10 minutes. Remove from the oven, slice the breast meat from the bones, and remove the thigh and drumstick intact.

6. While the chicken is roasting, and about 20 minutes before it's done, prepare the Guacamole, cover it tightly, and set aside.

7. As soon as you remove the chicken from the oven, prepare the Fried Tortilla Strips.

8. To serve, spread ½ cup of the Black Bean Chili on each of 4 dinner plates and arrange 1 chicken breast and 1 thigh/drumstick on top of the sauce. Mound ¼ cup of the Guacamole on the plate, and top the chicken with a handful of the Fried Tortilla Strips.

Tender Roast Chicken with Chestnut Corn-Bread Dressing

◆

Makes 2 feel-good dinner servings

Make this in the fall when chestnuts are in season. It will probably be the juiciest chicken you've ever eaten.

2 tablespoons olive oil, in all
¼ cup chopped onions
¼ cup chopped celery
¼ cup chopped carrots
½ cup chopped andouille or chorizo sausage
1 tablespoon minced garlic
6 roasted, peeled, and coarsely chopped chestnuts
1½ cups finely crumbled day-old plain corn bread or corn muffins (page 303)

¾ teaspoon salt, in all
9 turns freshly ground black pepper, in all
½ cup Basic Chicken Stock (page 6)
1 whole chicken (about 2½ pounds)
5 whole peeled garlic cloves
½ teaspoon Emeril's Creole Seasoning (page 3)

1. Preheat the oven to 400°F.

2. Heat 1 tablespoon of the oil in a large skillet over high heat. Add the onions, celery, and carrots and sauté for 2 minutes. Add the sausage and garlic and sauté for 1 minute. Remove from the heat.

3. Turn the contents of the skillet into a large bowl, add the chestnuts, corn bread, ¼ teaspoon of the salt, and 3 turns of the pepper, and toss until thoroughly combined.

4. Place the same skillet back over high heat, add the chicken stock, and deglaze the skillet, scraping up any browned bits clinging to the pan. Remove from the heat and pour into the mixture in the bowl. Stir until the dressing is evenly moistened. Makes about 1½ cups.

5. Push the garlic cloves under the skin of the chicken, and brush with the remaining 1 tablespoon oil. Sprinkle the chicken inside and out with the Creole Seasoning, the remaining ½ teaspoon salt, and the remaining 6 turns pepper. Using a large spoon, stuff the dressing into the cavity of the chicken. Place the chicken on a rack in a roasting pan and roast until juicy but done to the bone, about 1½ hours.

6. To serve, mound about ¾ cup of the dressing on each of 2 plates, and top with ½ chicken.

Piri Piri Chicken with Jícama Orange Salad

◆

Makes 4 main-course servings

I can't think of better eating on a warm summer evening than this light, easy-to-make dish. The unusual, tangy heat of the Piri Piri—a Portuguese/African rendition of the Creole or Cajun chile pepper condiment—is offset by the cool, refreshing flavors of the salad.

½ cup Piri Piri (page 4), in all
3 cups Jícama Orange Salad
  (page 113)
4 skinned and boned chicken breast
  halves (about 6 ounces each)

4 teaspoons Emeril's Southwest
  Seasoning (page 3), in all

1. Prepare the Piri Piri at least a week ahead.

2. Prepare the Jícama Orange Salad, and set aside.

3. Sprinkle 1 teaspoon Southwest Seasoning on each chicken breast, using your hands to coat both sides thoroughly.

4. Heat 1 tablespoon of the Piri Piri in a large skillet over high heat. Add the chicken and sauté until brown, for about 3 minutes on each side, then turn again and cook for another 2 minutes, for a total of 8 minutes. Remove from the heat, and remove the chicken with tongs.

5. Heat the remaining 7 tablespoons Piri Piri in a small saucepan until hot and bubbling, for about 2 minutes.

6. To serve, place 1 chicken breast on each of 4 plates and top with ¾ cup of the Jícama Orange Salad. Spoon 1½ tablespoons of the heated Piri Piri over all.

Chicken Pockets Stuffed with Goat Cheese, Chorizo, and Pine Nuts on a Bed of Southern-Style Black-Eye Peas

◆

Makes 4 main-course servings

Bite into this chicken, and a riot of flavors explodes in your mouth. I decided that the flavor teaming of goat cheese, chorizo, and pine nuts would work with chicken—and it does. This dish feels both new and old at the same time, since the stuffing in the chicken pockets is so current, and the black-eye peas fairly traditional.

8 ounces (1 cup) chopped chorizo, the casings removed and discarded
4 ounces (½ cup) goat cheese, such as Montrachet
¼ cup roasted pine nuts (page 14)
3 tablespoons chopped green onions
1 tablespoon minced garlic
1 tablespoon chopped fresh cilantro
1 teaspoon chili powder
1 teaspoon ground cumin

½ teaspoon salt
3 turns freshly ground black pepper
3 cups Southern-Style Black-Eye Peas (page 262)
4 skinned and boned chicken breast halves (about 6 ounces each), pounded very thin
4 teaspoons Emeril's Creole Seasoning (page 00), in all
2 teaspoons olive oil

1. Preheat the oven to 400°F. Line a baking sheet with parchment or wax paper.

2. Combine the chorizo, goat cheese, pine nuts, green onions, garlic, cilantro, chili powder, cumin, salt, and pepper in a bowl and mix until thoroughly blended. Makes 1½ cups of stuffing.

3. Prepare the Black-Eye Peas.

4. Spread the chicken breasts on a flat surface and sprinkle each, top side only, with ½ teaspoon Creole Seasoning. Place a heaping ⅓ cup of the stuffing on half of each chicken breast and fold the other half over the stuffing and pinch the edges together. Brush the tops with the oil, using ½ teaspoon on each, and sprinkle each with ½ teaspoon of the remaining Creole Seasoning.

5. Place the pockets on the baking sheet and bake until the chicken is golden brown, for about 18 minutes.

6. To serve, spread ¾ cup of the Black-Eye Peas on each of 4 plates, and top with 1 chicken pocket.

Panéed Chicken with Creamed Garlic Potatoes and Braised Kale

◆

Makes 4 main-course servings

When we pan-fry breaded chicken or veal in New Orleans, we call it "panéed," and it's truly a classic New Orleans preparation. Most people add dry herbs to the breading mixture, but I prefer using fresh herbs. If you fry these chicken breasts carefully in olive oil, they'll be wonderfully ungreasy, crisp, and delicious.

4 skinned and boned chicken breast halves (5 to 6 ounces each)
4 teaspoons Emeril's Creole Seasoning (page 3), in all
1 cup bread crumbs (page 17)
2 tablespoons coarsely grated fresh Parmesan cheese
1 teaspoon chopped fresh parsley
1 teaspoon chopped fresh basil
1 teaspoon chopped fresh thyme
1 teaspoon chopped fresh tarragon

1 teaspoon chopped fresh oregano
7 tablespoons olive oil, in all
½ teaspoon salt
3 turns freshly ground black pepper
½ cup all-purpose flour
1 large egg
½ cup milk
2 cups Braised Kale (page 279)
2½ cups Creamed Garlic Potatoes (page 272)

1. Pound the chicken breasts with a mallet between sheets of wax paper or plastic wrap until they're about ¼ inch thick. Sprinkle each chicken breast with ¼ teaspoon Creole Seasoning, using your hands to coat the meat.

2. In a bowl combine the bread crumbs with the Parmesan, parsley, basil, thyme, tarragon, oregano, 1 tablespoon oil, 1 teaspoon Creole Seasoning, salt, and pepper. In another bowl combine the flour with 1 teaspoon Creole Seasoning. In a third bowl beat the eggs with the milk and the remaining 1 teaspoon Creole Seasoning.

3. Prepare the Braised Kale and the Creamed Garlic Potatoes, and keep both warm.

4. Dredge the chicken in the seasoned flour, the egg wash, and then the bread-crumb mixture, coating each piece completely.

5. Heat the remaining 6 tablespoons oil in a large skillet over high heat. When the oil is hot, add the chicken breasts and sauté until golden brown, for about 2½ minutes on the first side and 2 minutes on the second side.

6. To serve, arrange 1 chicken breast, ½ cup of the Braised Kale, and a generous ½ cup of Creamed Garlic Potatoes on each of 4 dinner plates.

Pine Nut-Crusted Chicken with Roasted Poblano Sauce

◆

Makes 4 main-course servings

Pine nuts, piñon nuts, pignoli, pignons, Indian nuts—all refer to the small nuts most often used in pesto. There are two varieties: Portuguese, which are long and thin, and Chinese, which are short and stout. Try to get Portuguese pine nuts for this dish, because their flavor is sweeter and more delicate. The roasted poblano sauce, combined with the crunchy, juicy chicken, is pure heaven.

2 cups Roasted Poblano Sauce (recipe follows)

4 skinned and boned chicken breast halves (5 to 6 ounces each)

1 tablespoon plus 2 teaspoons Emeril's Southwest Seasoning (page 3), in all

½ cup all-purpose flour

1 large egg

¾ cup milk

2 cups finely chopped (in a food processor) pine nuts

¼ cup olive oil

¼ cup chopped fresh cilantro

1. Prepare the Roasted Poblano Sauce.

2. Sprinkle the chicken breasts on both sides with the Southwest Seasoning, using a total of 2 teaspoons, and pat it on with your hands.

3. In a bowl combine the flour with the remaining 1 tablespoon Southwest Seasoning. In another bowl beat the egg together with the milk. Place the chopped pine nuts in a third bowl.

4. Dredge the chicken in the seasoned flour, then the egg wash, then the pine nuts, pressing the nuts thickly onto the chicken all over.

5. Heat the oil in a large skillet over medium-high heat and sauté the chicken until golden, for about 5 minutes on each side.

6. To serve, pour ½ cup of the Poblano Sauce into each of 4 plates. Top with 1 chicken breast half and garnish with 1 tablespoon chopped cilantro.

ROASTED POBLANO SAUCE

◆

Makes 2 cups

1 tablespoon olive oil
½ cup (about 2 peppers) peeled,
   seeded, and chopped roasted
   poblano peppers (page 16)
½ cup (1 small onion) peeled and
   chopped Fire-roasted onions
   (page 16)

2 teaspoons minced garlic
1 teaspoon Emeril's Southwest
   Seasoning (page 3)
1 teaspoon salt
2 turns freshly ground black pepper
3 cups Basic Chicken Stock (page 6)
3 tablespoons heavy cream

1. Combine the oil, poblanos, onion, garlic, Southwest Seasoning, salt, and pepper in a medium saucepan over high heat and cook, stirring occasionally, for about 2 minutes.

2. Stir in the stock, bring to a boil, and cook over high heat for 18 minutes. Reduce the heat to medium. Stir in the cream and simmer for 2 minutes.

3. Remove from the heat and purée in a food processor or blender. Serve immediately or store, refrigerated, in an airtight container for up to 24 hours. Reheat in a saucepan over lowest heat.

Chicken Fricassee with Fried Polenta

◆

Makes 4 main-course servings

Let's really mix things up: fricassee, or stew, from France; polenta, which is a dish of cornmeal, from Italy; and Creole seasonings. New Orleans is a melting pot, too, and I like to let myself go really eclectic sometimes to gain new perspectives on food.

8 wedges Fried Polenta (page 285)
½ pound skinned and boned chicken breasts, cut into thin strips
1 tablespoon Emeril's Creole Seasoning (page 3)
¼ cup olive oil
1 onion, cut in half and sliced vertically
1 tablespoon minced garlic

½ cup peeled, seeded, and chopped Italian plum tomatoes
2 tablespoons chopped fresh basil
2 tablespoons chopped fresh sage
½ teaspoon salt
3 turns freshly ground black pepper
½ cup Basic Chicken Stock (page 6)
½ cup coarsely grated fresh Parmesan cheese

1. Prepare the Fried Polenta through Step 3.

2. In a bowl toss the chicken strips with the Creole Seasoning, using your hands to coat the meat well.

3. Heat the oil in a medium nonreactive skillet over high heat. Add the seasoned chicken and sauté, stirring, until the chicken is golden, for about 2 minutes. Add the onion, garlic, tomatoes, basil, and sage and sauté for 3 minutes. Add the salt, pepper, and stock and heat just until bubbles form around the edge, for about 1 minute. Remove from the heat and keep warm. Makes 2 cups.

4. Finish the Fried Polenta.

5. To serve, place 2 narrow wedges of the Fried Polenta on each of 4 plates and spoon ½ cup of the fricassee over them. Top each serving with 2 tablespoons Parmesan.

Chicken in Peanut Sauce

◆

Makes 4 first-course servings

In recent years, New Orleanians have become curious about all sorts of ethnic cooking. Indonesian food, however, has remained somewhat of a mystery, although the spices lend themselves to a certain Big Easy style of eating. Satay, which is a small skewer of bite-size meat—an Indonesian shish kebab—has, in some small culinary circles, gathered its own finger-licking following, especially if accompanied by a peanut sauce. A big lover of peanut butter, I was a natural to join the satay squad. The following is my version of this wonderful treat.

½ cup Basic Chicken Stock (page 6)
½ cup heavy cream
¼ cup chopped roasted unsalted peanuts
¼ cup smooth peanut butter
2 tablespoons sesame oil
1 tablespoon soy sauce
1 tablespoon minced garlic
1 tablespoon chopped fresh cilantro
½ teaspoon salt

¼ teaspoon cayenne pepper
2 turns freshly ground black pepper
½ pound skinned and boned chicken breasts, cut into long strips ¼ inch across
8 teaspoons Emeril's Creole Seasoning (page 3), in all
¼ cup finely chopped green onions
8 small wooden or metal skewers (about 8 inches)

1. In a medium saucepan over high heat, combine the stock, cream, peanuts, peanut butter, sesame oil, soy sauce, garlic, cilantro, salt, cayenne, and black pepper. Bring to a boil, reduce the heat, and simmer, stirring, for 3 minutes. Remove from the heat. Makes about 1½ cups.

2. Skewer the chicken pieces the long way, threading about 6 to 8 pieces per skewer. Sprinkle 1 teaspoon Creole Seasoning over each skewer of chicken, and use your hands to coat the meat.

3. Heat a large skillet over high heat and sear the chicken until brown, for about 1½ minutes on each of 4 sides, or a total of 6 to 8 minutes. Remove from the heat.

4. To serve, spoon a generous ⅓ cup of the sauce onto each of 4 plates, arrange 2 skewers on top, and sprinkle with 1 tablespoon of the green onions. Let your guests eat this as they wish, pushing the chicken off the skewers with a fork, or nibbling it right off the skewers.

Stuffed Chicken Legs in Pastry with Andouille Cream

◆

Makes 4 main-course servings

For a dish that's as visually exciting as it is wonderful tasting, you can't beat this one. It reflects the adventurous new direction food is taking in New Orleans. The most important ingredient here is a good butcher who's willing to bone your chicken legs—unless, of course, you happen to be adept at this tricky little operation. Once the legs are boned, the rest is a snap.

1½ cups Andouille Corn-Bread
   Stuffing (page 283)
1 recipe Basic Pie Dough (page
   313), rolled out into two 9-inch
   dough rounds, each cut in half
4 boned (except for the knuckle or
   joint at the bottom of the
   drumstick) chicken legs, the thigh
   and the drumstick all in 1 piece

2 teaspoons Emeril's Creole
   Seasoning (page 3), in all
1 large egg, lightly beaten
2 cups Andouille Cream
   (recipe follows)

1. Prepare the Andouille Corn-Bread Stuffing and the Basic Pie Dough.

2. Preheat the oven to 375°F. Line a baking sheet with parchment or wax paper.

3. Spread the meat of the chicken legs open and sprinkle the inside of each with ¼ teaspoon Creole Seasoning. Sprinkle the outside of each leg with another ¼ teaspoon Creole Seasoning, and use your hands to coat thoroughly.

4. Stuff the cavity of each leg with 6 tablespoons of the stuffing and close the skin around it. Brush the half-circles of dough with some of the beaten egg and place one leg on each piece with the joint sticking out. Fold the ends over to create a wrapper and place, seam side down, on the baking sheet. Brush the outside of each package with more of the beaten egg and bake until the crust is brown and the chicken tender, for about 35 minutes.

5. Prepare the Andouille Cream.

6. To serve, spoon ½ cup of the Andouille Cream onto each of 4 dinner plates, and place a baked chicken leg on each.

ANDOUILLE CREAM

◆

Makes 2 cups

1 teaspoon olive oil
2 ounces chopped andouille sausage,
  casings removed
3 tablespoons peeled and chopped
  Italian plum tomatoes
3 tablespoons chopped green onions
2 tablespoons chopped onions

1 tablespoon minced garlic
½ cup Basic Chicken Stock (page 6)
1½ cups heavy cream
2 teaspoons Emeril's Creole
  Seasoning (page 3)
½ teaspoon salt

1. Heat the oil in a nonreactive saucepan over high heat. Add the andouille and sauté, breaking up the sausage with the side of a spoon, for 1 minute. Add the tomatoes, green onions and onions, and garlic and stir-fry for 1 minute.

2. Stir in the stock and deglaze the bottom of the pot. Add the cream, Creole Seasoning, and salt, and bring to a boil, stirring occasionally. Reduce the heat and simmer, stirring occasionally, for 12 minutes. Remove from the heat. Serve immediately or store, refrigerated, in an airtight container for up to 2 days. Reheat in a saucepan over low heat.

Oyster-Stuffed Turkey Roll with Sage Reduction Sauce

◆

Makes 8 main-course servings

Loaded with oysters, andouille sausage, and fresh herbs, this turkey roll seems pretty indigenous to New Orleans. But add the sage reduction, and you've got something so special, it could become your favorite alternative to the usual Thanksgiving bird.

½ fresh uncooked turkey breast, with skin (about 4 pounds)
3 tablespoons Emeril's Creole Seasoning (page 3), in all
3 tablespoons chopped fresh sage, in all
3 tablespoons olive oil, in all
4 ounces (½ cup) chopped andouille sausage, casings removed
½ cup chopped onions
¼ cup chopped celery
¼ cup chopped green bell peppers
2 tablespoons minced garlic
¼ cup chopped fresh parsley

1 teaspoon Worcestershire sauce
½ teaspoon hot pepper sauce
½ teaspoon salt
3 turns freshly ground black pepper
½ cup Basic Chicken Stock (page 6)
3 cups diced day-old bread
1½ cups freshly shucked oysters with their liquor
¼ cup chopped green onions
2 cups Sage Reduction Sauce (recipe follows)
5 lengths butcher's twine (each about 2 feet long)

1. Preheat the oven to 400°F.

2. Place the turkey breast, skin side down, on a flat surface. Butterfly by making a series of small cuts vertically in the meat, without cutting all the way through. Place a sheet of plastic wrap over the turkey meat and pound it with a mallet until very thin and flat. Remove the plastic wrap and sprinkle the meat with 1 tablespoon Creole Seasoning and 1 tablespoon sage.

3. Heat 2 tablespoons of the oil in a large skillet over high heat. Add the andouille, onions, celery, and bell peppers and stir-fry for 1 minute. Add the garlic, parsley, and the remaining 2 tablespoons sage and stir-fry for 2 minutes.

4. Stir in the Worcestershire, hot sauce, salt, pepper, and 1 tablespoon Creole Seasoning, and simmer for 2 minutes. Add the stock and fold in the bread cubes and oysters and cook for 1 minute. Fold in the green onions, cook for 2 minutes, and remove from the heat. Makes about 3½ cups of stuffing.

5. Spread the stuffing over the turkey meat and roll up, tucking in the ends. Slide 4 pieces of twine under the roll crosswise and tie. Slide the last piece under lengthwise and tie. Sprinkle the skin with the remaining 1 tablespoon oil and 1 tablespoon Creole Seasoning.

6. Place the roll in a baking pan and roast until cooked through but tender, for about 1 hour, basting occasionally. Remove from the oven and allow to cool for about 15 minutes. Cut into 16 slices.

7. About 20 minutes before the meat is removed from the oven, prepare the Sage Reduction Sauce.

8. To serve, arrange 2 slices of stuffed turkey on each of 8 plates and drizzle ¼ cup Sage Reduction Sauce over each serving.

SAGE REDUCTION SAUCE
◆

Makes 2 cups

3 tablespoons chopped fresh sage
3 tablespoons minced shallots
2 tablespoons minced garlic
1 teaspoon salt
4 turns freshly ground black pepper
1 cup port wine

3 cups Brown Chicken Stock
   (page 7) or Basic Chicken Stock
   (page 6)
1 tablespoon cornstarch
2 tablespoons water

1. Combine the sage, shallots, garlic, salt, pepper, and port in a nonreactive saucepan over high heat. Bring to a boil, lower the heat, and simmer for 5 minutes.

2. Add the stock, bring to a boil, and cook for 15 minutes.

3. Meanwhile, combine the cornstarch with the water. Stir the mixture into the sauce, simmer for 2 minutes, and remove from the heat. Serve immediately or store, refrigerated, in an airtight container for up to 2 days. Reheat in a saucepan over low heat.

Roast Duck

◆

Makes 4 main-course servings

If you're not in the mood for fancy, this is a perfectly edible roast duck. You might want to give it some tasty side dishes, such as Candied Butternut Squash (page 274) and Fried Wild Mushroom Salad (page 105). Mainly, however, I've included this austere bird for use in recipes such as Duck and Pumpkin Risotto (page 95).

1 duck (4 to 5 pounds)
1 teaspoon salt

12 turns black pepper

1. Preheat the oven to 500°F.

2. Sprinkle the duck all over with the salt and pepper. Remove all visible fat, and with a fork prick the skin all over without piercing the meat.

3. Place on a rack in a roasting pan and roast for 40 minutes. Reduce the oven heat to 400°F and roast until the thigh juices run clear, for about 30 minutes. Remove from the oven and allow to cool before using in other recipes. Or carve into 4 pieces and serve immediately.

Tangerine Duck

◆

Makes 4 main-course servings

To me the aroma of tangerines is intoxicating. And with the start of tangerine season arriving just before Christmas, I always connect that wonderful smell to my favorite holiday. So it was natural that I created this dish—my answer to duck with orange sauce.

2 ducks (4 to 5 pounds each)
4 tangerines (2 peeled, peels
   reserved, and 2 unpeeled), in all
¼ cup granulated sugar
½ cup chopped onions, in all

½ cup chopped celery, in all
4 bay leaves, in all
2 teaspoons salt, in all
16 turns freshly ground black
   pepper, in all

1. The day before, clean the ducks, remove all visible fat, and refrigerate, uncovered, overnight.

2. Preheat the oven to 550°F. Remove the ducks from the refrigerator and with a fork prick the skin all over without piercing the meat.

3. In a bowl combine the 2 peeled tangerines with the sugar, and mash them with a potato masher until the sugar is thoroughly incorporated.

4. Using your fingers, lift the skin of each duck away from the breast meat and pack the pulp under each breast. Cut the 2 unpeeled tangerines in half, and rub the skin of the ducks all over with the cut sides of the fruit. Squeeze out the remaining juice from the halves, add to the tangerine/sugar mixture, and stuff the tangerine halves into the duck cavities. Pour half the remaining tangerine/sugar mixture into and over each duck.

5. Stuff *each* duck cavity with ¼ cup of the onions, ¼ cup of the celery, and 2 of the bay leaves. Sprinkle 1 teaspoon of the salt and 8 turns of the pepper over the skin and in the cavity of each duck; rub well into the skin. Sprinkle the reserved tangerine peels around a large roasting pan and place the ducks breast side up on a rack in the pan.

6. Roast the ducks for 20 to 22 minutes. Reduce the heat to 350°F, and roast for 35 minutes. Turn the oven heat up to 475°F, and roast until very dark and crisp, for about 20 minutes longer. Remove from the oven and drain the juices out of the cavity. Discard the juices.

7. To serve, cut off the wings at the second joint. Split each duck from the neck to the cavity, and serve one-half duck per portion.

Duck Roulades with Avocado, Pistachios, and Pistachio Armagnac Sauce

◆

Makes 4 main-course servings

Having a dinner party? Serve roulades. They're elegant, easy to make, and can be prepared ahead of time. Roulades, thin slices of meat rolled around a filling, are really an ONO dish—until you add the avocado, pistachios, and Armagnac, and then they become a NNO dish. You can get very creative with roulades, using various kinds of fowl, such as pheasant or goose, and there are infinite possibilities for filling combinations. So roll em' up ahead of time—and enjoy your party.

1 tablespoon minced shallots
1 teaspoon minced garlic
1 teaspoon chopped fresh tarragon
1 teaspoon chopped fresh basil
2 teaspoons Emeril's Creole
   Seasoning (page 3)
4 skinned and boned duck breast
   halves (from 2 ducks)
12 slices bacon

1 teaspoon salt, in all
8 turns freshly ground black pepper,
   in all
4 teaspoons chopped unroasted
   pistachio nuts, in all
½ medium avocado, peeled, pitted,
   and cut into 8 vertical slices, in all
1 cup Pistachio Armagnac Sauce
   (recipe follows)

1. Prepare a dry marinade by combining the shallots, garlic, tarragon, basil, and Creole Seasoning in a small bowl.

2. Place the duck breasts between sheets of plastic wrap and pound them with a meat mallet until they're very thin—$\frac{1}{16}$ to $\frac{1}{8}$ inch thick. Remove the plastic wrap, rub the dry marinade into both sides of each breast, place the breasts in a covered dish, and refrigerate for at least 1 hour or overnight, if possible.

3. Preheat the oven to 400°F. Line a baking sheet with parchment or wax paper.

4. Lay 3 slices of the bacon on a flat surface. Place 1 duck breast on top of the bacon along one end. Sprinkle the breast with ¼ teaspoon of the salt, 2 turns of the pepper, and 1 teaspoon of the pistachios. Arrange 2 avocado slices on top, and roll up—with the bacon—1 turn, or just until the bacon overlaps itself. Trim off the excess bacon and save it for the Pistachio Armagnac Sauce. Repeat the procedure to make the remaining roulades.

5. Place the roulades on a baking sheet and bake until the bacon is brown and crisp and the duck meat tender, for about 30 minutes. Remove from the oven. Using a very sharp knife, trim off the ends of each roulade and then cut each across into 4 slices.

6. While the roulades are baking, prepare the Pistachio Armagnac Sauce.

7. To serve, spoon ¼ cup of the Pistachio Armagnac Sauce on each of 4 plates and arrange 4 roulade slices on top.

PISTACHIO ARMAGNAC SAUCE

◆

Makes 1 cup

¼ cup coarsely chopped bacon
1 tablespoon minced shallots
½ teaspoon minced garlic
1 tablespoon Armagnac or cognac
2 cups Duck Glaze (page 13)
½ teaspoon sugar

½ teaspoon salt
2 turns freshly ground black pepper
1 tablespoon chopped unroasted
   pistachio nuts
1 teaspoon unsalted butter, at room
   temperature

1. Render the bacon in a saucepan over high heat, stirring occasionally, for about 2 minutes. Add the shallots, garlic, and Armagnac and cook for 1 minute.

2. Stir in the glaze, sugar, salt, pepper, and pistachios and bring to a boil. Reduce the heat and simmer for 20 minutes. Whisk in the butter and remove from the heat. Serve immediately or prepare without the butter and store, refrigerated, in an airtight container for up to 24 hours. Reheat in a small saucepan over low heat. When the sauce is at a simmer, whisk in the butter, and remove from the heat.

Quail Milton with Wild Mushroom Andouille Duxelles and Port Wine Sauce

◆

Makes 4 main-course servings

Quail Milton is a popular dish at Emeril's Restaurant. I've heard that customers who order it often rush home to look it up in some dictionary of gastronomy, only to find Escoffier left Milton out. The truth is, just before we opened, we prepared a preview luncheon for Councilman James Singleton, who did so much to promote the unique warehouse district of New Orleans, which is where we make our home. I created this dish for the luncheon and the councilman loved it. Now, for reasons unknown to us, Councilman Singleton's mother had long ago nicknamed her son Milton. And so it goes.

2 cups Wild Mushroom Andouille
   Duxelles (page 284)
8 quail, cleaned and boned by your
   butcher (leave only the leg
   bones in)

4 teaspoons olive oil, in all
4 teaspoons Emeril's Creole
   Seasoning (page 3), in all
1⅓ cups Port Wine Sauce
   (recipe follows)

1. Prepare the Wild Mushroom Andouille Duxelles.

2. Preheat the oven to 400°F. Line a baking sheet with parchment or wax paper.

3. Brush each quail with 1 teaspoon of the oil, ½ teaspoon inside the bird and ½ teaspoon over the skin. Sprinkle each quail with ½ teaspoon Creole Seasoning, ¼ teaspoon inside and ¼ teaspoon out.

4. Stuff each quail with ¼ cup of the duxelles and wrap the skin around the stuffing. Make an incision in the bony end of one leg of each bird and insert the other leg through the incision to keep the legs crossed and make a nifty presentation. Place the quail about an inch apart on the baking sheet.

5. Prepare the Port Wine Sauce. After you stir the stock into the sauce (see recipe), place the baking sheet in the oven and roast the quail until they're golden brown and crisp-skinned, for about 20 minutes.

6. To serve, arrange 2 quail on each of 4 dinner plates, and nap with ⅓ cup of the Port Wine Sauce.

PORT WINE SAUCE

◆

Makes 1⅓ cups

1 teaspoon olive oil
¼ cup minced shallots
1 tablespoon minced garlic
1 teaspoon salt
4 turns freshly ground black pepper

1 teaspoon sugar
1 cup port wine
3 cups Brown Chicken Stock
  (page 7)

Heat the oil in a large saucepan over high heat. When the oil is hot add the shallots, garlic, salt, and pepper and sauté for 1 minute. Stir in the sugar and port, bring to a boil, and cook for 3 minutes. Stir in the stock and cook over high heat, for about 20 minutes. Remove from the heat. Serve immediately or make up to an hour ahead, and keep warm.

THE LAST WORD

Duxelles is technically a dry mushroom paste used to flavor a stuffing, but I've taken a few liberties here, and call the stuffing itself ''dux-elles.''

CHAPTER 9

The New Meat Menu:
Beef, Veal, and Lamb

The thing about meat is, if you like yours rare, the person you're eating with probably prefers it well done. Or worse—burnt. It never fails. Somehow, though, if it's a good piece of meat, lovingly prepared, you won't mind terribly that the food comes out of the kitchen at different times. Usually the chef in a restaurant is happy to indulge the whims of his or her diners. But once I was in a small bistro in New York where the chef took unkindly to the order for steak au poivre—"well done, please"—from my dinner companion. He came storming out of the kitchen and went nose-to-nose with my friend, who stood his ground. The chef, who was clearly out of line, finally retreated to his kitchen; soon the steak appeared, scorched exactly the way my friend likes it.

Rare or well done, I've actually seen steak arrive at the table in several New Orleans restaurants swimming in a pool of butter. Or worse—buried under a gloppy, flour-thickened sauce. I could never understand it: Why would you ruin a good cut of meat by treating it so disrespectfully? My philosophy is to let meat taste like meat, even if there is a sauce or a stuffing. Even skillet steaks are cooked in 2 to 4 tablespoons of olive oil only. And sauces, some made with wine, some with intense meat glazes, are reduced. Never buttered; never floured. Beef, veal, and lamb are often accompanied by wild mushrooms, fresh corn, tasso or andouille, chile peppers, and herbs and seasonings such as cilantro, mint, rosemary, Creole or Southwest Seasoning, or curry.

Many of us eat more chicken and seafood these days, trying to cut down on fats in our diet, and I'm no exception. Even so, I've got to have my fix of red meat once a week, and my craving runs consistently toward steaks. My mom made lots of roasts and stews when I was a kid, but we only had steak on special occasions.

Some of the recipes here require special cuts and butchering techniques. Unless you're very knowledgeable and skilled, please have a good butcher help you.

Skillet Steak with Tasso Maque Choux and Fried Chanterelles

◆

Makes 4 main-course servings

*T*his dish is a union of some of the best things Louisiana has to offer, including spicy tasso, Creole seasonings, and *maque choux*. It also offers the Southern comfort of a fried steak, but it's the locally grown chanterelles that add that something special to satisfy even the most sophisticated palate.

2 cups Tasso Maque Choux
   (page 276)
4 boneless rib eye steaks, each
   1 inch thick (10 ounces each)
1 tablespoon olive oil
1 tablespoon plus 2 teaspoons
   Emeril's Creole Seasoning (page
   3), in all

3 cups vegetable oil
16 fresh chanterelles or 12 domestic
   mushrooms, rinsed just before
   using
½ cup all-purpose flour
½ teaspoon salt

1. Prepare the Tasso Maque Choux, and keep warm.

2. Trim the thinner layer of fat from one edge of the steak, leaving the thicker piece of fat attached, to help the meat keep its shape. Sprinkle the steaks with 2 teaspoons Creole Seasoning, allowing ½ teaspoon per steak. Pat on well with the side of a heavy knife or the palm of your hand.

3. Heat the olive oil in a large skillet over high heat. When the oil is smoking, add the steaks and sauté them for about 3 minutes on each side (rare), or 4 minutes on each side (medium rare). Remove from the heat and keep warm.

4. Start heating the vegetable oil in a medium saucepan over high heat.

5. While the oil is heating, combine the flour with the remaining 1 tablespoon Creole Seasoning in a bowl. Dredge the chanterelles in the seasoned flour, shaking off any excess. When the oil is smoking hot, add the chanterelles and fry until golden brown, for about 1 or 2 minutes. Remove the mushrooms with tongs, drain them on paper towels, and sprinkle them with the salt.

5. To serve, place ½ cup of the Tasso Maque Choux in each of 4 dinner plates. Place a steak on each portion of *maque choux*, and arrange 3 or 4 chanterelles or mushrooms on top.

Wild Mushroom-Smothered Steaks

◆

Makes 4 main-course servings

This easy one-skillet dish will delight anyone who's tired of eating "fancy," yet who must have *good* food.

4 boneless rib eye steaks, each
    1 inch thick (10 ounces each)
5 teaspoons Emeril's Creole
    Seasoning (page 3), in all
¼ cup olive oil
8 cups sliced assorted fresh wild
    mushrooms, such as shiitakes,
    chanterelles, oysters, or black
    trumpet mushrooms

½ cup chopped onions
½ cup chopped green onions
2 tablespoons minced garlic
1 teaspoon salt
6 turns freshly ground black pepper
8 tablespoons (1 stick) unsalted
    butter, cut up

1. Sprinkle each steak all over with 1 teaspoon Creole Seasoning and pound in once or twice with the side of a heavy knife or the palm of your hand.

2. Heat the oil in a large skillet over high heat. When the oil is very hot, add the steaks and sauté them on the first side, for about 4 minutes. Turn the steaks and sauté the second side for 2 minutes. Add the mushrooms, onions, green onions, garlic, salt, pepper, and the remaining 1 teaspoon Creole Seasoning and sauté for 2 minutes.

2. Turn the steaks back to the first side, dot with the butter pats, cover the skillet, and cook for 1 minute. Remove from the heat.

3. To serve, place 1 steak on each of 4 plates and cover each with ¾ cup mushrooms and their juices.

Southwest Cowboy Steak with Skillet Corn Sauce and Tortillas

◆

Makes 4 main-course servings

I can just see those ol' cowboys now, settin' around the campfire, eatin' steak and skillet sauce out of beat-up tin plates. I have a rather active imagination, but that's really what this dish makes me think of. So when I fix up some of this grub for myself, I kinda hunker down and sop up all that good sauce with my tortillas and thank my stars for my New New Cowboy Steak. This is great with Tin-Can Margaritas (page 171).

1 flank steak (about 2 pounds)
2 tablespoons olive oil
1 tablespoon Emeril's Southwest
  Seasoning (page 3)
¼ cup chopped fresh cilantro

1⅓ cups Skillet Corn Sauce
  (recipe follows)
12 Homemade Tortillas (page 306)
½ teaspoon salt

1. Rub the meat all over with the oil. Sprinkle it with the Southwest Seasoning and pack the cilantro leaves around the steak. Allow to marinate for 30 minutes.

2. Prepare the Skillet Corn Sauce, and keep warm.

3. Prepare the Homemade Tortillas through Step 1. Preheat the broiler.

4. Place the steak on a rack in a roasting pan and sprinkle the top side evenly with the salt. For medium-rare meat, set the pan on the lowest rack in the broiler (about 7 inches from heat) and broil for 5 to 7 minutes. Turn the meat over and broil for 5 minutes. Move to the middle rack (about 5 inches from heat) and broil for 5 minutes more. Remove from the broiler and slice diagonally against the grain in thin slices.

5. Ten minutes before the steak is done, finish the Homemade Tortillas.

6. To serve, spoon ⅓ cup of the Skillet Corn Sauce on each of 4 dinner plates. Arrange 4 slices of steak and 3 Homemade Tortillas on top of the sauce.

SKILLET CORN SAUCE

◆

Makes 1⅓ cups

2 ears corn, scraped, kernels only
½ teaspoon salt
2 turns freshly ground black pepper
¼ cup chopped onions
¼ cup chopped green onions

1 tablespoon minced garlic
2 cups Veal Stock (page 8)
2 tablespoons peeled, seeded, and
  chopped Italian plum tomatoes
2 tablespoons chopped fresh cilantro

1. Heat a medium nonreactive skillet over high heat until very hot. Add the corn, salt, and pepper and cook, shaking the skillet from time to time to char the corn evenly, for about 2 minutes. (The corn will pop a bit.) Add the onions, green onions, and garlic and char for 1 minute.

2. Add the stock and stir in the tomatoes and cilantro and bring to a boil. Reduce the heat and simmer for 15 minutes. Remove from the heat. Serve immediately, or prepare up to an hour ahead and keep warm.

Crawfish-Stuffed Filet Mignon with Crawfish Bordelaise Sauce

◆

Makes 4 main-course servings

The concept of surf' n' turf makes many people wince because they believe seafood and red meat don't belong together. But here in New Orleans we combine farm and bayou with outstanding results. The sauce is a classic French bordelaise, with which I've taken a little poetic license.

2 tablespoons olive oil, in all
1 teaspoon finely minced onions
1 teaspoon finely minced green onions
1 teaspoon finely minced celery
1 teaspoon finely minced green bell peppers
1 teaspoon finely minced garlic
¼ pound crawfish tails (page 24)

2 tablespoons Shrimp Stock (page 10)
2 tablespoons bread crumbs (page 17)
1 tablespoon Emeril's Creole Seasoning (page 3), in all
1½ cups Crawfish Bordelaise Sauce (recipe follows)
4 filet mignons (6 to 7 ounces each), well marbled, trimmed

1. Heat 1 tablespoon of the oil in a medium skillet over high heat. Add the onions and green onions, celery, bell peppers, and garlic and sauté for 1 minute. Add the crawfish tails, stock, bread crumbs, and 1 teaspoon Creole Seasoning and cook for 2 minutes. Remove from the heat and set aside to cool for at least 15 minutes. Makes 1 cup.

2. Prepare the Crawfish Bordelaise Sauce, and cover to keep warm.

3. Sprinkle the remaining 2 teaspoons Creole Seasoning over the meat, using ½ teaspoon on each steak and inside its pocket. Use your hands to coat the meat thoroughly, inside and out.

4. Using a small sharp knife, cut a slit about 2 inches long into the side of each steak and cut about 2 inches in to make a pocket. Stand the filets on their uncut edges and open the pockets. Using a spoon, fill each pocket with ¼ cup of the cooled stuffing.

5. Heat the remaining 1 tablespoon oil in a skillet over high heat. When the oil is hot, add the filets and sauté until rare, for about 3 minutes on each side, or medium rare, for about 4 minutes on each side. If you like your meat well done, you're on your own with the time.

6. To serve, place 1 filet on each of 4 dinner plates and cover with a generous ⅓ cup of the sauce.

CRAWFISH BORDELAISE SAUCE

Makes 1½ cups

1 tablespoon minced shallots
1 tablespoon minced garlic
1 teaspoon Emeril's Creole
  Seasoning (page 3)
½ cup dry red wine
¼ pound crawfish tails (page 24)
½ teaspoon salt

4 turns freshly ground black pepper
1½ cups Veal or Beef Glaze
  (page 13)
2 tablespoons unsalted butter, at
  room temperature
1 tablespoon chopped green onions

1. Combine the shallots, garlic, and Creole Seasoning in a small nonreactive saucepan and place over high heat and cook for 30 seconds. Watch carefully so it doesn't burn. Add the wine and bring to a boil. Add the crawfish, salt, and pepper and bring back to a boil.

2. Stir in the glaze and bring back to a boil. Reduce the heat and simmer, skimming off the fat and impurities several times for about 10 minutes. Turn up the heat to high, skim the remaining impurities from the top of the sauce, and cook for 1 to 2 minutes.

3. Whisk in the butter and continue to whisk until thoroughly incorporated, for about 30 seconds. Add the green onions and remove from the heat.

Carpetbag Steak with Tasso Hollandaise

◆

Makes 4 main-course servings

This steak, its deep pocket filled with a delicious oyster stuffing, resembles a carpetbag—a sacklike traveling case popular in the last century. The nippy Tasso Hollandaise adds a kick and is the perfect topping for this dish.

2 tablespoons olive oil, in all
¼ cup chopped onions
¼ cup chopped celery
¼ cup chopped green bell
   peppers
¼ cup chopped green onions
1 tablespoon minced garlic
4 bay leaves
2 tablespoons Emeril's Creole
   Seasoning (page 3), in all

1 cup freshly shucked oysters with
   their liquor plus ½ cup water
½ teaspoon salt
½ teaspoon Worcestershire sauce
¼ teaspoon hot pepper sauce
1 cup bread crumbs (page 17)
1⅓ cups Tasso Hollandaise
   (recipe follows)
4 (8 ounces each) filet mignons,
   about 1½ to 2 inches thick

1. Heat 1 tablespoon of the oil in a medium skillet over high heat. Add the onions, celery, bell peppers, and green onions and sauté for 1 minute. Stir in the garlic, bay leaves, and 2 teaspoons Creole Seasoning and sauté for 2 minutes.

2. Stir in the oysters, their liquor, and the water and cook, roughly chopping the oysters with a wooden spoon or spatula, for about 1 minute. Add the salt, Worcestershire, and hot pepper sauce; cook for 1 minute and remove from the heat. Turn into a bowl, add the bread crumbs, and mix until thoroughly incorporated. Makes 2 cups.

3. Prepare the Tasso Hollandaise, cover, and set aside.

4. Make a vertical incision in the side edge of each filet with a small sharp knife, and open up a pocket about three-quarters of the way into the meat. Sprinkle the remaining Creole Seasoning all over the steaks, using 1 teaspoon per filet, patting it in inside and out. Stuff each steak with ¼ cup of the oyster stuffing, packing it in.

5. Heat the remaining 1 tablespoon oil in a large ovenproof skillet over high heat. When the oil is hot, add the stuffed filets and sauté until brown, for about 3 minutes each top and bottom, then 3 minutes on one edge and another 3 minutes on the edge that's stuffed. That's a total of 12 minutes if you like your steaks rare as I do. If you prefer them medium rare to medium, preheat your oven to 400°F, and finish them in the oven for an additional 3 minutes.

6. Serve 1 filet on each of 4 plates and top with ⅓ cup of the Tasso Hollandaise.

TASSO HOLLANDAISE

Makes 1⅓ cups

4 large egg yolks
2 tablespoons freshly squeezed
  lemon juice
1 cup clarified butter (page 18), at
  room temperature
1 tablespoon plus 1 teaspoon water

2 ounces (¼ cup) finely minced
  tasso or spiced ham
1 teaspoon minced garlic
½ teaspoon hot pepper sauce
½ teaspoon Worcestershire sauce
1 teaspoon salt

1. In a stainless bowl set over a pot of simmering water on medium heat, whisk the egg yolks with the lemon juice—taking the bowl off the pot from time to time to temper the heat and keep the yolks from scrambling, but whisking constantly—until a ribbon forms when you lift the whisk.

2. Vigorously whisk in the butter a few drops at a time, alternating with a few drops of the water, until all is thoroughly incorporated. Whisk in the tasso, garlic, hot pepper sauce, Worcestershire, and salt. Serve immediately.

Spicy Beef Empanadas with Fire Sauce and Cilantro Cream

◆

Makes 4 main-course servings

With the border not too far away, Mexican food is a favorite of New Orleanians. I love it, too, and for me, one of the best south of the border treats is an empanada. In my version, these zippy little pies are baked in a peppery, cookie-textured cornmeal crust, drizzled with a killer Fire Sauce (aptly named), then cooled by cilantro cream. Wash them down with cold Tecata or Dos Equis beer.

1 recipe Empanada Dough
   (recipe follows)
½ pound lean, tender beef,
   preferably fillet, finely diced
1 tablespoon Emeril's Southwest
   Seasoning (page 3), in all
1 tablespoon olive oil
½ cup fresh corn kernels
¼ cup seeded and chopped poblano,
   New Mexican green, or Anaheim
   chile peppers
1 teaspoon salt

½ teaspoon crushed red pepper
   flakes
4 turns freshly ground black pepper
3 tablespoons minced shallots
1 tablespoon minced garlic
2 cups Beef Stock (page 8), in all
2 teaspoons cornstarch
1 large egg
2 tablespoons water
½ cup Cilantro Cream
   (recipe follows)

1. Prepare the Empanada Dough through Step 2.

2. While the dough is chilling, sprinkle the meat with 2 teaspoons Southwest Seasoning, and use your hands to coat it thoroughly.

3. Heat the oil in a large skillet over high heat. Add the seasoned beef and stir-fry for 1½ minutes. Stir in the corn, peppers, salt, red pepper flakes, black pepper, and the remaining 1 teaspoon Southwest Seasoning and sauté, stirring occasionally, for 1 minute. Add the shallots and garlic and stir-fry for 1½ minutes.

4. Stir in 1½ cups of the stock and bring to a boil. Combine the remaining ½ cup stock with the cornstarch and whisk this into the filling mixture in the skillet. Cook over high heat for 5 minutes. Remove from the heat and strain off the gravy. Makes 1½ cups of filling.

5. Return the gravy to a small saucepan over medium heat, bring to a boil, and cook for 5 minutes. Turn off the heat, cover, and keep warm. Makes about ⅔ cup of Fire Sauce.

6. Preheat the oven to 375°F. Line a baking sheet with parchment or wax paper.

7. Finish the Empanada Dough through Step 3.

8. Beat the egg with the water to make an egg wash and brush some of the wash on the top sides of the 4 Empanada Dough rounds. Mound a generous ⅓ cup of the filling in the middle of each round of dough, fold over to form a half-moon pie shape, and crimp the edges with a fork. Brush the tops of the empanadas with more egg wash, place them on the baking sheet, and bake for 35 minutes.

9. While the empanadas are baking, prepare the Cilantro Cream.

10. To serve, place 1 empanada on each of 4 plates and drizzle with 3 tablespoons of the Fire Sauce. Top with 2 tablespoons of Cilantro Cream.

EMPANADA DOUGH

◆

Makes enough dough for 4 empanadas

1 cup masa harina (see Note, page 29)
½ cup all-purpose flour
½ cup yellow cornmeal
½ teaspoon baking powder
½ teaspoon Emeril's Southwest Seasoning (page 3)

½ teaspoon salt
3 turns freshly ground black pepper
2 tablespoons solid vegetable shortening
1 cup warm water

1. Combine the masa harina, flour, cornmeal, baking powder, Southwest Seasoning, salt, and pepper in a bowl and mix thoroughly. Cream in the shortening and add the water a little at a time, working the mixture until all is completely incorporated.

2. Using your hands, form the dough into a log about 12 inches long by 3 inches across and refrigerate for about 20 minutes.

3. Remove from the refrigerator, divide the log into 4 equal sections about 3 inches long, and carefully roll each of them out between sheets of plastic wrap to an 8-inch circle, about ¼ inch thick. The dough must be handled with care to keep it from cracking.

CILANTRO CREAM

◆

Makes about ½ cup

½ cup sour cream
2 tablespoons chopped fresh cilantro
1 tablespoon water
1 teaspoon freshly squeezed lime
   juice

½ teaspoon salt
3 turns freshly ground black pepper

Combine all of the ingredients in a cup and mix thoroughly. Serve immediately or store, refrigerated, in an airtight container for up to 2 days. Stir before serving.

Portuguese Piri Piri Beef on a Stick with Cilantro Potato Salad

◆

Makes 4 main-course servings

For me, the greatest treat at the Portuguese festivals I attended as a child was *carne spart*, skewers of beef marinated in a fiery sauce and roasted over an open fire. I would take the money my mother gave me to the booth where the raw meat was marinated and then skewered. One of the men would give me a skewer of meat which I brought to the big pit where the fire was roaring. As I charred my beef I listened to the sounds of the traditional Portuguese music played by the bands of old-time musicians. The cooked meat was unskewered onto a small loaf of crusty Portuguese bread, and while the grown-ups got to wash it down with icy beer, I wasn't at all unhappy with my dinner. This recipe is my version of *carne spart*.

½ cup Piri Piri (page 4), prepared at
   least a week ahead
½ cup chopped fresh cilantro
1 tablespoon kosher salt
2 pounds sirloin or other lean,
   tender beef, trimmed and cut into
   2-inch cubes (about 20 cubes)

Cilantro Potato Salad (page 117)
1 loaf crusty peasant bread,
   preferably Portuguese
4 long wooden skewers

1. Combine the Piri Piri with the cilantro and kosher salt in a bowl, and marinate the meat in this mixture for 3 or 4 hours in your refrigerator.

2. About an hour before removing the marinade from the refrigerator, prepare the Cilantro Potato Salad, cover, and refrigerate.

3. Preheat the broiler and set the broiler rack 3 inches from the flame.

4. Thread the meat on the skewers, using 5 cubes of meat per skewer. Rest the skewers across a rack set in a pan and baste the meat with the Piri Piri marinade. Broil for 8 minutes, turn the skewers of meat over, baste, and broil for 5 minutes.

5. To serve, push the meat from the skewers onto the bread and eat sandwich-style with a generous cup of the Cilantro Potato Salad.

Monster Herbed Veal Chops with Rosemary Potato Crisps and Roasted Shallot Sauce

◆

Makes 4 main-course servings

Veal in New Orleans has often consisted of the ever-popular grillades (braised veal chunks under a blanket of sauce) and grits. Don't get me wrong; I like grillades. But the flavor of veal is so special, it seems a shame to cover it up. This big, juicy chop is a perfect guest-impresser at an elegant dinner party. In fact, it'll probably be the topic of conversation after the meal has been consumed, so forget the parlor games. And here's a big perk for you: The light, pungent sauce can be prepared ahead of time and the rest takes only 30 minutes or less.

½ cup (packed) chopped mixed fresh herbs (choose at least 4: tarragon, sage, basil, chives, thyme, lemongrass, oregano, parsley, or any other you particularly like)
2 tablespoons minced garlic
1 cup bread crumbs (page 17)
1 tablespoon Emeril's Creole Seasoning (page 3), in all

2 tablespoons plus 2 teaspoons olive oil, in all
1¼ cups Roasted Shallot Sauce (recipe follows)
4 servings Rosemary Potato Crisps (page 271)
4 large veal chops, 10 to 12 ounces each, 1½ inches thick

1. Preheat the oven to 400°F.

2. Combine the assorted herbs, garlic, bread crumbs, 1 teaspoon Creole Seasoning, and 2 tablespoons of the oil in a bowl, and mix until thoroughly blended. Makes about 2 cups.

3. Prepare the Roasted Shallot Sauce, and keep warm. While the sauce is cooking, prepare the Rosemary Potato Crisps through Step 2.

4. Sprinkle the chops with the remaining 2 teaspoons Creole Seasoning and use your hands to coat the meat on both sides. Heat the remaining 2 teaspoons oil in a large skillet over high heat. When the oil is hot, sear the chops until brown, for about 4 minutes on each side. Remove from the skillet.

5. Place the seared veal chops on top of the Rosemary Potato Crisps after they've been flipped. Pack the herb mixture on top of the veal chops, using about ½ cup for each. Place the baking sheet back in the oven and bake for 20 minutes (pink and juicy inside).

6. To serve, place a mound of the Rosemary Potato Crisps on each plate, top with a veal chop, and pour a generous ¼ cup of the Roasted Shallot Sauce over each chop, making sure each portion gets roasted shallots and garlic cloves.

ROASTED SHALLOT SAUCE

◆

Makes about 1¼ cups

16 roasted shallots (page 16)
8 roasted garlic cloves (page 16)
½ teaspoon salt
4 turns freshly ground black pepper

½ cup port or dry red wine mixed
   with 1 tablespoon sugar
2 cups Veal or Beef Stock (page 8)
   or Brown Chicken Stock (page 7)

1. Combine the shallots, garlic, salt, pepper, and port in a small nonreactive saucepan over high heat. Bring to a boil and cook for 5 minutes.

2. Stir in the stock and cook over high heat for 10 minutes. Reduce the heat to medium and cook for 20 to 25 minutes.

Veal with Artichokes and Wild Mushrooms

◆

Makes 4 main-course servings

Everyone who lives in New Orleans loves artichokes. We put artichokes in our soup, stuffing, sauces, stews, and salads. We boil them, fry them, and stuff them with spicy stuff. This is one of my favorite dishes using artichokes, because their distinctive flavor complements the veal and wild mushrooms so beautifully. In the New New Orleans (NNO) manner, the vegetables are crisp and the wine sauce made without flour.

8 veal medallions (2 to 3 ounces each), pounded about ¼ inch thick
2 teaspoons Emeril's Creole Seasoning (page 3)
1 tablespoon olive oil
1 tablespoon minced shallots
1 tablespoon minced garlic
2 cups sliced assorted fresh wild mushrooms
1 cup blanched quartered artichoke hearts (page 15)

¼ cup chopped green onions
1 teaspoon salt
6 turns freshly ground black pepper
1 tablespoon freshly squeezed lemon juice
¼ cup dry white wine
¼ cup heavy cream
4 tablespoons (½ stick) unsalted butter, cut up, at room temperature

1. Place the veal medallions on a flat surface, sprinkle them on both sides with the Creole Seasoning, and use your hands to coat the meat.

2. Heat the oil in a large nonreactive skillet over high heat. When the oil is hot, add the veal, shallots, garlic, mushrooms, artichoke hearts, green onions, salt, and pepper, and sauté for about 2 to 3 minutes.

3. Turn the veal, placing it on top of the vegetables. Stir in the lemon juice and the white wine and cook for 1 minute. Remove the veal and set aside. Cook the vegetables for 1 minute. Whisk in the cream and butter and bring to a boil. Return the veal to the skillet for 1 minute and remove from the heat. Remove the veal with tongs. You should have about 2 cups of sauce and vegetables.

4. To serve, place 2 veal medallions on each of 4 plates and smother with ½ cup of the sauce.

Curry-Crusted Lamb Chops with Garlic Wine Sauce and Potato Shallot Custards

◆

Makes 4 main-course servings

Curry is an acquired taste; but once you get it, you're going to love it. It's fantastic with lamb and in this creation is wonderfully enhanced by the fragrant wine sauce. This is a very popular dish at the restaurant and is a regular on the menu.

4 Potato Shallot Custards (page 267)
¾ cup Garlic Wine Sauce (recipe follows)
8 rib lamb chops (about 3 to 4 ounces each)
1 teaspoon salt, in all

16 turns freshly ground black pepper, in all
2 teaspoons Dijon mustard, in all
2 tablespoons plus 2 teaspoons curry powder, in all
2 tablespoons olive oil

1. Prepare the Potato Shallot Custards.

2. While the custards are cooling, prepare the Garlic Wine Sauce, and cover to keep warm. Sprinkle the chops with the salt and pepper, using 1 turn of the pepper on each side of each chop. With your hands, rub the chops all over with the mustard, using ¼ teaspoon on each side. Dust each side of each chop with ½ teaspoon of the curry powder.

3. Heat the oil in a large skillet over high heat until very hot. Add the chops and sauté for about 3 minutes on each side for rare, 4 minutes on each side for medium rare. For well done, you're on your own.

4. To serve, place one Potato Shallot Custard on each of 4 plates, cross 2 chops over the custard, and drizzle with 3 tablespoons of the Garlic Wine Sauce.

GARLIC WINE SAUCE

◆

Makes ¾ cup

3 tablespoons minced shallots
3 tablespoons minced garlic
½ teaspoon salt
4 turns freshly ground black pepper
1½ cups Lamb or Veal Stock (page 8)
  or Brown Chicken Stock (page 7)

½ cup dry red wine
2 tablespoons unsalted butter, at
  room temperature

Combine the shallots, garlic, salt, and pepper in a small nonreactive saucepan over high heat. Stir in the stock and the wine and bring to a boil. Cook over high heat for 15 minutes. Swirl in the butter, remove from the heat, and continue to whisk in the butter until thoroughly incorporated. Serve immediately, or prepare without the butter and store, refrigerated, in an airtight container for up to 24 hours. Reheat in a small saucepan over low heat. When the sauce comes to a simmer, swirl in the butter and proceed from there.

Lamb Shanks Braised in Wine Sauce with Mint Orzo

◆

Makes 4 main-course servings

Patient simmering in wine makes this lamb so tender it falls off the bone. The subtly minted orzo is a surprise—and the ideal accompaniment. As a meal, this tops the list of feel-good foods elegant enough for company. If you don't have a skillet that is large enough to hold the shanks, make this in two skillets.

8 lamb shanks (each piece about 2½ inches long) (have your butcher saw them for you)
2 tablespoons Emeril's Creole Seasoning (page 3)
2 tablespoons olive oil
1 cup chopped onions
1 cup chopped celery
1 cup chopped carrots
2 cups dry red wine

½ cup peeled, seeded, and chopped Italian plum tomatoes
¼ cup minced garlic
4 bay leaves
4 teaspoons chopped fresh thyme
2 teaspoons salt
4 turns freshly ground black pepper
7 cups Lamb or Beef Stock (page 8)
3 cups Mint Orzo (page 290)

1. Sprinkle the lamb shanks all over with the Creole Seasoning.

2. Heat the oil in a large nonreactive skillet over high heat and sear the shanks until brown on all sides, for about 4 minutes total. Add the onions, celery, and carrots and sauté for 1 minute. Stir in the wine, tomatoes, garlic, bay leaves, and thyme and simmer for 3 minutes.

3. Stir in the salt, pepper, and stock and bring to a boil. Reduce the heat to low, cover the skillet, and simmer until the meat is tender and the sauce syrupy, for about 1 hour. Baste occasionally.

4. While the lamb is simmering, prepare the Mint Orzo, and cover to keep warm.

5. To serve, spread ¾ cup of the Mint Orzo on each of 4 plates and top with 2 lamb shanks. Drizzle with some of the sauce from the pan, if there is any.

Rack of Lamb with Creole Mustard Crust, Rosemary Jus, and Apple Mint Relish

◆

Makes 4 to 6 main-course servings

Poor New Orleanians—many of them never even tasted lamb until they were adults. For some reason, Louisiana's low on lamb and consequently hundreds of thousands of would-be lamb lovers have never known the joy of a dish of broiled lamb chops or a juicy leg of lamb served at Sunday dinner. So, being a lamb lover myself, I looked around for the best I could find, and started importing it fresh from Colorado for the restaurant. I gave it a down-home touch with Creole mustard and seasonings, and now my New Orleans friends are no longer deprived.

1 cup bread crumbs (page 17)
1 tablespoon chopped fresh basil
1 teaspoon chopped fresh rosemary
1 teaspoon chopped fresh thyme
3 tablespoons olive oil
1 tablespoon Emeril's Creole
  Seasoning (page 3), in all
2 racks of lamb (about 8 bones
  each), trimmed, French-cut
  (have your butcher do this), each
  cut in half (you'll have 4 pieces,
  each with 4 bones)

2 cups Apple Mint Relish
  (page 291)
2 tablespoons Creole mustard
  (preferred), or any good
  whole-seed prepared mustard
1 cup Rosemary Jus (recipe follows)
4 mint sprigs

1. Make an herb/crumb mixture by combining the bread crumbs, basil, rosemary, thyme, oil, and 1 teaspoon Creole Seasoning in a small bowl. Set aside.

2. Sprinkle the 4 half racks with the remaining 2 teaspoons Creole Seasoning, using ½ teaspoon to season the meat on each half rack.

3. Heat a large skillet over high heat until hot for about 1 minute. Place 2 of the half racks, fat side down, in the skillet and sear them for 2 minutes, then turn and sear for 2 minutes on the second side. Remove and repeat with the remaining 2 half racks. Remove from the heat and allow to cool for about 15 minutes.

4. While the lamb is cooling, preheat the oven to 400°F. Line a baking sheet with parchment or wax paper.

5. Prepare the Apple Mint Relish, cover, and set aside.

6. When the lamb is cool, brush the fat side and edges of each half rack with 1½ teaspoons of the mustard, and dredge in the herbed crumbs, covering all but the bones. Dredge again in any remaining crumb mixture, using your hands to pack it on the meat. Place the lamb, fat side up, on the baking sheet and roast for 45 minutes for medium rare.

7. About 10 minutes before the lamb is done, prepare the Rosemary Jus.

8. To serve, cut each half rack into 4 chops and arrange them on dinner plates. Add ½ cup of the Apple Mint Relish and ¼ cup of the Rosemary Jus. Garnish with a mint sprig.

ROSEMARY JUS

◆

Makes about 1 cup

2 tablespoons minced shallots
1 tablespoon minced garlic
3 tablespoons chopped fresh
   rosemary
½ teaspoon salt

4 turns freshly ground black pepper
1½ cups Lamb or Veal Stock
   (page 8) or Brown Chicken Stock
   (page 7)

Combine the shallots, garlic, rosemary, salt, and pepper in a small saucepan, place over high heat, and cook for 30 seconds. Add the stock and bring to a boil. Reduce the heat and simmer for 6 minutes. Remove from the heat. Serve immediately or store, refrigerated, in an airtight container for up to 2 days. Reheat in a small saucepan over lowest heat.

Stuffed Leg of Lamb with Stewed Lentils

◆

Makes 8 main-course servings

This hearty dish reminds me of the legs of lamb my mother prepared for special Sunday dinners, although if hers were stuffed, they weren't stuffed with goat cheese. I have an aversion to mint jelly concoctions, but I like to use mint to heighten the flavor of the lamb, which is what the touch of mint does here.

1 boneless leg of lamb (4 to 5 pounds trimmed)
¼ cup Emeril's Creole Seasoning (page 3), in all
3 tablespoons olive oil, in all
¼ cup chopped onions
2 tablespoons minced garlic

4 turns freshly ground black pepper
2 cups chopped fresh spinach
¼ cup chopped fresh mint
4 ounces (½ cup) goat cheese, such as Montrachet
6 cups Stewed Lentils (page 265)

1. Preheat the oven to 400°F. Cut 7 lengths of butcher's twine, each 2 feet long.

2. Open up the leg of lamb so that the inside is facing up, and butterfly the meat by cutting a series of small slits vertically, without cutting all the way through. Trim off and reserve extra pieces of meat until the leg is fairly smooth and flat. Reserve the extra meat, about 8 ounces.

3. Place a sheet of plastic wrap over the lamb and pound it out with a meat mallet until it's about ¼ inch thick. Use a sharp knife to poke holes all over the meat without cutting through. Sprinkle just the top side of the meat with 2 tablespoons Creole Seasoning, and set aside.

4. Cut the reserved lamb into ½-inch dice. Heat 2 tablespoons of the oil in a large skillet over high heat. Add the chopped lamb, sprinkle it with 1 tablespoon Creole Seasoning, and brown for about 3 minutes. Add the onions, garlic, and black pepper and sauté, shaking the skillet, for 1 minute. Turn off the heat. Fold in the spinach and mint and turn the mixture into a bowl. Makes 4 cups of stuffing.

5. Spread about half the stuffing lengthwise along one side of the lamb, dot with the goat cheese, and top with the remaining stuffing. Roll the lamb up around the stuffing and tuck in the ends. Slide 6 pieces of the twine under the roll and tie them, starting at the outside ends and working your way in. Use the last piece to tie the roll lengthwise. Sprinkle the outside of the roll with the remaining 1 tablespoon Creole Seasoning.

6. Prepare the Stewed Lentils.

7. While the lentils are cooking, heat the remaining 1 tablespoon oil in a large skillet over high heat. Add the stuffed lamb roll and sear for 1½ minutes on each of 4 sides, a total of 6 minutes.

8. Place the lamb in a roasting pan and roast until brown and tender, for about 30 minutes for rare, 35 for medium rare, and 40 for medium. Baste occasionally. Remove from the oven, discard the strings, and cut into 16 slices.

9. To serve, spoon ¾ cup of the Stewed Lentils onto each of 8 dinner plates and top with 2 slices of stuffed lamb.

Beggars' Purses of Lamb, Goat Cheese, and Pine Nuts on a Bed of Rosemary Lentils

◆

Makes 4 main-course servings

*T*hese are dramatic-looking, delicious, and fun to eat. Yet they're so easy to make, you'll make them often.

3 cups Rosemary Lentils
  (page 266)
1 boneless loin of lamb (about 1
  pound), trimmed and cut into 4
  medallions
2 teaspoons Emeril's Creole
  Seasoning (page 3)
12 12- × 17-inch sheets frozen
  phyllo dough, thawed (page 51)
4 tablespoons olive oil

4 cups rinsed and stemmed spinach
  leaves, loosely packed
4 teaspoons minced shallots
4 teaspoons minced garlic
4 tablespoons pine nuts
4 ounces (½ cup) goat cheese, such
  as Montrachet
½ teaspoon salt
8 turns freshly ground black pepper
4 tablespoons chopped fresh basil

1. Prepare the Rosemary Lentils, and cover to keep warm.

2. Preheat the oven to 375°F. Line a baking sheet with parchment or wax paper.

3. Sprinkle the lamb with the Creole Seasoning and use your hands to coat the meat.

4. Heat a large dry skillet over high heat. When the skillet is very hot, add the seasoned lamb. Sear, turning every 2 minutes, until the meat is brown on all sides, for about 6 minutes total. Remove from the heat.

5. Make a stack of 3 phyllo sheets (keeping the remaining sheets covered to prevent them from drying) and brush the top sheet with 2 teaspoons of the oil. Place ½ cup of the spinach in the center, and sprinkle with 1 teaspoon of the shallots, 1 teaspoon of the garlic, and 1 tablespoon of the pine nuts. Place 1 tablespoon of goat cheese on top, a lamb mignon on the goat cheese, and another tablespoon of goat cheese on top of the meat. Sprinkle with ⅛ teaspoon of the salt and 2 turns of the pepper. Spread 1 tablespoon of the basil on top and add ½ cup spinach. Pull up the 4 corners of the phyllo to meet one another and twist the top to create a sack like a party favor. Drizzle with 1 teaspoon oil, and use your fingers to rub it all over carefully. Repeat this procedure 3 more times, making a total of 4 "purses."

6. Place the purses on a baking sheet and bake until they're golden brown, about 18 minutes.

7. To serve, place ¾ cup of the Rosemary Lentils on each of 4 dinner plates, and top with a beggar's purse.

Herbed Lamb Patties with Creole Ratatouille and Rosemary Jus

◆

Makes 4 main-course servings

So here's the story: My good friend and customer Mike Pulaski comes in for lunch one day and tells me he wants lamb, but not chops. I thought it over and put together some lean ground lamb with fresh herbs, shallots, and garlic, and then whipped up a fresh ratatouille to go with it. Mike fell hard for this dish and asks for it often. When you make it, be sure to buy only a quality cut of lamb that's very lean and fresh. This is a great example of how a few simple ingredients can make a memorable meal.

1½ pounds lean ground lamb
2 tablespoons minced shallots
2 tablespoons minced garlic
2 tablespoons chopped fresh basil
1 tablespoon chopped fresh thyme
2 teaspoons Emeril's Creole
   Seasoning (page 3)
2 teaspoons ground cumin

1 teaspoon ground chili powder
1 teaspoon salt
6 turns freshly ground black pepper
1 large egg
1 cup Rosemary Jus (page 239)
3 tablespoons olive oil
2 cups Creole Ratatouille (page 275)

1. Combine the lamb, shallots, garlic, basil, thyme, Creole Seasoning, cumin, chili powder, salt, pepper, and egg in a bowl, and work gently with your hands until thoroughly blended. Form into 12 small patties.

2. Prepare the Rosemary Jus, and cover to keep warm. Prepare the Creole Ratatouille.

3. Heat the oil in a large skillet over high heat. Add the patties and sauté until brown, for about 3 minutes on each side.

4. To serve, place 3 lamb patties on each of 4 plates, add ½ cup of the Creole Ratatouille, and drizzle with ¼ cup of the Rosemary Jus.

CHAPTER 10

Pig Heaven: Pork

Before I moved to New Orleans, my idea of a southern pork dinner was either pork chops smothered in a thick, heavy gravy or a big, baked ham. With gravy. When I arrived at Commander's Palace, I saw this wasn't necessarily the case; there was an awareness of and appreciation for a variety of dishes using pork. Unfortunately, many were still masked with floury sauces and gravies.

What to do? How to satisfy diners who love the flavor of pork, but fear the typically heavy, fatty dishes that feature it? Knowing that lean pork is as tasty as fatty pork, I've devised some lean pork creations for the contemporary palate. Some are light, such as Pork and Eggplant Cutlets with Olive Tomato Sauce and New New Creole Pork Chops with White Beans; some elegant, such as Pork Roulades with Andouille Corn-Bread Stuffing, Sage Jus, and Mango Chutney and Pork Wellington with Onion Applesauce and Candied Butternut Squash; and some exciting because of their flavor intensity, such as Glazed Baby Back Ribs with Plum Sauce and Cilantro Potato Salad and Tamarind-Glazed Pork Chops with Mole Cream and Roasted Sweet Potatoes.

Pork specials appear regularly on the menu at the restaurant, because we have regular customers who are pork lovers. Because of its savory goodness, its popularity isn't surprising, despite some bad press it's received in recent years. If you buy only lean, top-quality pork to prepare the dishes in this chapter, you'll get plenty of juicy flavor with a minimum of fat. And you'll enjoy pork as never before.

Pork Medallions with Braised Red and Green Cabbages and Roasted Shallots

◆

Makes 4 main-course servings

At Mardi Gras parades in New Orleans, the float riders throw beads, doubloons, plastic cups, and other collectibles to the eager crowd. But if you line up for the Saint Patrick's Day parade in the Big Easy, you're likely to go home with a cabbage—a far more practical reward. Of course, the paraders don't throw the cabbages—they hand them to lucky spectators. One of my favorite cabbage dishes is a traditional New England boiled dinner; another is this newer dish, which uses both green and red cabbages in sweet and tangy supporting roles.

16 Roasted Shallots (page 16)
2 cups Braised Red Cabbage
   (page 280)
2 cups Braised Green Cabbage
   (page 281)

8 pork loin medallions (2 to 3
   ounces each)
2 teaspoons Emeril's Creole
   Seasoning (page 3)
1 tablespoon olive oil

1. Prepare the Roasted Shallots. Prepare the Braised Red Cabbage and the Braised Green Cabbage, and cover them separately to keep warm.

2. Sprinkle the pork with the Creole Seasoning on both sides.

3. Heat the oil in a large skillet over high heat. When the oil is hot, add the pork medallions and sauté until brown, for about 2 to 3 minutes on each side.

4. To serve, mound ½ cup of the Braised Red Cabbage on one side of each of 4 dinner plates, and mound ½ cup of the Braised Green Cabbage on the other side. Place one pork medallion on each mound of cabbage and arrange 4 Roasted Shallots around each portion.

Pork and Eggplant Cutlets with Olive Tomato Sauce

◆

Makes 4 main-course servings

Although people often pair pork with side dishes such as cabbage or apples and anything with sage, I've discovered that eggplant and pork make wonderful running mates, and this rich, spicy sauce gives both an uncommon denominator. This dinner is a snap to make and could easily be whipped up even on a weekday worknight.

2 cups Olive Tomato Sauce (recipe follows)
5 tablespoons olive oil, in all
8 vertical ½-inch slices peeled eggplant (about 1 large or 2 medium eggplants)

8 boneless pork loin cutlets (about 3 ounces each and ½ inch thick)
4 teaspoons Emeril's Creole Seasoning (page 3)

1. Prepare the Olive Tomato Sauce, and cover to keep warm.

2. Heat 2 tablespoons of the oil in a large skillet over high heat. Add 4 slices of the eggplant and sauté until golden brown, for about 2½ minutes on each side. Remove the eggplant with tongs, add 2 tablespoons of the oil to the skillet, and when it's hot, repeat the process with the remaining 4 slices of eggplant. Remove the eggplant with tongs, and drain on paper towels.

3. Sprinkle the pork with the Creole Seasoning, using ¼ teaspoon per side of each cutlet.

4. Heat the remaining 1 tablespoon oil in the same skillet over high heat. Add the cutlets and sauté until brown, for about 2 minutes on each side.

5. To serve, arrange 2 slices of eggplant with 2 pork cutlets on each of 4 plates and nap with ½ cup of the Olive Tomato Sauce.

OLIVE TOMATO SAUCE

◆

Makes about 2 cups

1 tablespoon olive oil
½ cup peeled, seeded, and chopped
   Italian plum tomatoes
½ cup pitted and halved black Greek
   or Niçoise olives
½ cup halved green pimiento-stuffed
   olives
¼ cup chopped onions
¼ cup chopped green onions
¼ cup chopped fresh basil

1 tablespoon minced garlic
1 teaspoon Emeril's Creole
   Seasoning (page 3)
½ teaspoon salt
4 turns freshly ground black pepper
¼ cup heavy cream
8 tablespoons (1 stick) unsalted
   butter, at room temperature, cut
   up

1. Heat the oil in a medium nonreactive saucepan over high heat. Add the tomatoes, black and green olives, onions and green onions, basil, and garlic and stir-fry for 3 minutes.

2. Stir in the Creole Seasoning, salt, pepper, and cream and simmer for 2 minutes. Stir in the butter and turn off the heat as soon as it begins to melt. Keep stirring until the butter is thoroughly incorporated.

Pork Cutlets with Onion Applesauce and Couscous Jambalaya

◆

Makes 4 main-course servings

1⅔ cups Onion Applesauce
(recipe follows)
5 cups Couscous Jambalaya
(page 268)
8 boneless pork cutlets
(about ½ inch thick)

2 tablespoons plus 2 teaspoons
Emeril's Creole Seasoning
(page 3), in all

1. Prepare the Onion Applesauce, and set aside. Prepare the Couscous Jambalaya, and keep warm.

2. Sprinkle each of the cutlets with Creole Seasoning, using ½ teaspoon per side.

3. Warm a large heavy dry skillet over high heat until very hot. Sear the cutlets for 3 minutes on each side. Remove from the heat.

4. To serve, spread 1¼ cups of the Couscous Jambalaya on each of 4 plates. Arrange 2 pork cutlets on each bed of couscous and spoon a generous ⅓ cup of the Onion Applesauce over the pork.

ONION APPLESAUCE

◆

Makes 1⅔ cups

1 tablespoon olive oil
1 cup peeled and quartered onions
1 cup peeled and coarsely chopped
Granny Smith apples

1 teaspoon minced garlic
½ teaspoon salt
3 turns freshly ground black pepper
2 cups Basic Chicken Stock (page 6)

1. Heat the oil in a saucepan over high heat. Add the onions and stir-fry for 2 minutes. Add the apples, garlic, salt, and pepper and stir-fry for 1 minute.

2. Stir in the stock and bring to a boil. Reduce the heat and simmer for 20 minutes. Remove from the heat, and serve warm. Serve immediately or store, refrigerated, in an airtight container for up to 24 hours. Reheat in a saucepan over low heat.

New New Creole Pork Chops with White Beans

◆

Makes 4 main-course servings

In New England pork and beans is a tradition. In New New Orleans this version may well become a tradition.

2½ cups Creole White Beans
 (page 264)
4 large pork loin chops, trimmed
 (about 8 ounces each and 2 inches
 thick)

4 teaspoons Emeril's Creole
 Seasoning (page 3)
1 tablespoon olive oil

1. Prepare the Creole White Beans, and cover to keep warm.

2. Sprinkle the chops with the Creole Seasoning, using ½ teaspoon per side, and with your hands coat the meat.

3. Heat the oil in a large skillet over high heat. Add the chops and sauté them for 7 minutes on each side; stand them on their fat edge and cook for another 4 minutes. The pork will be very dark on the outside, pink and juicy on the inside.

4. To serve, spread a heaping ½ cup of the Creole White Beans on each of 4 plates and top with a pork chop.

Unstuffed Pork Chops with Herbed Shallot Sauce

◆

Makes 4 main-course servings

Well, these chops *do* have a sweet apple stuffing, one that's laced with pecans, bacon, and sage. But the chops aren't stuffed—they *sit* on the stuffing. They're finished with an aromatic sauce of sage and sweet roasted shallots—a great partner for the juicy pork chops and their unstuffing.

6 cups Apple Pecan Stuffing
   (page 282)
4 pork loin chops, trimmed (about
   10 ounces each and 2 inches
   thick)
4 teaspoons Emeril's Creole
   Seasoning (page 3)

1 tablespoon plus 1 teaspoon olive
   oil, in all
2 cups Herbed Shallot Sauce
   (recipe follows)

1. Preheat the oven to 400°F. Line a baking sheet with parchment or wax paper.

2. Prepare the Apple Pecan Stuffing.

3. Sprinkle the chops with the Creole Seasoning using ½ teaspoon on each side, and using your hands coat the meat well.

4. Heat 1 teaspoon of the oil in a large skillet over high heat. Add the chops and sear them until brown, for 3 minutes on each side, and for 2 minutes standing on their fat edges. Remove from the heat.

5. Spread the remaining 1 tablespoon oil on the baking sheet and cover the oil with the Apple Pecan Stuffing. Arrange the chops on the stuffing and bake for 20 to 25 minutes.

6. While the chops are baking, prepare the Herbed Shallot Sauce.

7. To serve, mound 1½ cups of the Apple Pecan Stuffing on each of 4 plates and top with a chop. Spoon ½ cup of the Herbed Shallot Sauce over each serving.

HERBED SHALLOT SAUCE

◆

Makes 2 cups

1 teaspoon olive oil
15 Roasted Shallots (page 16)
1 tablespoon chopped fresh sage
1 teaspoon Emeril's Creole
  Seasoning (page 3)

½ teaspoon salt
2 turns freshly ground black pepper
2 cups Veal Stock (page 8) or Brown
  Chicken Stock (page 7)

1. Heat the oil in a medium saucepan over high heat. Add the shallots and sauté, shaking and stirring, for about 30 seconds.

2. Add the remaining ingredients and bring to a boil. Reduce the heat and simmer for 20 minutes. Remove from the heat. Serve immediately or store, refrigerated, in an airtight container for up to 2 days. Reheat in a saucepan over low heat.

Glazed Baby Back Ribs with Plum Sauce and Cilantro Potato Salad

◆

Makes 4 main-course servings

As an unrepentant rib lover, I've experimented over the years, trying to develop the Ultimate Rib Experience. Here's the winning recipe—a heavenly concoction of plums and shallots, honey, molasses, soy sauce, and mustard. The secret ingredient (don't tell anyone!) is liquid crab boil—something most of us in Louisiana are intimately familiar with. You can buy liquid crab boil in specialty food stores and supermarkets in almost any state, but if you have trouble finding it, you can order it by mail (page 19). The ribs are precooked with the crab boil for a Cajun twist on an American classic.

8 peeled fresh plums, pitted and
  diced
12 whole Roasted Shallots (page 16)
2 tablespoons minced garlic
2 cups Brown Chicken Stock
  (page 7)
½ cup ketchup
¼ cup dark molasses
6 tablespoons honey
3 tablespoons plus 1 teaspoon
  distilled white vinegar
2 tablespoons soy sauce
2 teaspoons dry mustard

4 teaspoons salt, in all
18 turns freshly ground black
  pepper
2 racks baby back ribs, trimmed of
  excess fat (3 to 4 pounds each)
1 teaspoon Emeril's Creole
  Seasoning (page 3)
2 tablespoons liquid crab boil
  (page 59)
4 bay leaves
5 cups Cilantro Potato Salad
  (page 117)

1. Preheat the oven to 375°F.

2. Combine the plums, shallots, garlic, stock, ketchup, molasses, honey, vinegar, soy sauce, mustard, 1 teaspoon of the salt, and 6 turns of the pepper in a medium saucepan over high heat and bring to a boil. Reduce the heat and simmer, stirring occasionally, for 15 minutes. Remove from the heat and purée in a food processor. Makes 2⅔ cups.

3. Place the ribs in a large stockpot with 4 quarts of water, the Creole Seasoning, crab boil, bay leaves, and 2 teaspoons of the salt. Bring to a boil and cook over high heat for 10 minutes.

4. Remove the ribs from the pot and place on a rack in a large roasting pan. Brush on the glaze to coat. Sprinkle with the remaining 1 teaspoon salt, using ¼ teaspoon for each side of each rack, and the remaining 12 turns pepper, allowing 3 turns for each side of each rack.

5. Roast, turning and basting every 10 to 15 minutes, until dark brown, crusty, and caramelized, for about 1 hour 25 minutes. Remove from the oven. When cool enough to handle, cut into individual ribs.

6. While the ribs are roasting, prepare the Cilantro Potato Salad, and refrigerate until the ribs are ready.

7. To serve, arrange 4 to 5 ribs on each plate, with a generous cup of the Cilantro Potato Salad.

Pork Roulade with Andouille Corn-Bread Stuffing, Sage Jus, and Mango Chutney

◆

Makes 6 to 8 main-course servings

This dish seems to be French, Indian, and Louisianan all at once. Although chutneys are traditionally Indian, I don't believe they have to be confined to accompanying just Indian food. In fact—not to be too immodest—I think my own mango chutney is great with this spicy, andouille-seasoned pork.

1 tablespoon unsalted butter
½ cup chopped onions
¼ cup chopped celery
¼ cup chopped green bell peppers
12 ounces (1½ cups) chopped andouille sausage
¼ cup chopped green onions
1 tablespoon minced garlic
1 cup Basic Chicken Stock (page 6)
½ teaspoon salt
6 turns freshly ground black pepper

4 cups crumbled Jalapeño Corn Muffins (page 303), about 5 muffins
1 rolled lean pork roast, unrolled and pounded flat between sheets of plastic wrap to about ½ inch thickness (4 to 5 pounds)
1 tablespoon plus 1 teaspoon Emeril's Creole Seasoning (page 3), in all
1½ cups Sage Jus (recipe follows)
2 cups Mango Chutney (page 287)

1. Preheat the oven to 375°F.

2. In a large skillet over high heat, melt the butter. When the butter sizzles, add the onions, celery, and bell peppers and sauté for 1 minute. Add the andouille and sauté for 1 minute. Add the green onions and garlic and sauté for 1 minute. Stir in the stock, salt, and pepper, and turn off the heat. Turn the mixture into a very large bowl, crumble in the Jalapeño Corn Muffins, and stir until thoroughly incorporated. The mixture should be moist but not wet.

3. Remove the pounded meat from the plastic wrap, place on a flat surface, and sprinkle the top side with 1 tablespoon Creole Seasoning. Spread about half of the stuffing mixture vertically down the center. Roll up and place the stuffed pork roll, seam side down, in a roasting pan. Sprinkle the outside of the roll with the remaining 1 teaspoon Creole Seasoning. Roast until the meat is brown and juicy, for about 55 to 60 minutes.

4. While the pork roll is roasting, prepare the Sage Jus, and cover to keep warm. Prepare the Mango Chutney, and set aside.

5. To serve, cut the pork roll into 6 or 8 slices. Place 1 slice on each plate, and spoon 3 or 4 tablespoons of the Sage Jus on top. Add a mound of the Mango Chutney (⅓ cup for 6 servings, ¼ cup for 8).

SAGE JUS

◆

Makes about 1½ cups

3 cups Basic Chicken Stock (page 6)	1 teaspoon minced garlic
2 tablespoons chopped fresh sage	½ teaspoon salt
1 teaspoon minced shallots	3 turns freshly ground black pepper

In a small saucepan over high heat, combine all of the ingredients and bring to a boil. Reduce the heat and simmer for 25 to 30 minutes. Remove from the heat. Serve immediately or store, refrigerated, in an airtight container for up to 2 days. Reheat in a saucepan over low heat.

Tamarind-Glazed Pork Chops with Mole Cream and Roasted Sweet Potatoes

◆

Makes 4 main-course servings

In Mexico, a green mole (MOH-lay) sauce is like a pesto, blending chile peppers, pumpkin seeds, nuts, and spices. The flavors and textures of this dish are so indescribable, they're guaranteed to bring forth a string of "omigoshes." You can thank the tamarind, that homely brown legume, for the savory richness that brings the mole, sweet potatoes, and pork into heavenly alignment. It's a new idea—and a serious investment in pork futures.

½ cup Green Mole Sauce
   (recipe follows)
4 Roasted Sweet Potatoes (page 273)
2 tablespoons tamarind paste
   (see Note)
1 tablespoon minced garlic
3 tablespoons dark cane syrup (or
   corn syrup, if you can't find cane)
3 tablespoons dark molasses
2 tablespoons ketchup

2 tablespoons water
3 turns freshly ground black pepper
2 tablespoons plus 1 teaspoon
   Emeril's Southwest Seasoning
   (page 3), in all
4 large pork loin chops (each about
   8 to 10 ounces and 2 inches thick)
1 tablespoon olive oil
1 cup Mole Cream (recipe follows)

1. Prepare the Green Mole Sauce up to a week ahead.

2. Prepare the Roasted Sweet Potatoes, and keep warm.

3. Preheat the broiler.

4. To prepare the glaze, combine the tamarind paste, garlic, syrup, molasses, ketchup, water, pepper, and 1 tablespoon Southwest Seasoning in a food processor or blender. Purée until pasty. Makes ¾ cup.

5. With your hands, rub the pork chops on both sides with the remaining 4 teaspoons Southwest Seasoning, using 1 teaspoon per chop. Heat the oil in a large skillet over high heat. Add the chops and sear for 4 minutes on each side and 2 minutes on the fat edge.

6. Arrange the chops on a rack in a baking pan and place on the middle rack of the broiler, about 5 inches from the flame. Broil for 5 minutes on the first side. Brush both sides of each chop with some of the tamarind paste, turn the chops to the second side, and broil for 5 minutes. Turn the chops again, baste with the paste, and broil until brown and gooey, for about 5 minutes longer—a total of about 15 minutes.

7. While the chops are broiling, prepare the Mole Cream.

8. To serve, spoon ¼ cup of the Mole Cream on each of 4 plates, add 1 pork chop, and brush with the tamarind glaze. Add a Roasted Sweet Potato to each plate.

Note: Tamarind paste can be purchased in Latin American, Indian, or Indonesian specialty stores.

GREEN MOLE SAUCE

◆

Makes about 1½ cups

½ cup shelled pumpkin seeds
¼ cup shelled pistachio nuts
¼ cup roasted pine nuts (page 14)
1 tablespoon tamarind paste
¼ cup (about 1 pepper) roasted, peeled, and chopped poblano, New Mexican green, or Anaheim chile pepper (page 16)

1 teaspoon chili powder
1 teaspoon ground cumin
½ teaspoon salt
1 tablespoon dark cane or corn syrup
1 teaspoon distilled white vinegar
1 cup olive oil

In a food processor or blender, combine all of the ingredients, and purée until creamy, stopping once to scrape the sides of the bowl. This sauce can be refrigerated in an airtight container for up to a week, or frozen for up to a month.

MOLE CREAM

◆

Makes 1 cup

½ cup Basic Chicken Stock (page 6)   ¼ cup heavy cream
½ cup Green Mole Sauce (preceding
   recipe)

Combine all of the ingredients in a small saucepan and bring to a boil, stirring constantly, over high heat. Continue to cook over high heat for 2 minutes. Remove from the heat. Serve immediately or store, refrigerated, in an airtight container for up to 24 hours. Reheat in a small saucepan over low heat.

Pork Wellington with Onion Applesauce and Candied Butternut Squash

◆

Makes 4 main-course servings

One doesn't readily connect the traditional beef Wellington to New Orleans food, but using pork rather than the expected beef, Creole seasonings, and local culinary techniques, it assumes a down-home attitude with a "nouvellington" twinkle. My version consists of a tender pork roast smeared with a paste of goat cheese, nuts, and basil before being wrapped in a blanket of flaky pastry and baked.

2 ounces (¼ cup) goat cheese, such
   as Montrachet
¼ cup roasted walnut pieces
   (page 14)
2 tablespoons chopped fresh basil
2 tablespoons minced shallots
1 tablespoon minced garlic
1 tablespoon walnut oil
½ teaspoon salt
2 turns freshly ground black
   pepper

1 boneless loin of pork, trimmed
   (1 to 1½ pounds, 6 inches long ×
   3 inches across)
1 tablespoon Emeril's Creole
   Seasoning (page 3)
1 10-inch square sheet frozen puff
   pastry, thawed
1 large egg, lightly beaten
1 cup Onion Applesauce (page 249)
3 cups Candied Butternut Squash
   (page 274)

1. Preheat the oven to 400°F. Line a baking sheet with parchment or wax paper.

2. Combine the goat cheese, walnuts, basil, shallots, garlic, walnut oil, salt, and pepper in a food processor and purée until grainy. Makes about ½ cup.

3. Using your hands, rub the pork with the Creole Seasoning until coated. Heat a large heavy dry skillet over high heat and sear the meat for 3 minutes on the first side, 3 on the second, and 1 minute on each end. Remove from the skillet and allow to cool for a minute or two.

4. Brush the pastry sheet with some of the beaten egg. Place the pork in the middle of the sheet and pack with the goat cheese paste. Wrap the pastry around the pork and seal the edges tightly, pressing with moistened fingers. Place the package, seam side down, on the baking sheet, and brush with more of the egg. Bake until golden brown and puffy, for about 35 to 40 minutes. Remove from the oven, let cool a minute or two, and cut into 4 thick slices.

5. While the meat is baking, prepare the Onion Applesauce and the Candied Butternut Squash.

6. To serve, spoon ¾ cup of the Candied Butternut Squash onto each of 4 plates. Add 1 slice of pork and drizzle with ¼ cup of the Onion Applesauce.

CHAPTER 11

—————◆—————

Choosing Sides:
Vegetables, Legumes,
Potatoes, and Relishes

Whether I'm dining in a restaurant or at someone's home, I'm always amazed when a spectacular main course arrives at the table accompanied by something slapped on as an afterthought. Sometimes the offending side dish is clearly there for a touch of color; at other times it's a cursory nod toward the old four food groups. In a very popular restaurant in New Orleans, for example, I was once served a saucer of gray-green canned peas along with an excellent lasagna.

Why go to the trouble of preparing a wonderful dinner if all you're going to do is throw some white rice, a plain baked potato, or soggy vegetables on the plate next to the main attraction? The side dish is as important as the main dish if your goal is to create an exciting, satisfying meal.

Use your head when planning. If you're preparing a main dish with two side dishes, the three dishes should complement one another rather than fight for the spotlight. In other words, don't team up Lobster with Champagne Vanilla Sauce with Apple Mint Relish and Tomato Corn Salsa. You get my drift.

In the following pages I've designated the sides for the mains they're meant to accompany, according to the Book of Emeril. Switch them around if you prefer different combinations, but always keep in mind their relative compatibility.

Southern-Style Black-Eye Peas

◆

Makes 3 cups

As every Southerner knows, black-eye peas can happily complete most meals from fried chicken to ribs to pot roast. Try them with Chicken Pockets Stuffed with Goat Cheese, Chorizo, and Pine Nuts (page 202) for an unusual and wonderful combination of tastes and textures.

1 tablespoon olive oil
¼ cup chopped onions
2 ounces (¼ cup) chopped tasso or
  other spiced ham
1 tablespoon minced garlic

1½ cups dried black-eye peas
1 teaspoon Emeril's Creole
  Seasoning (page 3)
4 cups Basic Chicken Stock (page 6)
1 teaspoon salt

1. Heat the oil in a saucepan over high heat. Add the onions and sauté for 1 minute. Add the tasso, garlic, peas, and Creole Seasoning and stir-fry for 1 minute.

2. Add the stock and bring to a boil. Reduce the heat to medium, cover, and cook for 15 minutes. Uncover, stir once, re-cover, and simmer for 15 minutes. Add the salt, stir, cover again, and simmer for a final 10 minutes, or until the peas are tender. Remove from the heat.

Black Bean Chili

◆

Makes 2 cups

...broiled fish moves South of the ...brimming with fresh cilantro and ...(page 198) and Grilled Tuna with ...169).

teaspoon Emeril's Southwest
 Seasoning (page 3)
1 teaspoon chili powder
1 teaspoon ground cumin
½ teaspoon salt
3 turns freshly ground black pepper
¼ cup coarsely chopped fresh
 cilantro

1 tablesp...
 juice

1. Drain and rinse the beans. Heat the oil in a large skillet over high heat. Add the onions, garlic, jalapeños, and beans and sauté, stirring occasionally, for 2 minutes. Add the stock, lime juice, Southwest Seasoning, chili powder, and cumin. Bring to a boil, lower the heat, and simmer for 50 to 60 minutes, or until the beans are tender.

2. Stir in the salt, pepper, and cilantro and simmer for about 5 minutes longer. Remove from the heat. Serve immediately or store, refrigerated, in an airtight container for up to 2 days. Reheat in a saucepan over low heat, stirring occasionally.

Creole White Beans

◆

Makes 2½ cups

I could sit down and eat a big bowl of these zippy beans and nothing else, because they make my mouth so happy, but I like them best with New New Creole Pork Chops (page 250).

2 cups dried white navy beans, soaked overnight, rinsed well and then cooked in fresh water to cover until tender (about 1 hour)
1 tablespoon olive oil
2 ounces (¼ cup) tasso, spiced ham, or bacon
¼ cup chopped onions
1 teaspoon Emeril's Creole Seasoning (page 3)
¾ teaspoon salt

¼ teaspoon cayenne pepper
¼ cup chopped green onions
1 tablespoon minced garlic
12 ounces beer
3 tablespoons Creole or other whole-seed mustard
1 teaspoon Worcestershire sauce
½ teaspoon hot pepper sauce
1 tablespoon unsalted butter, at room temperature

1. Drain the beans.

2. Heat the oil in a large skillet over high heat. Add the tasso and sauté for 30 seconds. Add the onions and stir-fry for 30 seconds. Add the Creole Seasoning, salt, and cayenne pepper; fold in the beans and stir-fry for 1 minute.

3. Stir in the green onions, garlic, beer, mustard, Worcestershire, and hot sauce. Bring to a boil and cook over high heat, stirring occasionally, for 6 minutes. Fold in the butter and cook, stirring constantly, for 1 minute. Remove from the heat. Keeps up to 2 days, refrigerated, in an airtight container. To prepare ahead, cook without adding the butter; reheat in a saucepan over low heat. When the sauce comes to a simmer, fold in the butter and proceed.

Stewed Lentils

◆

Makes 6 cups

A serious foundation for a serious and grand dish—Stuffed Leg of Lamb (page 240).

1 tablespoon olive oil
1 smoked ham hock (about
  6 ounces)
2½ cups (1 pound) lentils
¼ cup chopped onions

2 tablespoons minced garlic
3 bay leaves
6½ cups Basic Chicken Stock
  (page 6)
1 teaspoon salt

1. Heat the oil in a large saucepan over high heat. Add the ham hock and sauté, browning on all sides, for about 1 minute. Add the lentils, onions, garlic, and bay leaves and stir-fry for 1 minute.

2. Stir in the stock and bring to a boil. Reduce the heat to medium and simmer for 8 minutes. Cover the pot and simmer, uncovering once or twice to stir, until the lentils are firm-tender, about 30 minutes. Add the salt, stir, remove from the heat. Remove the ham hock before serving.

Rosemary Lentils

◆

Makes 3 cups

*S*erve this fragrant dish with Beggars' Purses of Lamb, Goat Cheese, and Pine Nuts (page 242).

1 teaspoon olive oil
4 strips bacon, diced
½ cup chopped onions
1 tablespoon minced garlic
1½ cups lentils
1 tablespoon chopped fresh
   rosemary

1 teaspoon Emeril's Creole
   Seasoning (page 3)
4 cups Basic Chicken Stock
   (page 6) or Brown Chicken Stock
   (page 7)
1 teaspoon salt
4 turns freshly ground black pepper

1. Combine the oil and bacon in a large pot over high heat and sauté for 2 minutes. Add the onions, garlic, and lentils and stir-fry for 1 minute. Stir in the rosemary and Creole Seasoning and stir-fry for 1 minute more.

2. Stir in the stock and bring to a boil. Reduce the heat to medium and simmer until the lentils are just tender, for about 30 minutes. Stir in the salt and pepper. Remove the pot from the heat and allow to sit for 15 minutes.

Potato Shallot Custards

◆

Makes 4 side servings

These delicate custards are a little bit of heaven with any roast or broiled meat. I serve them with Curry-Crusted Lamb Chops with Garlic Wine Sauce (page 235).

1 large baking potato
2 tablespoons butter, sliced into 8 thin pats
¾ teaspoon salt, in all
10 turns freshly ground black pepper, in all

1 shallot, thinly sliced
⅔ cup heavy cream
1 large egg
1 tablespoon minced garlic
¼ teaspoon ground nutmeg

1. Preheat the oven to 350°F.

2. Peel and thinly slice the potato.

3. Place 1 pat of the butter in the bottom of each of 4 ramekins. Press 2 slices of the potato on top of the butter, and sprinkle all 4 ramekins with a total of ¼ teaspoon of the salt and 1 turn each of pepper. Add 2 slices of the shallot, 2 slices potato, 1 slice shallot, 1 slice potato, and 1 pat butter on each. Add another ¼ teaspoon salt on all 4, and 1 turn each of pepper.

4. In a bowl, combine the cream with the egg, garlic, nutmeg, the remaining ¼ teaspoon salt and 2 turns black pepper. Whisk until thoroughly blended. Divide among the ramekins, pouring this custard over the potatoes and shallots.

5. Place the ramekins in a 2-inch-deep roasting pan. Place the pan on the oven rack and carefully pour 1 inch of water around the ramekins. Bake until golden brown, for about 1 hour. Remove from the oven and cool to room temperature, for about 20 minutes. Slip the tip of a sharp knife around the side of each custard and turn the ramekins over to unmold. Serve immediately.

Couscous Jambalaya

◆

Makes about 5 cups

This dish could be called "Africajun," since it combines the best of two cuisines. Pork Cutlets with Onion Applesauce (page 249) plays off this side dish beautifully, combining the diverse flavors and textures with great results. This is also great all by itself, served as a light dinner with a salad.

12 raw shrimp (about ¾ pound), peeled and chopped
1 small chicken breast boned, skinned, and chopped (generous ½ cup)
1 tablespoon Emeril's Creole Seasoning (page 3)
¼ cup olive oil, in all
4 ounces (½ cup) chopped andouille sausage
¼ cup chopped onions
¼ cup chopped green bell peppers

¼ cup chopped celery
2 tablespoons minced garlic
½ cup peeled, seeded, and chopped Italian plum tomatoes (about 2)
3 bay leaves
1 teaspoon Worcestershire sauce
1 teaspoon hot pepper sauce
1 cup Basic Chicken Stock (page 6)
1 teaspoon salt
3 turns freshly ground black pepper
1½ cups couscous

1. In a bowl combine the shrimp, chicken, and Creole Seasoning and use your hands to blend thoroughly.

2. Heat 2 tablespoons of the olive oil in a large nonreactive skillet over high heat. Add the seasoned shrimp and chicken and stir-fry for 1 minute. Add the andouille, onions, bell peppers, celery, and garlic and stir-fry for 1 minute.

3. Stir in the tomatoes, bay leaves, Worcestershire, hot sauce, stock, salt, and pepper and bring to a boil. Cook for 10 minutes, stir in the couscous, and turn off the heat. Cover the skillet and allow to sit for 5 minutes. Remove the cover and stir in the remaining olive oil. Serve immediately.

Apple Mint Couscous

◆

Makes 2½ cups

Oh, what a fantastic side dish for lamb—from chops to stew to a roast leg. But, being the perverse soul that I am, I decided to try it with Sautéed Escolar with Curry Oil (page 172). I was rewarded with extraordinarily delicious results.

1 tablespoon plus 1 teaspoon
   unsalted butter, in all
½ cup peeled and finely chopped
   sweet apples
1 tablespoon minced shallots
1 teaspoon minced garlic
3 tablespoons chopped fresh mint

1 teaspoon salt
9 turns freshly ground black pepper
1 cup couscous
1 tablespoon olive oil
1 cup Basic Chicken Stock (page 6)
Mint sprigs, for garnish

1. Melt 1 tablespoon of the butter in a large skillet over high heat. Add the apples, shallots, garlic, mint, salt, and pepper and sauté for 2 minutes. Add the couscous and the olive oil and sauté, stirring, for about 3 minutes.

2. Stir in the stock and bring to a boil, stirring, for about 2 minutes. Reduce the heat to medium and cook, stirring constantly, for 1 minute. Stir in the remaining 1 teaspoon butter and turn off the heat. Cover and allow to sit for about 2 minutes.

3. To serve, press into lightly oiled half-cup molds and unmold immediately onto plates. Garnish with a fresh mint sprig. Serve immediately.

Twice-Fried Vinegar Chips

◆

Makes 6 cups

*T*hese chips make an irresistible snack—just try eating only two handfuls. The method of twice-frying makes them wonderfully delicious and perfectly perfect. They're great with steaks, chops, and any kind of fish, but I really created them for Beer-Battered Fish with Twice-Fried Vinegar Chips and Basil Mayonnaise (page 166). If you're making the Beer-Battered Fish, do the second frying of the potatoes after the fish.

8 to 10 cups vegetable oil
6 cups very thinly sliced unpeeled
   red potatoes

2 tablespoons white vinegar
1 teaspoon salt

1. Heat the oil in a large pot over high heat. When the oil is very hot (375°F), add the potatoes slowly, separating the slices with a spoon, and fry for 2 minutes. Reduce the heat to 350°F, or medium, and fry for 3 minutes, stirring to keep the slices separated and frying evenly. Remove the slices to a basket and shake the excess oil back into the pot and turn off the heat. Spread the potato slices on a baking sheet and allow them to cool for about 10 minutes.

2. Turn the heat up to high under the oil. When the oil is very hot (375°F), add the potatoes and fry for 1 minute. Reduce the heat to 350°F, or medium, and fry until crisp and golden brown, for about 6 minutes. Remove the potatoes with a slotted spoon and drain on paper towels. Sprinkle with the vinegar and salt and serve.

Rosemary Potato Crisps

◆

Makes 4 side servings

*S*erve these habit-forming crisps with roast chicken, grilled fish, steak, and Monster Herbed Veal Chops (page 232).

**12 small unpeeled red potatoes,
  sliced almost 1/16 inch thin
4 tablespoons olive oil**

**2 teaspoons chopped fresh rosemary
1 teaspoon salt
6 turns freshly ground black pepper**

1. Preheat the oven to 400°F.

2. Toss the potato slices in a bowl with the oil, rosemary, salt, and pepper. Spread on a baking sheet in a single layer and bake for 15 to 20 minutes. Remove from the oven, and turn with a spatula.

3. If you're serving these with Monster Herbed Veal Chops, follow the finishing directions on page 233. If you're preparing the potatoes to serve with another dish, bake them until golden brown and crisp, for about 15 minutes longer. Remove from the oven and serve immediately.

Creamed Garlic Potatoes

◆

Makes about 2½ cups

These potatoes are sinfully delicious. You can serve them with almost anything—especially chicken, and *most* especially Panéed Chicken (page 203).

2 cups diced peeled potatoes (½-inch dice)	4 cloves lightly roasted garlic (page 16)
3 cups water	½ teaspoon white pepper
2 teaspoons salt, in all	2 tablespoons unsalted butter
1 cup heavy cream	

1. In a medium saucepan, combine the potatoes, water, and ½ teaspoon of the salt and bring to a boil over high heat. Reduce the heat to medium-high and cook until tender, for 8 to 10 minutes. Remove from the heat and drain in a colander.

2. Place the potatoes back in the pot over medium heat, add the cream, roasted garlic, the remaining 1½ teaspoons salt, and the white pepper and mash vigorously with a potato masher until fairly smooth, for about 4 minutes. Whisk in the butter and remove from the heat. Serve immediately.

Saffron Potatoes

◆

Makes 4 side servings

These potatoes are subtly flavored. They go especially well with Roasted Shrimp and Tomato Mirliton Relish (page 288).

12 peeled small to medium red potatoes	1 teaspoon salt
1 teaspoon saffron threads	½ teaspoon ground white pepper
	6 cups Shrimp Stock (page 10)

1. Combine all of the ingredients in a saucepan over high heat and bring to a boil. Reduce the heat and simmer until the potatoes are firm-tender, for about 12 to 14 minutes.

2. Remove the pot from the heat and allow the potatoes to sit in the broth for 2 to 3 minutes to soak up the flavors. Remove the potatoes with a slotted spoon and serve immediately. Allow the broth to cool and then refrigerate or freeze it for later use.

Roasted Sweet Potatoes

◆

Makes 4 side servings

Wonderful with roast turkey or chicken, these simply prepared sweet potatoes are just right with Tamarind-Glazed Pork Chops with Mole Cream (page 256).

4 medium sweet potatoes, scrubbed	2 turns freshly ground black pepper, in all
2 tablespoons olive oil	
½ teaspoon salt, in all	

1. Preheat the oven to 400°F. Line a baking sheet with parchment or wax paper.

2. Rub the potato skins with the oil and sprinkle with salt and pepper. Place the potatoes on the baking sheet and roast until fork-tender, for 45 to 50 minutes. Remove from the oven, split them, and serve warm.

Candied Butternut Squash

◆

Makes 3 cups

This sweet side dish goes with pork or turkey and is incredibly good with Pork Wellington with Onion Applesauce (page 258).

3 cups peeled and diced butternut squash, about 1 large squash (½-inch dice)
3 tablespoons unsalted butter
1 tablespoon sugar

½ teaspoon ground cinnamon
¼ teaspoon ground nutmeg
½ teaspoon salt
2 turns freshly ground black pepper

1. In a pot of boiling water over high heat, cook the squash with 1 teaspoon of salt until the squash is tender, for about 7 minutes. Remove from the heat and drain.

2. Melt the butter in a large skillet over high heat. Add the squash and the remaining ingredients and glaze the squash, shaking the pan and stirring, for about 2 minutes. Remove from the heat.

Creole Ratatouille

◆

Makes about 2 cups

This ratatouille, unlike many I've sampled, has crisp vegetables with lots of character. If you prefer your ratatouille as a mush, don't bother with this one. It was created especially for Herbed Lamb Patties (page 243), but it makes a great side dish for almost any roast or broiled meat or fish.

3 tablespoons olive oil
1 cup peeled and diced eggplant
   (½-inch dice)
½ cup chopped onions
½ cup diced yellow squash
   (½-inch dice)
½ cup diced zucchini (½-inch dice)

½ cup peeled, seeded, and chopped
   Italian plum tomatoes (about 2)
¼ cup chopped fresh basil
2 tablespoons minced garlic
1 teaspoon salt
4 turns freshly ground black pepper

Heat the oil in a large skillet over high heat. When the oil is hot, add the remaining ingredients and stir-fry for 5 to 8 minutes or until the vegetables are tender. Remove from the heat and serve.

Tasso Maque Choux

◆

Makes about 2 cups

Pronounced mock SHOO, *maque choux* is a spicy Cajun dish of corn and seasonings. Every family has its own variations; Hazel Prudhomme, Paul's mama, liked to make chicken or crawfish *maque choux*. Mine gets its flavor not only from very fresh corn but also from tasso, or Cajun spiced ham. I love it best of all with Skillet Steak (page 220).

2 tablespoons olive oil
3 ounces (⅓ cup) diced tasso or
    Cajun spiced ham
1½ cups fresh corn, scraped from
    the cob (about 2 ears)
⅓ cup chopped onions

1 tablespoon minced garlic
1 teaspoon salt
1 turn freshly ground black pepper
1 cup heavy cream
⅓ cup minced red bell peppers
⅓ cup chopped green onions

1. Heat the oil in a large skillet over high heat. When the oil is hot, add the tasso and sauté for 30 seconds. Add the corn and cook, shaking and flipping the skillet several times, for about 1 minute.

2. Add the onions and sauté for 30 seconds. Add the garlic, salt, and pepper and cook for 1 minute. Stir in the cream, red peppers, and green onions and simmer until heated through, for about 2 minutes. Remove from the heat.

Onion Crisps

◆

Makes about 2 cups

An elegant substitute for their less refined, pudgy cousin, the french-fried onion ring, these delicate crisps nonetheless satisfy the same urge for a crunchy, tangy treat. You could serve them with steak or even a burger, but if you're feeling daring, try them with Roast Smothered Monkfish (page 161).

4 cups vegetable oil
1 cup all-purpose flour
1 tablespoon plus 1 teaspoon
   Emeril's Creole Seasoning
   (page 3)

2 cups thinly shaved onion slices,
   separated into rings
1 large egg, beaten with 3
   tablespoons water
½ teaspoon salt

1. Start heating the oil in a large pot over high heat.

2. Combine the flour with the Creole Seasoning in a bowl. Dip the onions in the egg wash and toss in the seasoned flour.

3. When the oil is very hot (about 375°F), fry the onions in batches until golden and crisp, for about 2 to 3 minutes. Remove with a slotted spoon, drain on paper towels, and sprinkle with the salt. Serve immediately or keep warm on a baking sheet in a 250°F oven.

Stir-Fried Sesame Vegetables

◆

Makes about 2 cups

Have everything sliced, diced, and ready *before* you start this dish, because you must cook it fast to keep the vegetables crisp. Serve it over rice for a delicious vegetarian lunch or team it up with Steamed Ginger Shrimp Dumplings (page 186).

2 tablespoons sesame oil, in all
½ cup sliced fresh broccoli florets
¼ cup diagonally sliced celery
2 cups chopped bok choy, stems and leaves
½ cup thinly sliced onions
½ teaspoon salt

4 turns freshly ground black pepper
½ cup red bell pepper strips
½ cup fresh bean or sunflower sprouts
½ cup water
1 teaspoon soy sauce

Heat 1 tablespoon of the sesame oil in a large skillet over high heat. Add the broccoli and stir-fry for 30 seconds. Add the celery and stir-fry for 30 seconds. Add the bok choy, onions, salt, and pepper and stir-fry for 30 seconds. Add the bell peppers and bean sprouts and stir-fry for 1 minute. Stir in the water, soy sauce, and the remaining 1 tablespoon sesame oil, and remove from the heat. Serve immediately.

Fried Arugula

◆

Makes 4 side servings

You haven't lived until you've tasted fried arugula, especially as it appears with Tipsy Snapper with Ginger Sake Sauce (page 158). Don't miss it.

2 tablespoons olive oil   **8 cups arugula**

Heat the oil in a large skillet over high heat until hot and smoking, for about 2 minutes. Drop the arugula into the oil and move away quickly because the oil will spit and spatter for a second or two. Stir-fry the arugula for 30 seconds, remove from the oil with a slotted spoon, and drain on paper towels. Serve immediately.

Braised Kale

◆

Makes 4 side servings

Here's a great vegetable side dish, with the sparkling green color only fresh kale has. Serve it with pork, fish, or chicken. The tough, center kale stem should be removed before it is cooked.

1 tablespoon olive oil
2 cups thinly sliced onions
1 teaspoon salt
12 turns freshly ground black
   pepper

2 tablespoons minced garlic
8 cups (firmly packed) torn and
   stemmed kale pieces
2 cups Basic Chicken Stock
   (page 6)

Heat the oil in a large skillet over high heat. Add the onions, salt, and pepper and stir-fry for 2 minutes. Add the garlic, kale, and stock and cook, stirring occasionally, for 3 minutes. Remove from the heat. Serve immediately.

Braised Red Cabbage

◆

Makes about 2 cups

This is a super side dish, especially with pork. For a beautiful contrast, serve it alongside Braised Green Cabbage (recipe follows). Both cabbages are featured in Pork Medallions with Braised Red and Green Cabbages and Roasted Shallots (page 246).

1 ½ teaspoons olive oil
¼ cup chopped onions
4 cups coarsely shredded red
   cabbage (about ½ head)
¼ teaspoon salt
2 turns freshly ground black pepper

¼ cup apple cider vinegar
2 bay leaves
2 whole cinnamon sticks
¼ teaspoon ground allspice
½ cup water
3 tablespoons sugar

1. Heat the oil in a large nonreactive skillet over high heat. When the oil is hot, add the onions, cabbage, salt, and pepper and stir-fry for 1 minute. Add the vinegar, bay leaves, cinnamon, allspice, and water, and stir and simmer for 3 minutes. Stir in the sugar and cook, stirring and folding the ingredients through the cabbage, for 2 minutes.

2. Cover the pot and cook over high heat for 3 minutes. Reduce the heat to medium and cook for 15 minutes. Uncover, turn the heat up to high and cook, stirring from time to time, until the cabbage is tender, for about 15 minutes. Serve immediately.

Braised Green Cabbage

◆

Makes about 2 cups

1½ teaspoons olive oil
3 strips thick-sliced bacon, chopped
¼ cup chopped onions
7 cups coarsely shredded green
   cabbage (about ½ large head)
½ teaspoon salt

4 turns freshly ground black pepper
2 bay leaves
¾ cup beer
1½ teaspoons Creole or other
   whole-seed mustard

1. Heat the oil in a large skillet over high heat and add the bacon. Cook the bacon until golden brown, for about 1½ minutes. Add the onions, cabbage, salt, and pepper and stir-fry for 1 minute. Stir in the bay leaves, beer, and mustard and simmer, folding the ingredients through the cabbage, for 3 minutes.

2. Cover the pot and cook over high heat for 3 minutes. Reduce the heat to medium and cook for 10 minutes. Uncover, turn the heat up to high and cook, stirring from time to time, until the cabbage is tender, for about 10 minutes. Serve immediately.

Apple Pecan Stuffing

◆

Makes 6 cups

This easy-to-make stuffing may become your favorite in turkeys, chickens, and such. But you'll also want to use it to "unstuff" pork chops in Unstuffed Pork Chops with Herbed Shallot Sauce (page 251).

2 teaspoons olive oil
1 cup diced lean bacon
½ cup chopped onions
½ cup chopped celery
1 cup peeled and diced apples, such as Granny Smiths
½ cup pecan pieces
6 tablespoons chopped fresh parsley
¼ cup chopped fresh sage

1 teaspoon salt
12 turns freshly ground black pepper
4 cups cubed day-old bread (1-inch cubes)
1 teaspoon Emeril's Creole Seasoning (page 3)
2 cups Basic Chicken Stock (page 6)

1. Combine the oil and bacon in a large skillet over high heat and stir-fry for 3 minutes. Add the onions, celery, apples, pecans, parsley, sage, salt, and pepper and stir-fry for 2 minutes.

2. Stir in the bread cubes, Creole Seasoning, and stock; bring to a simmer, and remove from the heat. Use immediately.

Andouille Corn-Bread Stuffing

◆

Makes 1½ cups

The taste of andouille is so distinctively delicious, you absolutely can't eat just one bite. That's why this stuffing makes a hit of any roast chicken, pork, or turkey. But if you wanna wow 'em, put it together with Stuffed Chicken Legs in Pastry with Andouille Cream (page 208).

1 tablespoon olive oil
¼ cup chopped onions
4 ounces (½ cup) chopped andouille
  sausage
¼ cup chopped green onions
2 tablespoons chopped celery
2 tablespoons chopped green bell
  peppers
1 tablespoon minced garlic

1 teaspoon Emeril's Creole
  Seasoning (page 3)
½ teaspoon salt
3 turns freshly ground black pepper
1 cup coarsely crumbled Jalapeño
  Corn Muffins (page 303)
½ cup Basic Chicken Stock
  (page 6)

1. Heat the oil in a large skillet over high heat. Add the onions and andouille and sauté for 1 minute. Add the green onions, celery, bell peppers, and garlic and stir-fry for 1 minute.

2. Stir in the Creole Seasoning, salt, pepper, corn muffins, and stock and cook, stirring and shaking the skillet, for 2 minutes. Remove from the heat. Use immediately.

Wild Mushroom Andouille Duxelles

◆

Makes about 2 cups

Get your duxelles in a row and be sure to pronounce them doo-ZELL. This wild and wonderful mixture would be happy stuffing steaks, veal chops, or a chicken, but is thrilled when bursting from Quail Milton served with Port Wine Sauce (page 216).

3 cups chopped assorted fresh wild
   mushrooms, such as shiitakes,
   chanterelles, black trumpets, or
   lobster mushrooms
4 ounces (½ cup) diced andouille
   sausage
¼ cup chopped onions
1 tablespoon minced garlic

1 tablespoon olive oil
1 teaspoon Emeril's Creole
   Seasoning (page 3)
½ teaspoon salt
3 turns freshly ground black pepper
½ cup port wine
¾ cup bread crumbs (page 17)

1. Combine the mushrooms, andouille, onions, and garlic in the bowl of a food processor and pulse about 10 times, until the mixture forms a coarse paste.

2. Turn the mixture into a medium skillet over high heat and stir in the oil, Creole Seasoning, salt, and pepper. Sauté, stirring occasionally, for about 4 minutes. Stir in the port and cook for 1 minute.

3. Reduce the heat to medium, add the bread crumbs, and cook, stirring constantly, for 2 minutes. Remove from the heat and allow to cool.

Fried Polenta

◆

Makes 8 wedges

Used extensively in northern Italy, polenta is cornmeal that is usually cooked up as a mush or pudding and topped with a variety of sauces, cheeses, or sausages. Such homey dishes have recently become chic. In this case, I don't mind, since polenta is so delicious, and it adds a fresh touch to more traditional Creole dishes. I love it cut in wedges and fried, then served like crisp bread with Chicken Fricassee (page 206).

5 tablespoons plus 1 teaspoon olive oil, in all
¼ cup chopped onions
1 tablespoon minced garlic
2 tablespoons chopped fresh basil
½ teaspoon salt

3 turns freshly ground black pepper
1½ cups milk
¼ cup freshly grated Cheddar cheese
¼ cup coarsely grated fresh Parmesan cheese
¾ cup yellow cornmeal

1. Grease a 9-inch tart or cake pan with a removable bottom with 1 teaspoon of the oil.

2. Heat 2 tablespoons of the oil in a large pot over high heat. When the oil is hot, add the onions, garlic, and basil and sauté for 30 seconds. Add the salt and pepper and sauté for another 30 seconds.

3. Stir in the milk and bring to a boil. Reduce the heat to medium and whisk in the Cheddar and Parmesan, just until the cheeses melt. Whisk in the cornmeal *slowly,* a little at a time, until the mixture has the consistency of a thick roux. Remove from the heat, and working quickly, spoon the mixture into the greased pan, spreading it and packing it down before it sets. Refrigerate for 1 hour.

4. Remove the polenta from the refrigerator, remove it from the pan, and cut it into 8 wedges. Heat the remaining 3 tablespoons oil in a large skillet over high heat. When the oil is hot, add the wedges of polenta and fry until golden brown, for about 1 minute on each side. Remove and drain on paper towels. Serve immediately.

Guacamole

◆

Makes 1 cup

This popular avocado dip is just one of the many Southwestern foods New Orleanians have come to love. This is the definitive guacamole for Albuquerque Roast Chicken (page 198).

1 ripe avocado, peeled and pitted
2 tablespoons peeled and finely
  chopped Italian plum tomatoes
2 teaspoons seeded and minced
  jalapeño peppers
2 tablespoons chopped onions
½ teaspoon minced garlic
2 tablespoons chopped fresh cilantro
1 tablespoon freshly squeezed lime
  juice

1 teaspoon freshly squeezed lemon
  juice
½ teaspoon Worcestershire sauce
¼ teaspoon hot pepper sauce
½ teaspoon salt
3 turns freshly ground black pepper
2 tablespoons sour cream

In a bowl mash all of the ingredients together with a fork or potato masher until thoroughly blended and somewhat chunky. Cover tightly by laying a sheet of plastic wrap directly on the surface of the guacamole and gently squeezing out any air bubbles. Seal the wrap to the edges of the bowl and refrigerate until ready to use, up to 8 hours.

Mango Chutney

◆

Makes 2 cups

This Indian-style relish is a great partner for pork or chicken. Try it with Pork Roulades with Andouille Corn-Bread Stuffing (page 254).

1 tablespoon olive oil
¼ cup chopped onions
2 teaspoons seeded and minced jalapeño peppers
2 cups peeled and diced mangoes
¼ cup chopped green onions
½ cup plus 2 teaspoons water, in all
1 teaspoon freshly squeezed lime juice

1 teaspoon freshly squeezed lemon juice
1 tablespoon distilled white vinegar
2 tablespoons sugar
½ teaspoon salt
4 turns freshly ground black pepper
1 teaspoon cornstarch

1. Heat the oil in a large pot over high heat. Add the onions, jalapeños, and mangoes and sauté for 30 seconds. Stir in the green onions, ½ cup of the water, the lime and lemon juices, vinegar, sugar, salt, and pepper. Bring to a boil, lower the heat, and simmer for 5 minutes.

2. Meanwhile, combine the cornstarch with the remaining 2 teaspoons water. Stir the cornstarch mixture into the pot, bring to a boil, and cook for 1 to 2 minutes. Remove from the heat. Serve immediately or store, refrigerated, in an airtight container for up to 24 hours. Reheat in a saucepan over low heat.

Tomato Mirliton Relish

◆

Makes 1⅔ cups

The mirliton is a mild-mannered squash whose acquaintance I made when I moved to Louisiana. Its delicate flavor is a great counterpoint for some of the spicier dishes we serve, and its versatility makes it any cook's good friend. Whip up this relish in minutes and enjoy it with Roasted Shrimp with Saffron Potatoes (page 182).

**1 medium mirliton or 1 large
  cucumber
¼ cup peeled, seeded, and diced
  Italian plum tomatoes**

**¼ cup finely chopped red onions
2 teaspoons finely chopped fresh dill
¾ teaspoon salt
8 turns freshly ground black pepper**

1. Drop the mirliton in boiling water and simmer until tender, for about 35 to 45 minutes; then peel, seed, and dice. (If using a cucumber, simmer until fork-tender, for about 20 minutes, then peel, cut in half vertically, remove the seeds, and dice.)

2. In a bowl, combine all of the ingredients and blend thoroughly.

Pecan Crab Relish

◆

Makes 2 cups

*T*his quick and easy relish is a perfect accompaniment for almost any fish dish, but beware: It may outshine everything else on the table. Pecan-Crusted Lemonfish (page 155) is a wonderful exception. The two complement each other beautifully.

½ pound (1 cup) lump crabmeat, picked over for shells and cartilage
½ cup roasted pecan halves (page 14)
¼ cup chopped green onions

2 tablespoons minced red bell peppers
1 teaspoon freshly squeezed lemon juice
½ teaspoon salt
3 turns freshly ground black pepper

In a small bowl, combine all of the ingredients and toss gently to keep from breaking up the crabmeat lumps. Refrigerate until ready to serve, up to 24 hours.

Mint Orzo

◆

Makes about 3 cups

This is a knockout side dish, especially with Lamb Shanks Braised in Wine Sauce (page 237).

2 tablespoons olive oil
½ cup finely chopped onions
1 tablespoon minced garlic
1 cup (½ pound) orzo
  (a rice-shaped pasta)
1 teaspoon salt

4 turns freshly ground black pepper
¼ cup chopped fresh mint
3 cups Basic Chicken Stock
  (page 6)
1 tablespoon unsalted butter, at
  room temperature

1. Heat the oil in a saucepan over high heat. Add the onions, garlic, orzo, salt, and pepper and stir-fry for 2 minutes. Stir in the mint and stock and bring to a boil.

2. Reduce the heat to medium and cook, stirring occasionally, for 20 minutes. Remove from the heat and fold in the butter until thoroughly incorporated. Serve immediately.

Apple Mint Relish

◆

Makes about 2 cups

One of lamb's best friends is fresh mint. Combine it with sweet apples and serve it with Rack of Lamb with Creole Mustard Crust (page 238).

2 cups water
1 lemon, juice only
2 cups peeled and finely diced sweet
  apples (about 2 apples)

1 teaspoon sugar
3 tablespoons chopped fresh mint

1. In a bowl combine the water and lemon juice. Add the chopped apples and soak them for 20 minutes. Drain the apples, reserving 3 tablespoons of the lemon water.

2. Combine the apples, sugar, mint, and the 3 tablespoons lemon water, and mix until thoroughly blended. Serve immediately or store, refrigerated, in an airtight container for up to 2 days. Stir well before serving.

Fava Bean Relish

◆

Makes about 1⅔ cups

Less common and therefore more interesting than a lot of other beans, the fava should be added to your bean repertoire. Favas must be removed from their pods, blanched, and then peeled. Serve them with Spicy Salt Cod Cakes with Fondue Piquante (page 126).

1 tablespoon olive oil
8 ounces (1 cup) chopped andouille
    sausage
½ cup fresh or frozen (and thawed)
    fava beans, blanched in salted
    water for 1 minute, and peeled
¼ cup chopped onions

¼ cup peeled, seeded, and chopped
    Italian plum tomatoes
1 tablespoon minced garlic
1 tablespoon chopped fresh cilantro
½ teaspoon salt
2 turns freshly ground black pepper

Heat the oil in a large nonreactive skillet over high heat. Add the andouille and sauté, stirring occasionally, for 2 minutes. Add the beans, onions, tomatoes, garlic, and cilantro, and sauté, stirring and shaking the skillet occasionally, for 2 minutes. Remove from the heat. Season with salt and pepper.

White Bean Relish

◆

Makes about 2 cups

When you live in Louisiana, you eat a lot of beans. Red, black, white, green, round, kidney shaped—we love 'em all. The trick to buying navy beans is to remember they're white—not navy blue. This spicy relish goes beautifully with Crab-Stuffed Shrimp with Tomato Butter (page 184).

1 cup dried white navy beans, soaked overnight, rinsed well, then cooked in fresh water to cover until tender (about 1 hour)
2 tablespoons olive oil
2 ounces (¼ cup) diced andouille sausage
¼ cup chopped green onions
¼ cup chopped celery

2 tablespoons minced red bell peppers
2 tablespoons peeled, seeded, and chopped Italian plum tomatoes
2 teaspoons minced garlic
1 teaspoon Emeril's Creole Seasoning (page 3)
½ teaspoon salt
3 turns freshly ground black pepper

1. Drain the beans.

2. Heat the oil in a medium skillet over medium-high heat. When the oil is hot, add the sausage, green onions, celery, bell peppers, tomatoes, garlic, and Creole Seasoning and sauté for 2 minutes. Stir in the beans, salt, and pepper; sauté for 1 minute and remove from the heat. This can be stored, refrigerated, in an airtight container for up to 2 days. Reheat in a saucepan over low heat.

CHAPTER 12

Your Daily Bread:
Breads, Breadsticks,
Biscuits, and Muffins

Carrera's Bakery, which later became the Moonlight Baking Company, was a hangout for me when I was a little boy. I would go every day after school and tell the old Portuguese men who worked there how much I wanted to be a baker. I'm sure they finally gave me a job to stop me from hassling them. Of course, my first assignment was as a pan washer, not a baker. But soon I graduated to baking simple things like cookies and cupcakes, and I was very proud of myself.

Mom and Dad would deliver my dinner—piping hot and wrapped in foil—to the bakery, where the old bakers and I sat on steel flour bins, eating over the wooden baking tables. They conducted their men's conversation and jokes in Portuguese, but they would talk shop in broken English so I could pick up the inside skinny on how to be a successful baker. This information was driven into my head as I picked my way through their heavy accents. And even though it wasn't easy for us to communicate, the love of baking made us close and kept us together. I was so crazy about baking and about the men at the bakery that, although weekends were for music and play, I could hardly wait for Monday so I could get back to work.

In New Orleans, bread is often baked so it can be used later in a bread pudding or in *pain perdu,* which literally means lost bread, and is actually French toast. The most popular local breads have always included yeast rolls and corn bread—with or without jalapeño peppers. The breads I bake today are reminiscent of some of those more traditional recipes, but I've taken liberties with them by adding fresh herbs, olives, cracked pepper, sun-dried tomatoes, and Parmesan cheese. In some cases, I've created newer textures and shapes, like the flatbreads.

Remember that bread almost always tastes better when it's warm, and you might even want to finely chop some fresh herbs into the softened butter you serve with it.

Black Pepper Bread

◆

Makes 1 loaf

This bread is intense in flavor and not for the faint of heart. Of course, if you like your food pungent and peppery and you don't mind a little heat, you'll love this *pain au poivre*.

5 tablespoons plus 2 teaspoons melted unsalted butter, in all
3 tablespoons plus 2 teaspoons freshly cracked or ground black pepper, in all
2 teaspoons active dry yeast

1 cup warm water (about 110°F)
1 tablespoon sugar
1 teaspoon salt
1 large egg
3¾ cups all-purpose flour

1. Grease the bottom and sides of a loaf pan with 2 teaspoons of the butter, and dust with 1 tablespoon of the pepper, tapping out any excess.

2. In a large bowl dissolve the yeast in the water. Add the sugar, salt, egg, and 2 tablespoons of the pepper and whisk until thoroughly blended. Add the flour and 4 tablespoons of the butter and mix gently with your hands just until you have a smooth ball of dough. Press the dough gently into the loaf pan, cover with a towel, place in a warm spot, and allow to rise for 1 hour. The dough will have risen up over the rim of the pan.

3. Preheat the oven to 350°F.

4. Make a shallow slit in the dough lengthwise down the center, drizzle with the remaining 1 tablespoon butter, and sprinkle the top of the loaf with the remaining 2 teaspoons pepper. Bake until brown and firm, for about 30 minutes. Remove from the oven and the pan and allow to cool on a rack before serving.

Black and Green Olive Bread

◆

Makes 1 round peasant loaf

This bread—both dense and intense—is fantastic thickly sliced and dipped in olive oil. We also tried it spread with cream cheese and loved it that way, too.

1 tablespoon active dry yeast
2½ cups warm water (about 110°F)
3½ cups whole wheat flour
3 cups plus 1 handful all-purpose flour, in all
2 teaspoons salt

3 turns freshly ground black pepper
2 tablespoons olive oil
2 cups mixed halved black and green olives
¼ cup chopped fresh basil

1. Dissolve the yeast in the water in a bowl, stirring. Add the whole wheat flour and 3 cups of the all-purpose flour, and mix by hand. Add the salt, pepper, olive oil, olives, and basil. Blend well with your hands. Knead and form into a round ball of dough. Place in a clean oiled bowl, cover with a towel, and place in a warm spot to rise for 30 minutes.

2. Line a baking sheet with parchment or wax paper. When the dough has risen to double in size, sprinkle with the remaining handful of all-purpose flour. Fold the sides of the dough up over the flour, turning the dough and continuing to fold the sides over.

3. About 15 minutes before baking, preheat the oven to 350°F.

4. Place the dough on the baking sheet and bake until firm and crusty, for about 45 minutes. Remove from the oven and allow to cool until just warm before serving.

Rosemary Flatbread

◆

Makes 6 wedges

Flatbread is fun to eat, and I always enjoy experimenting with it. This one's pretty basic, but the fragrant, fresh rosemary makes it special. If you prefer, substitute fresh basil or sage for the rosemary.

1 teaspoon active dry yeast	1 tablespoon minced garlic
¾ cup warm water (about 110°F)	2 cups all-purpose flour
4 tablespoons olive oil, in all	½ teaspoon salt
2 tablespoons roughly chopped fresh rosemary	1 handful cornmeal (about ¼ cup)
	1 teaspoon kosher salt

1. Line 2 baking sheets with parchment or wax paper.

2. In a bowl dissolve the yeast in the water. Add 3 tablespoons of the olive oil, the rosemary, garlic, flour, and salt. Mix and knead well by hand until you have a smooth ball of dough.

3. Spread the cornmeal on a flat surface. Place the dough on the cornmeal and cover with a warm, damp dish towel. Allow the dough to rise until double in size, for about 50 minutes.

4. About 15 minutes before baking, preheat the oven to 400°F.

5. With a rolling pin, flatten the dough into a round and cut it into 6 equal wedges. Flatten each wedge with your fingers, pounding it out very thin. (Don't worry about holes—they add character.) Spread on the baking sheets and bake until golden brown, for about 10 minutes. Brush each piece of flatbread with ½ teaspoon of the remaining 1 tablespoon olive oil, and sprinkle lightly with the kosher salt. Serve warm.

Sun-Dried Tomato Flatbread

◆

Makes 8 wedges

Arrange two wedges of this pungent, crackery bread on a plate with a mixed greens salad, and you've got a sophisticated, delicious first course or side dish.

1 teaspoon active dry yeast
¾ cup warm water
   (about 110°F)
5 tablespoons olive oil, in all
¼ cup chopped fresh basil
½ teaspoon salt
1 tablespoon minced garlic

½ cup chopped sun-dried tomatoes,
   preferably homemade (page 16),
   drained, or storebought (packed in
   oil), drained
2¼ cups plus 1 handful all-purpose
   flour, in all
1 teaspoon kosher salt

1. In a bowl dissolve the yeast in the water, and add 3 tablespoons of the olive oil, the basil, salt, garlic, sun-dried tomatoes, and 2¼ cups of the flour. Mix and knead into a ball of dough and set aside to rise, covered, in a warm place, for 1 hour.

2. Preheat the oven to 350°F.

3. Sprinkle the remaining handful of flour on a flat surface and flatten the dough on it. Cut it into 8 wedges.

4. Spread 1 tablespoon of the olive oil on 2 baking sheets. Pull and flatten each of the 8 pieces of bread until very thin and place them on the baking sheets. Brush the bread with the remaining 1 tablespoon olive oil and sprinkle it with the kosher salt. Bake until brown and crisp, for about 20 to 25 minutes. Remove from the oven and allow to cool before serving.

Albuquerque Cakebread

◆

Makes 1 round loaf

We call this a cakebread because of its texture. It's loaded with the familiar Southwestern flavors of jalapeño peppers, fresh cilantro, chili powder, and cornmeal. A warm, buttered slice of this scrumptious bread is terrific with an omelet or salad.

2 teaspoons active dry yeast
1 cup warm water (about 110°F)
1 tablespoon seeded, chopped
    jalapeño peppers
¼ cup chopped fresh cilantro
1 teaspoon minced garlic
1 teaspoon Emeril's Southwest
    Seasoning (page 3)
1 teaspoon chili powder

½ teaspoon salt
½ cup grated jalapeño
    pepper~flavored Jack cheese
1 tablespoon Piri Piri (page 4) or
    olive oil
1 cup all~purpose flour
½ cup masa harina
    (see Note, page 29)
1 cup yellow cornmeal, in all

1. Line a baking sheet with parchment or wax paper.

2. In a bowl dissolve the yeast in the water. Add the jalapeños, cilantro, garlic, Southwest Seasoning, chili powder, salt, cheese, Piri Piri, masa harina, and ½ cup of the cornmeal. Knead with your hands into a smooth ball of dough. Cover the bowl with a towel, set in a warm place, and allow to rise for about 45 minutes.

3. About 15 minutes before baking, preheat the oven to 350°F.

4. Spread 1 handful of cornmeal on the baking sheet, place the ball of dough on top, and sprinkle with the remaining cornmeal. Bake until golden, for about 40 minutes. Remove from the oven and cool before serving.

Parmesan Fennel Breadsticks

◆

Makes 8 breadsticks

These were created especially for Fennel Tomato Soup (page 62), but are a wonderful accompaniment to almost any meal.

1 teaspoon active dry yeast
½ cup warm water (about 110°F)
½ teaspoon salt
½ teaspoon sugar
¼ cup grated Parmesan cheese
1 teaspoon minced garlic
1 tablespoon chopped fresh fennel
   leaves

1 teaspoon Emeril's Creole
   Seasoning (page 3)
1 cup plus 1 tablespoon all-purpose
   flour
1 tablespoon olive oil
½ teaspoon kosher salt

1. Line a large baking sheet with parchment or wax paper.

2. In a bowl dissolve the yeast in the water. Add the salt, sugar, Parmesan, garlic, fennel leaves, and Creole Seasoning, and mix until thoroughly blended. Using a wooden spoon, mix in the flour until thoroughly incorporated into a ball of dough. Don't overmix.

3. Preheat the oven to 300°F.

4. On a lightly floured surface, pat out the dough with your hands until you have a rough square about 8 by 8 inches. Use a pastry cutter to cut 8 equal strips of the dough, and roll each one out into a skinny log about 13 to 14 inches long.

5. Place the sticks on the baking sheet, brush them with the olive oil, sprinkle them lightly with the kosher salt, and bake until brown, for about 30 minutes. Remove from the oven and serve warm.

Buttermilk Biscuits

◆

Makes 12 mini biscuits

These very southern biscuits, prepared in their mini size, are meant to accompany André's Barbecued Shrimp (page 180). If you make them larger, increase the baking time slightly. Double the recipe to make more biscuits, or flavor them: Try a teaspoon of your favorite fresh herb, especially thyme, tarragon, basil, cilantro, or dill; or make cheese biscuits using a tablespoon of grated Parmesan cheese.

1 cup all-purpose flour, sifted	¼ teaspoon salt
1 teaspoon baking powder	2 tablespoons unsalted butter
⅛ teaspoon baking soda	¼ cup plus 1 teaspoon buttermilk

1. Preheat the oven to 375°F. Line a baking sheet with parchment or wax paper.

2. In a bowl combine the dry ingredients and blend thoroughly. Cream in the butter with your fingers or a fork, until the mixture resembles coarse crumbs. Add the buttermilk a little at a time and, using your hands or a fork, work it in just until it's thoroughly incorporated and you have a smooth ball of dough. Don't overwork or overhandle the dough.

3. On a lightly floured surface, roll out the dough with a rolling pin to a circle about 7 inches in diameter, ½ inch thick. Using a small round cookie cutter or the rim of a shot glass, press out twelve 1-inch rounds. If you like, you can reroll the leftover dough to make more, but the texture of these will be denser than the others.

4. Place the dough rounds on the baking sheet and bake until golden on top and brown on the bottom, for about 15 minutes. Serve warm.

Rosemary Biscuits: Follow the recipe above but substitute ¼ cup milk for the buttermilk and add 1 tablespoon chopped fresh rosemary. Serve them with Rosemary Lamb Stew (page 75). Follow the same method for other herbed biscuits.

Jalapeño Corn Muffins

♦

Makes 12 muffins

You could bake these and crumble them up for a stuffing. But if you do, make an extra batch to butter and enjoy. For regular corn muffins, just omit the jalapeños.

1 tablespoon softened butter
4 large eggs
2 tablespoons seeded and minced jalapeño peppers
2 cups fresh corn kernels, scraped from 3 or 4 blanched ears of corn (page 16)

1 cup all-purpose flour
1 cup yellow cornmeal
1 tablespoon baking powder
1 teaspoon salt
¾ cup milk
1 tablespoon vegetable oil

1. Preheat the oven to 375°F. Grease a 12-cup muffin tin with the softened butter.

2. In a large bowl whisk the eggs with the jalapeños and corn. Stir in the flour, cornmeal, baking powder, and salt. Beat in the milk and oil. Pour the batter into the muffin tin.

3. Bake until golden, for about 25 minutes. Remove from the oven and cool slightly before serving.

Pumpernickel Rolls

◆

Makes about 18 rolls

Don't be thrown by the chocolate and the mashed potatoes in this recipe—it makes pumpernickel taste like you've never tasted it before.

2 teaspoons active dry yeast
1 scant cup warm water (about
  110°F)
1 tablespoon melted unsalted butter
1 teaspoon sugar
6 tablespoons dark molasses
1 tablespoon caraway seeds

½ cup mashed cooked potatoes
1 tablespoon finely chopped
  semisweet chocolate
2 cups rye flour
½ cup whole wheat flour
¼ cup cornmeal
1 handful all-purpose flour

1. Line a baking sheet with parchment or wax paper.

2. In a large bowl dissolve the yeast in the water. Add the butter, sugar, and molasses and mix well. Stir in the caraway seeds, potatoes, chocolate, rye and wheat flours, and the cornmeal. Using your hands, mix the ingredients together, and knead until you have a smooth ball of dough.

3. Cover the bowl with a towel, place in a warm spot in your kitchen, and allow to rise for about 1¼ hours.

4. About 15 minutes before baking, preheat the oven to 350°F.

5. Spread the all-purpose flour on a flat surface and using your hands, flatten the dough into a circle about 1 inch thick. Cut the dough into 18 pieces and form each into a roll about 3 inches in diameter. Place the rolls on the baking sheet and bake until they are brown and firm, for about 30 minutes. Remove from the oven and set aside to cool.

Herbed Profiteroles

◆

Makes 16

Profiteroles are for dessert, right? Not necessarily. You're probably accustomed to having your profiteroles filled with custard or ice cream and topped with chocolate sauce. But I decided to fill them with savory foods, such as seviche and duck mousse. So try these profiteroles with Smoked Duck Mousse Profiteroles with Chile Pepper Glaze (page 42) and Scallops Seviche in Herbed Profiteroles (page 39). They're fun to make, and the result is spectacular.

8 tablespoons (1 stick) unsalted
   butter
1 cup milk
½ teaspoon salt
2 turns freshly ground black pepper
1 cup all-purpose flour

5 large eggs
½ teaspoon baking powder
1 tablespoon assorted chopped fresh
   herbs (basil, parsley, thyme,
   tarragon)

1. Preheat the oven to 375°F. Line a baking sheet with parchment or wax paper.

2. In a saucepan over high heat, combine the butter and milk, and whisk until the butter has melted and the mixture has come to a boil. Stir in the salt and pepper. Add the flour all at once and stir vigorously until the mixture comes away from the sides of the pan and forms a ball of dough. Remove from the heat and turn the mixture into the bowl of an electric mixer.

3. Beat in the eggs, one at a time, until each is well incorporated. Add the baking powder and herbs and beat until the herbs are thoroughly distributed.

4. Using a pastry bag without a tip, squeeze 16 generous golf ball-size blobs of the dough onto the baking sheet. Bake until golden brown, smooth on the bottom, and dry inside, for about 25 to 30 minutes. Remove from the oven and allow the profiteroles to cool on a rack before filling.

THE LAST WORD

Don't refrigerate profiteroles once they've been baked, or they'll become mushy. Store them at room temperature in an airtight container or covered with plastic wrap.

Homemade Tortillas

◆

Makes 12 tortillas

*T*hese are very much like the rustic tortillas you might be served in Mexico or New Mexico, so don't expect the big soft tortillas you get at your local Tex-Mex. For best results, use a tortilla press; but if you can't find one, press them out with a heavy pie pan or skillet bottom. If you must buy tortillas instead of making them yourself, buy only fresh ones from a Latin American food market.

2 cups masa harina (see Note, page 29)

1 cup warm water
3 teaspoons butter, softened

1. In a bowl work the masa harina together with the water until it becomes a cohesive dough. Don't overwork it. With wet hands, divide the dough into 12 balls and place 2 pieces of plastic wrap on each, top and bottom. Flatten each in a tortilla press or with a rolling pin, heavy pie pan, or skillet.

2. Heat a heavy dry 9-inch skillet over medium heat, and brown the tortillas for about 1 minute on each side. Just before serving, rub each tortilla all over with ¼ teaspoon softened butter and reheat in a hot skillet over high heat, for about 15 seconds on each side.

Aioli Crostini

◆

Makes about 12

Crostini, which literally means "little crusts" in Italian, are delightful party munches—crisp toasts baked with a variety of interesting spreads calculated to kick the appetite into gear. They're dynamite baked with aioli, as they are here, and set afloat on a bouillabaisse, cioppino, or Portuguese Seafood Stew (page 74).

½ cup roasted garlic (page 16)
1 large egg
½ teaspoon salt
3 turns freshly ground black pepper

½ cup olive oil
12 slices (each 2 to 3 inches in diameter) crusty Portuguese or Italian bread

1. Preheat the oven to 375°F.

2. In the bowl of a food processor, combine the garlic, egg, salt, and pepper. Turn on the machine and slowly stream in the oil. Continue to process until the mixture is thoroughly emulsified, stopping once to scrape down the sides of the bowl. Makes about ⅔ cup of aioli.

3. Place the bread slices in a single layer on a baking sheet and spread each with about 1 tablespoon of the aioli. Bake until just golden, for about 2 to 3 minutes. Watch them carefully to see that they don't burn.

CHAPTER 13

Sweet Revolution: Desserts

Ah, dessert in New Orleans: rich bread puddings, dramatic Bananas Foster, mile-high pies, sugary beignets, chewy pralines, custards, cakes, and more. So what's new? Just my own sweet take on the subject—the desire to dazzle every diner in my restaurant with an irresistible creation, just when he or she thinks the party's over.

The dessert must of course taste good, but to coax a reluctant customer into indulging in the first place, it must also be attractive. When I was a kid I enrolled in a cake-decorating class in a Continuing Education program at night. I was the only male and by far the youngest in the class. Every week we whipped up frostings and practiced making buttercream roses and violets. I was amazed when I took first prize in our class competition. Encouraged, I entered a big wedding cake contest and won grand prize for the American Northeast region.

Throughout my training and early career, I was influenced by a number of talented pastry chefs. But when I started working at Commander's Palace, I finally met the dessert maker's dessert maker, Lou Lynch. Mr. Lou, as we call him, is the best pastry chef—or baker, as he prefers to be known—I've ever worked with. He's a warm, genuine person with natural talent, who often worked on new dessert projects for me after hours at Commander's. Mr. Lou is now the backbone of the bakery at Emeril's, where he inspires the young cooks and shares with them—and with me—his considerable knowledge.

Many of the recipes in this chapter appear on the menu at Emeril's, such as Banana Cream Pie, J.K.'s Chocolate Chocolate Soufflés, Banana Chocolate Bread Pudding with Mint Crème Anglaise, and New Orleans Goat Cheesecake. All of my chocolate desserts are prepared with Ghirardelli chocolate, but Lindt or Toblerone would do just as well. I hope every dessert you make from this book dazzles both you and your guests. And may all your dinner parties be sweet.

Banana Cream Pie with Banana Crust and Caramel Drizzles

◆

Makes one 9-inch pie

As I planned the opening of the restaurant, I wanted to create a signature dessert that would represent the flavors of my childhood in Massachusetts as well as those of my adopted home, New Orleans. I had thought of and discarded many ideas and was about to go bananas before finally hitting on the fruit of the same name. In fact, the word *banana* is said to have roots in the Portuguese language. More importantly, I have fond childhood memories of creamy-soft banana pies served on special occasions. As for New Orleans, one of its most popular desserts is Bananas Foster, a flambéed treat of bananas, rum, and ice cream. So I feel cross-culturally vindicated. There are three secrets to this pie: the bananas in the crust, the old-fashioned pastry cream, and the whole vanilla bean.

1 Banana Piecrust (recipe follows)
3 cups heavy cream, in all
1 small vanilla bean, split and scraped (page 14)
1 tablespoon unsalted butter
¾ cup cornstarch
2½ cups sugar
½ teaspoon salt

5 large egg yolks
4 ripe bananas
¾ cup Caramel Drizzle Sauce (recipe follows)
2 cups heavy cream whipped with ½ teaspoon vanilla and 2 teaspoons sugar
Shaved chocolate

1. Prepare the Banana Piecrust, and allow it to cool completely.

2. Heat 2 cups of the cream in a large saucepan over high heat. Stir in the paste scraped from inside the vanilla bean, and the butter, and bring to a simmer.

3. Meanwhile, in a small bowl, combine the remaining 1 cup cream with the cornstarch and stir until thoroughly blended and smooth. When the mixture in the saucepan begins to boil, stream in the cream/cornstarch mixture, whisking constantly until all is thoroughly incorporated. Remove from the heat.

4. In a bowl combine the sugar and salt, and whisk this dry mixture vigorously into the saucepan until the cream is thick and the dry ingredients are thoroughly incorporated. Over low heat, whisk in the egg yolks one at a time. Remove from the heat and whisk the pastry cream until smooth and creamy.

5. Peel the bananas and cut them crosswise into ¼-inch slices. Spread about ⅓ of the pastry cream in the piecrust and arrange ½ of the banana slices over the cream. Spread on another ⅓ of the pastry cream and arrange the remaining banana slices over that. Cover with the remaining pastry cream and smooth out the top. Refrigerate for at least 2 hours or until firm.

6. About 20 minutes before serving, prepare the Caramel Drizzle Sauce.

7. To serve, cut the pie into wedges and drizzle on the warm Caramel Drizzle Sauce. Top with the whipped cream and shaved chocolate.

BANANA PIECRUST

◆

Makes one 9-inch crust

2 cups graham cracker crumbs
¼ cup light brown sugar
8 tablespoons (1 stick) unsalted
   butter, at room temperature

1 very ripe banana, mashed

1. Preheat the oven to 375°F.

2. In a bowl cream the ingredients together with your hands. Press the mixture into a 9-inch pie pan, and bake until brown, for about 15 minutes. Remove from the oven and allow to cool completely before filling.

CARAMEL DRIZZLE SAUCE

◆

Makes about ¾ cup

1 cup sugar
¼ cup water

1 cup heavy cream

1. In a saucepan, combine the sugar and water, and bring it to a boil, stirring often. Cook, stirring occasionally, until the mixture is a deep nutty-brown color and the consistency of thin syrup, for about 10 to 15 minutes. Turn off the heat.

2. Stir in the cream, turn the heat back on to high, and boil the sauce for about 2 minutes. Remove from the heat. Use immediately.

Peanut Butter Cream Pie

◆

Makes one 9-inch pie

I'm mad about peanut butter and was delighted to discover that peanut butter pie is a favorite in New Orleans. So I have to please my customers—right?

1 baked Graham Cracker Crust (recipe follows)	2 tablespoons chopped roasted peanuts
8 ounces cream cheese, at room temperature	4 cups heavy cream, whipped until thick, in all
¾ cup confectioners' sugar	½ cup chopped salted peanuts
½ cup smooth peanut butter	½ cup chocolate shavings and curls
2 tablespoons milk	

1. Prepare the Graham Cracker Crust, and allow it to cool completely.

2. Using an electric mixer, beat the cream cheese with the confectioners' sugar until creamy. Add the peanut butter, milk, and peanuts and beat well.

3. Fold half the whipped cream into the peanut butter mixture and spoon this into the piecrust, smoothing out the top. Refrigerate for at least 1 hour until set.

4. To serve, spoon some of the remaining whipped cream over each wedge of pie, and top with 1 tablespoon of peanuts and 1 tablespoon of chocolate curls.

GRAHAM CRACKER CRUST

◆

Makes one 9-inch crust

1½ cups graham cracker crumbs	¼ cup smooth peanut butter
4 tablespoons (½ stick) unsalted butter, melted (¼ cup)	

1. Preheat the oven to 350°F.

2. In a bowl combine the ingredients thoroughly, and press the mixture into a 9-inch pie pan. Bake until golden and crisp, for about 6 to 8 minutes. Remove from the oven and allow the crust to cool completely before filling.

Basic Pie Dough

◆

Makes two 9-inch crusts

Did you know you can freeze pie dough? If you only need a single crust, cut the ball of dough in half and freeze what you don't immediately need. Defrost the frozen dough thoroughly before rolling it out. Or halve this recipe if you want to make a single crust without freezing another.

2¼ cups all-purpose flour
1 teaspoon salt

⅔ cup (10⅔ tablespoons) very cold unsalted butter, cut up, or solid vegetable shortening, or lard
4½ tablespoons ice water

1. In a bowl combine the flour and salt. Add the butter or shortening and work it through with your hands until the mixture resembles coarse crumbs.

2. Using the tines of a fork, stir in the water 1 tablespoon at a time and work it in with your hands just until you have a smooth ball of dough. (Don't overhandle the dough.) Wrap in plastic and refrigerate for 20 minutes.

3. Remove the dough from the refrigerator, and place on a floured surface. If you're making 2 crusts, cut the dough in half and put the second half back in the refrigerator.

4. For each crust, roll out the dough on a floured surface into a circle about 14 inches in diameter and ⅛ inch thick. Gently fold the circle of dough in half and then in half again so that you can lift it without tearing it, and unfold it into a 9-inch pie pan. Crimp the edges, or pinch in a decorative border. Fill and bake as directed in the recipe.

Note: For a baked pie crust, preheat the oven to 425°F. Prick the bottom of the pie all over with a fork, and bake for 18 to 20 minutes, or until lightly browned. Remove, cool thoroughly, and then fill as directed in the recipe.

Perfect Pecan Pie

◆

Makes one 9-inch pie

Pecan pie is a New Orleans tradition, and I guess I've eaten it more times than I can count. Everyone here who makes pecan pie thinks his or hers is the best. But mine is.

½ recipe Basic Pie Dough
  (page 313)
4 large eggs
¾ cup sugar
½ teaspoon salt

1½ cups light corn syrup
1 tablespoon melted butter
1 teaspoon pure vanilla extract
1½ cups pecan pieces
Vanilla ice cream (optional)

1. Preheat the oven to 350°F.

2. Prepare the Basic Pie Dough and line a pie pan. Refrigerate until ready to fill.

3. In a bowl beat the eggs together with the sugar and salt. Add the corn syrup, butter, and vanilla and whisk until all is thoroughly incorporated and the mixture is frothy.

4. Spread the pecans in a layer on the bottom of the pastry shell, and pour in the filling. Bake until firm, for about 1 hour.

5. Serve warm, cut into wedges, with or without vanilla ice cream.

Cranberry Apple Pie with Sweet Walnut Topping

◆

Makes one 9-inch pie

This pie is as New England as can be. But my friends in New Orleans love it. In the autumn, drive east from Fall River, and you'll know you're approaching Cape Cod when you see zillions of cranberries floating in the watery bogs. Apples and walnuts, of course, trigger thoughts of the Thanksgiving and Christmas holidays in the head of this All-American boy, so here's that boy's entry for this year's holiday pie.

½ recipe Basic Pie Dough (page 313)
1¾ cups light brown sugar
5 tablespoons cornstarch
1 tablespoon ground cinnamon
1 teaspoon ground nutmeg
1 teaspoon salt
1 pound Granny Smith apples, peeled, cored, and cut into ¼-inch slices (about 4 cups)
2 cups fresh cranberries, rinsed and picked over

2 tablespoons freshly squeezed lemon juice
10 tablespoons unsalted butter, in all
¾ cup granulated sugar
2 tablespoons heavy cream
1 teaspoon pure vanilla extract
1 cup walnut pieces
Ice cream (optional)

1. Preheat the oven to 350°F.

2. Prepare the Basic Pie Dough and line pie pan. Refrigerate until ready to fill.

3. In a bowl combine the brown sugar, cornstarch, cinnamon, nutmeg, and salt, and mix well. In another bowl combine the apples, cranberries, and lemon juice, and toss well. Pour the dry mixture over the fruit. Melt 2 tablespoons of the butter, pour it over all, and mix thoroughly.

4. Turn the mixture into the pie shell and bake the pie until the fruit is tender, for about 1 hour. Remove from the oven and set the pie on a rack to cool.

5. In a large skillet over medium heat, melt the remaining 8 tablespoons butter with the granulated sugar. Cook, stirring, until the mixture is bubbling and the consistency of a thick roux, for about 5 to 6 minutes. Stir in the cream, vanilla, and walnuts and cook, stirring constantly, for 4 minutes. Remove from the heat and cool for 20 minutes. Spoon the topping over the cooled pie and refrigerate overnight.

6. To serve, cut the pie into wedges, and add a scoop of ice cream, if you like.

Chocolate Chip Pie with Bourbon Cream

◆

Makes one 9-inch pie

This cookie-style pie's for the kid in all of us, but the bourbon makes it grow up in a hurry.

½ recipe Basic Pie Dough (page 313)
8 tablespoons (1 stick) unsalted
    butter
1½ cups sugar
3 large eggs
2 cups all-purpose flour

2 teaspoons bourbon
1 cup chopped walnuts
8 ounces bittersweet chocolate,
    chopped
3 cups Bourbon Cream
    (recipe follows)

1. Preheat the oven to 350°F.

2. Prepare the Basic Pie Dough and line a pie pan. Refrigerate until ready to fill.

3. In a bowl cream together the butter, sugar, and eggs. Stir in the flour and bourbon, and fold in the walnuts and chocolate. Pour into the pie shell. Bake until golden brown, for about 1 hour. Remove from the oven and allow to cool.

4. When the pie is almost cool, prepare the Bourbon Cream.

5. To serve, spread about ⅓ cup of the Bourbon Cream in each plate and top with a wedge of the pie.

BOURBON CREAM

◆

Makes 3 cups

2 cups heavy cream
¼ cup confectioners' sugar

2 teaspoons bourbon

In a large bowl whip the cream and sugar with an electric beater until thick. Beat in the bourbon, and continue to beat until soft peaks form. Serve immediately.

Serendipity Apple Tart

◆

Makes one 9-inch tart

We were kitchen-testing the Pork Wellington (page 258), and I realized there was some puff pastry left over. I used it to put together an apple tart, and the result was so good, we decided to put it in the book. The beauty of it is it's easier to make than pie and is as elegant as a tarte Tatin.

1 sheet frozen puff pastry, about 10
  by 10 inches, thawed
1 large egg, lightly beaten
3 tablespoons granulated sugar, in all
1¼ teaspoons cinnamon, in all
¼ teaspoon plus a pinch of nutmeg,
  in all

2 tablespoons unsalted butter, in all
2 cups peeled and thinly sliced
  Granny Smith apples (½ pound)
2 tablespoons confectioners' sugar
Whipped cream

1. Preheat the oven to 400°F.

2. Use the bottom of a 9-inch false-bottomed tart or springform cake pan to trace and cut out a 9-inch circle on the puff pastry. Replace the bottom in the pan, place the round of pastry dough into it, and brush some of the beaten egg over it.

3. Using a small sharp knife or pastry cutter, cut out a ½-inch strip of dough around the original circle and place this strip in the tart pan on top of the bottom crust around its edge to form a lip or border. Use a knife or fork to crimp a design in this border. Perforate the bottom crust all over with the tip of a knife.

4. Sprinkle the bottom crust with 1 tablespoon of the sugar, ½ teaspoon of the cinnamon, and ¼ teaspoon of the nutmeg. Dot it with 1 tablespoon of the butter. Meanwhile, in a small saucepan over low heat, melt the remaining 1 tablespoon butter.

5. Toss the apple slices with the remaining 2 tablespoons granulated sugar, ¾ teaspoon cinnamon, a pinch of nutmeg, and the melted butter. Blend until the mixture is thoroughly incorporated.

6. Arrange the apple slices like spokes on top of the crust, without covering the crimped border. Pour the accumulated juices from the bowl over the apples. Bake until the pastry is brown and puffy, for about 40 minutes. Remove the tart from the oven and allow it to cool slightly. Remove it from the pan to a serving dish.

7. To serve, sift the confectioners' sugar over the tart, mound the whipped cream in the center, and cut into wedges.

New Orleans Goat Cheesecake

◆

Makes one 9-inch cheesecake

Look out, New York. I'm tired of hearing about New York cheesecake. I think *we* now have a shot at immortality in the cheesecake department. Endowing the old standby with creamy goat cheese gives it new life, new texture, and a wonderfully subtle, savory flavor. Look out, world—for New Orleans cheesecake.

4 tablespoons (½ stick) unsalted
    butter, melted (¼ cup), plus 1
    teaspoon unsalted butter, at room
    temperature
1 cup graham cracker crumbs
2 pounds cream cheese, at room
    temperature
1½ cups sour cream, in all

12 ounces (1½ cups) soft goat
    cheese, such as Montrachet
2 large eggs
2 cups sugar
1 tablespoon pure vanilla extract
2 tablespoons freshly squeezed lime
    juice
2 tablespoons Grand Marnier

1. Preheat the oven to 350°F. Grease the sides of a 9-inch springform pan with 1 teaspoon of butter.

2. In a bowl combine the graham cracker crumbs and the melted butter until thoroughly blended, and press the mixture into the bottom of the springform pan.

3. In another bowl beat the cream cheese with an electric mixer until thick, smooth, and creamy, for about 5 minutes. Beat in 1 cup of the sour cream, the goat cheese, eggs, and sugar, and continue beating until the mixture is very smooth and creamy, for about 4 to 5 minutes. Add the vanilla and lime juice and beat until thoroughly incorporated, for about 2 minutes.

4. Pour the filling over the crust in the springform pan and bake until brown and springy-firm, for about 1½ hours. Remove from the oven and allow to cool to room temperature. If you refrigerate the cake, remove from the refrigerator and allow it to come to room temperature (about 2 hours) before serving. Run a knife around the perimeter and release the cake from the springform ring.

5. In a small bowl combine the Grand Marnier with the remaining ½ cup sour cream and beat with an electric mixer on medium speed until smooth and creamy, for about 2 minutes. Spread on top of the cooled cake.

6. To serve, cut wedges of the cheesecake with a warm knife.

Note: To cut cheesecake successfully, keep a tall glass of warm water at hand, and dip your knife in the water between slices.

Chocolate Fantasy Cake

◆

Makes one 9-inch cake

This flourless chocolate cake is a regular on the restaurant's dessert menu, and the remarks it evokes usually include "sinful," "decadent," "morally corrupt," and "ridiculously wonderful." Our Victorian antecedents would probably be shocked unless they lived in New Orleans. For best results, serve it to your favorite chocoholic.

8 tablespoons (1 stick) plus 1 tablespoon softened unsalted butter, in all
8 ounces semisweet chocolate, coarsely chopped
5 large eggs, at room temperature, separated, in all

¾ cup sugar
2 teaspoons pure vanilla extract
½ teaspoon salt
1½ cups Chocolate Ganache Icing (recipe follows)
Fresh raspberries
Whipped cream

1. Preheat the oven to 350°F. Grease a 9-inch springform pan with 1 tablespoon of the butter, and dust with the flour, tapping out any excess.

2. In a metal bowl set over a pot of simmering water, melt the chocolate with the remaining 8 tablespoons butter and stir occasionally until smooth and creamy. Remove from the heat.

3. In another bowl use an electric mixer to beat the egg yolks together with the sugar and vanilla until thick, stopping to scrape the sides of the bowl once or twice, for about 3 minutes. In a third bowl whisk the egg whites with the salt until stiff, for about 2 minutes. Slowly and gently fold the chocolate into the yolk mixture, adding just a little chocolate at a time to keep the eggs from scrambling. Fold in the egg whites.

4. Pour the batter into the springform pan, and bake in the center of the oven until spongy, for about 40 minutes. Remove from the oven, remove the springform ring, and place the cake on a rack to cool completely.

5. When the cake is cool, prepare the Chocolate Ganache Icing.

6. To serve, spread the Chocolate Ganache Icing over the cake. Top with raspberries and serve a small wedge of cake with a dollop of whipped cream.

CHOCOLATE GANACHE ICING

◆

Makes 1½ cups

8 ounces semisweet chocolate,
chopped

½ cup heavy cream

In a metal bowl set over a pot of simmering water, melt the chocolate with the cream, stirring constantly until smooth. Don't let the mixture boil. Remove from the heat. Use immediately or store, refrigerated, in an airtight container for up to 24 hours. Reheat in the top of a double boiler.

Raspberry Chocolate Cheesecake

◆

Makes one 9-inch cheesecake

New Orleans meets Nashville in this exceptional cheesecake. The recipe was adapted from one Kathy Grossman, a good foodie friend of mine in Nashville, Tennessee. Kathy has a fantastic produce company in Nashville; even more important, she makes a dynamite raspberry chocolate cheesecake.

5 tablespoons plus 1 teaspoon (⅓ cup) melted unsalted butter, in all
8 ounces chocolate wafer or icebox cookies
½ cup plus 2 tablespoons granulated sugar, in all
1½ pounds cream cheese, at room temperature
6 ounces bittersweeet chocolate, melted

½ cup raspberry liqueur, such as Chambord
4 large eggs
½ cup heavy cream
1 cup sour cream
½ cup confectioners' sugar
1 pint fresh raspberries

1. Preheat the oven to 350°F. Butter the sides and bottom of a 9-inch springform pan with 1 teaspoon of the butter.

2. In a food processor grind the chocolate wafers into fine crumbs. Add the remaining 5 tablespoons melted butter and 2 tablespoons of the granulated sugar and blend thoroughly. Press evenly into the bottom and partway up the sides of the springform pan.

3. In a bowl beat the cream cheese with an electric mixer at high speed until smooth and creamy, for about 5 minutes. Beat in the melted chocolate and the remaining ½ cup granulated sugar until thoroughly blended. Beat in the raspberry liqueur and continue beating until the mixture is very smooth, for about 4 minutes.

4. Set the mixer at low speed and add the eggs one at a time, beating each until incorporated but taking care not to overbeat. Add the heavy cream and beat just until incorporated, for about 30 seconds.

5. Pour the mixture into the crust in the springform pan and bake until firm, for about 50 minutes. The filling should seem soft in the middle; don't overbake. Remove from the oven and allow to cool to room temperature.

6. In a small bowl whisk the sour cream together with the confectioners' sugar until smooth and creamy. Spread this topping over the cooled cake and then refrigerate for at least 4 hours. Remove from the refrigerator and remove the springform ring.

7. To serve, top the cake with the raspberries and cut it into wedges.

Chocolate Pecan Cake with White Chocolate Mocha Sauce

◆

Makes 12 servings

In my early days at Commander's Palace, my sous chef was Peter Oldfield, who'd worked for about a year at Jacques Cagna's restaurant in Paris. Since chocoholics abounded among our customers, Peter helped me create a rich chocolate dessert based on Cagna's well-known "Queen of Sheba." Ours was called Chocolate Sheba and caused a sensation among the chocolate lovers. When I opened Emeril's, it evolved into this flourless cake which has a rich, fudgy consistency yet somehow manages to be light.

8 tablespoons (1 stick) plus 2 teaspoons unsalted butter, at room temperature, in all
1¾ pounds bittersweet chocolate
10 large eggs, separated, in all
½ cup sugar, in all
1½ cups Roasted Pecans (page 14), in all

2½ cups White Chocolate Mocha Sauce (recipe follows)
1 cup heavy cream, whipped
¼ cup chocolate-covered coffee beans

1. Grease a 10-inch cake pan with 2 teaspoons of the butter.

2. In a metal bowl set over a simmering pot of water, melt the chocolate with the remaining 8 tablespoons butter and stir occasionally until smooth and creamy. Remove from the heat.

3. In another bowl beat the egg yolks with ¼ cup of the sugar until pale and thick. In a third bowl beat the egg whites together with the remaining ¼ cup sugar until stiff peaks form.

4. Slowly beat the chocolate into the egg yolk mixture, then gently fold in the egg whites. Spread 1 cup of the pecans in the buttered cake pan and pour the chocolate mixture over them. Sprinkle the remaining ½ cup pecans over the top, and refrigerate overnight.

5. Just before serving, prepare the White Chocolate Mocha Sauce. Remove the terrine from the refrigerator.

6. To serve, spoon some of the White Chocolate Mocha Sauce onto each plate and add a slice of the terrine. Top with a dollop of whipped cream and several coffee beans.

WHITE CHOCOLATE MOCHA SAUCE

◆

Makes 2½ cups sauce

1 cup strong brewed coffee
2 cups heavy cream

8 ounces white chocolate pieces

In a saucepan over high heat, combine the coffee and cream and bring to a boil. Reduce the heat to medium. Stir in the chocolate, whisking as it melts, and simmer for 20 minutes. Serve immediately or store, refrigerated, in an airtight container for up to 24 hours. Reheat in a double boiler.

Fruit Terrine with Almond Cream and Three Fruit Coulis

◆

Makes 8 servings

Don't turn the page! This is not a difficult recipe—it just seems long because it has three basic steps: the genoise, or cake; the almond cream; and the assembly. But anyone can do it, and the results make the time spent more than worthwhile. A coulis, or light smooth sauce, is a relative newcomer in New Orleans. It can help move any dessert from the ONO list to a place of honor on the NNO roster. Use whatever seasonal fruits are available or whichever are your favorites. Don't feel as if you're stuck with the three fruits I've used; you can change them to make them wild or mild, using blueberries or passion fruit, pears or mangoes. Adjust the amount of sugar in the coulis, depending on the natural sweetness of the fruit. If you prepare these sauces ahead of time, you can refrigerate them and then thin them with a little water before serving.

8 tablespoons (1 stick) plus 1 teaspoon unsalted butter, cut up, at room temperature, in all
9 large eggs, in all
1¼ cups sugar, in all
1 tablespoon plus 1 teaspoon pure almond extract, in all
½ cup all-purpose flour
¼ teaspoon baking powder
1½ cups almonds, toasted (page 14), and finely chopped in a food processor, in all

¼ cup Frangelica (hazelnut liqueur), in all
1 cup fresh blackberries, in all
1 cup halved large fresh strawberries, in all
1 cup thinly sliced peeled fresh peaches, in all
1 cup thinly sliced peeled fresh kiwi fruit, in all
Three Fruit Coulis (recipe follows)

1. Preheat the oven to 375°F. Grease a 6-cup loaf pan with 1 teaspoon of the butter.

2. To make the almond genoise (the cake part): In a metal bowl set over a pot of simmering water, whisk 6 of the eggs with ¾ cup of the sugar and 1 tablespoon of the almond extract. Whisk constantly, occasionally removing the bowl from the heat when the mixture threatens to get too hot and scramble the eggs. Whisk until a 3-second ribbon forms (lift the whisk and the mixture will fall from it like a ribbon that lasts 3 seconds), for about 5 minutes.

3. Remove the bowl from the heat and beat the mixture with an electric mixer until thick and frothy, for about 3 minutes. In a bowl combine the flour, baking powder, and 1 cup of the almonds, and mix well. Gently fold the dry ingredients into the egg mixture, about ½ cup at a time, until thoroughly incorporated.

4. Pour the batter into the loaf pan and bake until spongy, for about 25 to 30 minutes. Remove from the oven and allow to cool. Run a small knife around the inside of the pan and turn the genoise out onto a rack to cool. Using a sharp bread knife, slice the genoise into 3 equal, horizontal layers, and set aside.

5. To make the almond cream: In a metal bowl set over a pot of simmering water, whisk together the remaining 3 eggs, the remaining ½ cup sugar, and the remaining 1 teaspoon almond extract. Reduce the heat to medium and whisk constantly, removing the mixture from the heat occasionally to ensure that the eggs don't scramble, until you get a 3-second ribbon. Remove the bowl from the heat and beat the mixture with an electric mixer until it's thick and frothy, for about 5 minutes. Beat in the remaining ½ cup almonds and the remaining 8 tablespoons butter. Makes about 1½ cups.

6. Line the loaf pan with long pieces of plastic wrap overhanging the sides and place 1 layer of the cake in the bottom. (Save the best-looking layer for the top.) Sprinkle the bottom layer with 1 tablespoon of the Frangelica. Spread about ½ cup of the cream over the layer and arrange half the fruit in layers over the cream. Add the next layer of cake, sprinkle with another tablespoon Frangelica, and spread another ½ cup of the cream. Layer the remaining fruits over the top and spread the remaining ½ cup cream over the fruit. Sprinkle the underside of the top layer with 1 tablespoon of the Frangelica and turn it over on the last layer of cream. Sprinkle the top of the cake with the remaining 1 tablespoon Frangelica. Wrap the plastic wrap tightly over the cake and press gently but firmly into the loaf pan. Refrigerate overnight.

7. Prepare the Three Fruit Coulis. Remove the terrine from the refrigerator and unwrap it. Carefully turn the cake out onto a platter and cut 8 slices.

8. To serve, place 1 slice of the terrine on each plate and spoon a pool of each of the Three Fruit Coulis onto the plate on each of 3 sides.

THREE FRUIT COULIS

◆

1 cup Blackberry Coulis

1½ cups fresh blackberries or
   seasonal fruit

1 cup water
¼ cup sugar

◆

1½ cups Strawberry Coulis

2 cups hulled fresh strawberries
1 cup water

2 tablespoons sugar

◆

1½ cups Peach Coulis

2 cups sliced peeled fresh peaches
1 cup water

1 tablespoon sugar

1. For each coulis, combine the ingredients in a small saucepan over high heat. Cook, stirring, for 12 to 15 minutes. Remove from the heat and allow to cool for about 15 minutes.

2. Pour the mixture into the bowl of a food processor. Pulse several times, then purée, and serve.

Note: Strain the coulis if there are seeds, such as blackberry or raspberry.

Banana Chocolate Bread Pudding with Mint Crème Anglaise

◆

Makes 15 servings

Bread pudding is the beloved dessert of New Orleans, usually served with cream, whipped or not. To give this favorite treat a new new taste, I add fresh, ripe bananas and chocolate chunks, and serve it on a silky puddle of Mint Crème Anglaise.

4 tablespoons (½ stick) unsalted butter, melted (¼ cup), in all
4 large eggs, lightly beaten
1 cup light brown sugar
3 cups heavy cream
1 cup milk
1 teaspoon pure vanilla extract
½ teaspoon ground cinnamon
2 ripe bananas, mashed
½ cup pecan pieces

6 cups day-old bread cubes (½-inch)
6 ounces bittersweet chocolate, chopped
2½ cups Mint Crème Anglaise (recipe follows)
1 cup heavy cream, whipped with ½ teaspoon vanilla and 2 teaspoons granulated sugar
Confectioners' sugar

1. Preheat the oven to 350°F. Brush a baking dish (about 10 × 14 inches) with 2 tablespoons of the butter.

2. In a large bowl whisk together the eggs, brown sugar, cream, and milk. Add the vanilla, cinnamon, bananas, pecans, bread, and chocolate and stir to blend thoroughly.

3. Stir the remaining 2 tablespoons butter into the pudding mixture and pour into the baking dish. Bake until firm, for about 1 hour. Remove from the oven and allow the pudding to cool on a rack until just warm before cutting into squares.

4. To serve, spread about 2 tablespoons of the Mint Crème Anglaise on each plate and top with a square of the pudding. Add a dollop of whipped cream, and dust with confectioners' sugar.

MINT CRÈME ANGLAISE

◆

Makes 2½ cups

2 cups heavy cream
½ cup sugar
1 vanilla bean, split and scraped
  (page 14)

2 tablespoons chopped fresh mint
1 tablespoon crème de menthe
5 large egg yolks

1. In a saucepan over high heat, whisk the cream together with the sugar, vanilla bean paste, mint, and crème de menthe. Bring to a simmer and remove from the heat.

2. In a bowl beat the egg yolks until thick and frothy. Temper the egg yolks by stirring just 1 tablespoon of the sauce into the yolks, then another, then another, until all is incorporated. Turn the egg yolk mixture into the sauce (off the heat) and stir until thoroughly blended.

3. Return the saucepan to low heat and cook 2 to 4 minutes, stirring often to prevent scorching. Remove from the heat. Strain through a fine mesh sieve.

Pumpkin Walnut Bread Pudding with Kentucky Bourbon Sauce

◆

Makes 8 generous servings

In the fall a young man's fancy turns to thoughts of pumpkins and walnuts. No? Well, anyway, if the guy's a chef, they do. This recipe was pure serendipity. I had some pumpkin left over the day we were testing the pumpkin soup, so I created this bread pudding especially for this book. The bourbon was an afterthought that turned out to be a brainstorm. It's exactly right for this pudding.

1 tablespoon plus 2 teaspoons
  unsalted butter, at room
  temperature, in all
1 cup half-and-half
1½ cups heavy cream
5 large eggs
½ teaspoon grated orange zest
5 tablespoons granulated sugar
6 tablespoons light brown sugar,
  in all
1 tablespoon minced fresh ginger

1 teaspoon ground cinnamon
½ teaspoon ground nutmeg
1 teaspoon pure vanilla extract
2 tablespoons Grand Marnier
2 cups cooked and mashed pumpkin
8 slices white bread, with crusts,
  torn into 2-inch pieces
½ cup chopped walnuts
2 cups Kentucky Bourbon Sauce
  (recipe follows)
Fresh mint sprigs

1. Preheat the oven to 350°F. Lightly grease an 8-cup ovenproof casserole or mold with 2 teaspoons of the butter.

2. In a large bowl whisk together the half-and-half, cream, eggs, and orange zest. Add all of the granulated sugar, 4 tablespoons of the brown sugar, the ginger, cinnamon, nutmeg, vanilla, and Grand Marnier, and whisk vigorously until thoroughly blended. Add the pumpkin and whisk until incorporated. Fold in the bread and walnuts and mix thoroughly.

3. Pour the mixture into the casserole, dot the top with the remaining 1 tablespoon butter, and sprinkle with the remaining 2 tablespoons brown sugar. Place the casserole in a water bath (a larger baking dish with about an inch of hot water). Bake until golden brown and puffy, for about 1 hour 15 minutes.

4. About 15 minutes before the pudding is finished baking, prepare the Kentucky Bourbon Sauce.

5. Serve warm or at room temperature. To serve, spoon the pudding into bowls or wineglasses, add 2 tablespoons of the Kentucky Bourbon Sauce, and top with a mint sprig.

KENTUCKY BOURBON SAUCE

◆

Makes 2 cups

1 ½ cups heavy cream
1 cup half-and-half
2 teaspoons pure vanilla extract

¼ cup sugar
1 tablespoon cornstarch
3 tablespoons bourbon

1. Heat the cream, half-and-half, vanilla, and sugar in a saucepan over high heat, whisking, for 3 minutes. Dissolve the cornstarch in the bourbon.

2. When bubbles form around the edges of the cream, whisk in the bourbon mixture. As the cream boils up, remove the pot from the heat and continue whisking vigorously until thoroughly blended and slightly thickened. Place over low heat and simmer for 1 minute. (This is not a thick cream sauce; it's meant to be fairly thin.) Serve immediately or store, refrigerated, in an airtight container for up to 24 hours. Reheat in a double boiler.

Lemon Pudding with Blackberry Coulis

◆

Makes 8 servings

New Orleanians are fans of lemon desserts; years ago a dessert called lemon icebox pie was all the rage. So as I was opening Emeril's, Mr. Lou and I poked around for something lemony and spongy-light. The following is the delicious result.

1 teaspoon unsalted butter, at room temperature
½ cup all-purpose flour
1¾ cups sugar, in all
4 tablespoons (½ stick) unsalted butter, melted (¼ cup)
¾ cup freshly squeezed lemon juice
1 tablespoon freshly grated lemon zest

3 large eggs, separated
2¼ cups buttermilk
1 cup Blackberry Coulis (page 326)
1 cup heavy cream, whipped with ½ teaspoon vanilla and 2 teaspoons sugar
Confectioners' sugar

1. Preheat the oven to 350°F. Lightly butter a 9- × 5-inch loaf pan.

2. In a large bowl combine the flour and 1½ cups of the sugar, and mix well. Add the melted butter, lemon juice, lemon zest, and the 3 beaten egg yolks. Stir in the buttermilk.

3. Beat the 3 egg whites with the remaining ¼ cup sugar until stiff, and gently fold into the first mixture. Pour into the loaf pan, place the pan in a water bath (a larger baking dish with about an inch of hot water), and bake until brown on top and puffed above the rim of the loaf pan, for about 1 hour.

4. About 10 minutes before the pudding is finished baking, prepare the Blackberry Coulis.

5. Serve warm or at room temperature. To serve, spoon the pudding onto plates, add 2 tablespoons Blackberry Coulis around the pudding, and top with whipped cream and confectioners' sugar.

J.K.'s Chocolate Chocolate Soufflés with Chocolate Grand Marnier Sauce

◆

Makes 4 individual soufflés

The favorite dessert at Commander's was a bread pudding soufflé, but occasionally I slipped in a favorite of my own—chocolate soufflé. John Kushner, who was a regular customer, fell in love with this indulgent creation and always called me out of the kitchen to put in a special request for it. When Emeril's opened, John started showing up three or four times a week, needing a chocolate soufflé fix at least once a week. I felt compelled to name this dessert after John, so J.K.'s Chocolate Chocolate Soufflé it became.

2 teaspoons unsalted butter, softened
½ cup sugar, in all
8 ounces semisweet chocolate, finely chopped
4 large egg whites

3 large egg yolks
¼ cup Grand Marnier
¾ cup Chocolate Grand Marnier Sauce (recipe follows)
Confectioners' sugar

1. Preheat the oven to 400°F. Using the butter, grease 4 individual ramekins and sprinkle them with about 1 teaspoon sugar per ramekin.

2. In a large metal bowl set over a pot of simmering water, melt the chocolate, stirring it with a whisk from time to time. Remove the bowl of melted chocolate from the heat.

3. In another bowl beat the egg whites with ¼ cup of the sugar until stiff and glossy.

4. Whisk the egg yolks into the chocolate one at a time, add the Grand Marnier, and whisk in the remaining 2 tablespoons sugar. Fold in the egg whites and whisk until thoroughly blended.

5. Pour the chocolate mixture into the prepared ramekins, place on a baking sheet, and bake until they're puffed and somewhat firm, for about 20 to 25 minutes. Remove from the oven.

6. While the soufflés are baking, prepare the Chocolate Grand Marnier Sauce, and cover to keep warm.

7. To serve, place a ramekin on each of 4 plates and sift powdered sugar over the top of each soufflé. Break the tops of the soufflés and spoon in the warm Chocolate Grand Marnier Sauce, allowing it to drip over the sides.

CHOCOLATE GRAND MARNIER SAUCE

◆

Makes about ¾ cup

¼ cup heavy cream
1 ½ teaspoons Grand Marnier
¾ teaspoon sugar

¾ ounce semisweet chocolate, finely
chopped

Heat the cream in a small saucepan over high heat. Add the Grand Marnier and sugar. Start whisking in the chocolate and bring to a boil, whisking constantly. Remove from the heat. Serve immediately or store, refrigerated, in an airtight container for 24 hours. Reheat in a double boiler.

Frozen Chestnut Soufflés with Brandied Berry Sauce

◆

Makes 5 servings

Chestnuts always make me think of late-autumn afternoons in New York City—vendors hunched over their stoves selling brown paper bags of chestnuts to shoppers, the pungent, smoky aroma filling the air. As we're reminded every Christmas, they're terrific roasting on an open fire, but chestnuts' special texture and nutty-sweet flavor also make them fantastic in frozen soufflés. These soufflés are nothing short of spectacular, so serve them to guests you want to wow.

2 teaspoons unsalted butter, softened
¼ cup sugar, in all
2 large egg whites
10 cooked, peeled, and chopped chestnuts (see Note)
1 cup heavy cream
1 teaspoon grated orange zest
½ teaspoon pure vanilla extract

1 tablespoon plus 1 teaspoon Grand Marnier
1 teaspoon ground cinnamon
¼ teaspoon ground nutmeg
1⅓ cups Brandied Berry Sauce (recipe follows)
Confectioners' sugar

1. Grease five ½-cup ramekins with the butter, and sprinkle them with about 1 teaspoon of sugar per ramekin.

2. In a bowl beat the egg whites with an electric mixer until stiff.

3. In another bowl combine the chestnuts, cream, orange zest, vanilla, Grand Marnier, cinnamon, nutmeg, and the remaining 2 tablespoons sugar, and beat with an electric mixer until thick and firm, but not hard. The trick is not to overbeat. Fold in the egg whites.

4. Spoon the mixture into the 5 prepared ramekins and freeze for at least 2 hours.

5. A few minutes before removing the soufflés from the freezer, prepare the Brandied Berry Sauce. Remove the soufflés from the freezer and allow them to sit for about 10 minutes, while the sauce is resting.

6. To serve, place the ramekins on serving plates and cut a "cap" out of the center of each soufflé with a spoon. Spoon some of the Brandied Berry Sauce over the top and into the soufflé, allowing it to drip down the sides. Replace the cap of soufflé on the top. Sift confectioners' sugar over each soufflé.

BRANDIED BERRY SAUCE

◆

Makes 1⅓ cups

1 cup fresh blackberries or
   raspberries
2 tablespoons sugar

⅓ cup Grand Marnier
½ cup heavy cream

1. In a saucepan over high heat, combine all of the ingredients except the cream, and bring to a boil. If you tilt the pot the mixture may flame, so be careful not to burn yourself.

2. Add the heavy cream, and while mashing the berries with a potato masher, cook over high heat, stirring, for about 3 minutes. Remove from the heat, strain, and let the sauce rest for about 10 minutes before serving. Serve immediately.

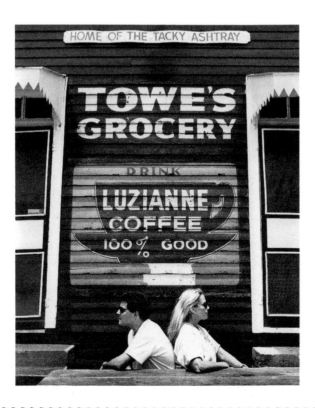

Jilly's Chocolate Chunk Cookies

◆

Makes a double baker's dozen (26 large cookies)

My youngest daughter, Jilly, who is 11 going on 30, is a big fan of chocolate chip cookies. She and I have made batches and batches of them both at home and at the restaurant, in pursuit of pure perfection. Here it is. Mrs. Fields, watch out!

½ pound (2 sticks) unsalted butter, softened
¾ cup granulated sugar
¾ cup brown sugar
1 teaspoon pure vanilla extract
1 large egg
2¼ cups all-purpose flour
1 teaspoon baking powder

½ teaspoon baking soda
½ teaspoon salt
1 cup chopped nuts (mix 2 of your favorites, half-and-half: pecans, walnuts, almonds, macadamias)
8 ounces semisweet chocolate, chopped

1. Preheat the oven to 350°F.

2. In a large bowl cream together the butter, granulated and brown sugars, vanilla, and the egg. Mix the flour, baking powder, baking soda, and salt together and add to the other ingredients, and mix just until the dough is stiff.

3. Stir in the nuts and chocolate, form the cookies with 2 soup spoons, and place them 2 inches apart on ungreased cookie sheets. Bake until light brown, for about 20 to 25 minutes, and remove from the oven.

Jessica Lagasse's Black-and-White Brownies

◆

Makes about 16 brownies

I love brownies, and so does my daughter, Jessica. She's a teenager now, but when she was little she'd come into the kitchen and help me bake them. Then we'd eat them all, so we'd have to bake another batch for whomever we were baking them for in the first place. This white and dark chocolate variation is Jessica's favorite.

10 tablespoons (1 stick) unsalted
    butter, in all
8 ounces white chocolate pieces
2 large eggs, lightly beaten
½ cup sugar
1 cup all-purpose flour

½ teaspoon pure vanilla extract
½ teaspoon salt
½ cup pecan pieces
6 ounces semisweet chocolate,
    chopped

1. Preheat the oven to 350°F. Using 2 tablespoons of the butter, grease an 8-inch-square baking pan.

2. In a metal bowl set over a pot of simmering water, melt the remaining ½ cup butter with the white chocolate.

3. In a medium bowl whisk together the eggs and sugar. Add the flour, vanilla, and salt and mix well. Fold in the pecans and the melted white chocolate.

4. Spread the brownie mixture in the buttered pan and sprinkle the chopped semisweet chocolate over the top. Bake until firm, for about 25 minutes. Remove from the oven and allow to cool on a rack before cutting into squares.

Feel-Good Rice Pudding

◆

Makes 6 servings

Many of the best restaurants in New England have rice pudding on their menus, but in New Orleans you will find it in very few restaurants. This is especially surprising when you realize how much rice is grown in Louisiana. None of the better restaurants seem to care. Except one.

4 large eggs
1 cup heavy cream
½ cup milk
1 teaspoon cornstarch
1 teaspoon ground cinnamon
½ teaspoon ground nutmeg
½ cup sugar

2 teaspoons pure vanilla extract
2 cups cooked long-grain rice
½ cup raisins
1 cup heavy cream whipped with ½ teaspoon vanilla and 1 teaspoon sugar

1. Preheat the oven to 350°F.

2. In a bowl beat the eggs until frothy. Whisk in the cream, milk, cornstarch, cinnamon, and nutmeg, and beat until thoroughly blended. Whisk in the sugar and vanilla.

3. Combine the rice with the raisins and add them to the custard mixture. Blend thoroughly and pour into a 5-cup casserole. Bake until the pudding is set, for about 40 minutes. Don't overbake or the pudding will be dry.

4. Serve warm or at room temperature. To serve, spoon the pudding into stem goblets and top with sweetened whipped cream.

Banana Loaf

◆

Makes 1 loaf

This sounds plain, but it's loaded with flavor and is versatile, too. Slice it to serve with ice cream, use it to make an English trifle, or save it for breakfast or brunch.

12 tablespoons (1½ sticks) unsalted
    butter, melted (¾ cup), in all
2 cups plus 1 tablespoon all-purpose
    flour, in all
2 ripe bananas, mashed
1 cup sugar

2 large eggs
2 teaspoons baking soda
3 tablespoons buttermilk
    (see The Last Word)
1 cup roasted pecan pieces
    (page 14)

1. Preheat the oven to 350°F. Grease a standard loaf pan (8 × 4 × 3 inches deep) with 1 tablespoon of the butter. Dust the pan with 1 tablespoon of the flour and tap out the excess.

2. In a bowl combine the bananas with the sugar and eggs until well blended. Stir in the remaining 2 cups flour, baking soda, buttermilk, and the remaining 11 table-spoons butter. Fold in the pecans and mix well.

3. Pour the batter into the loaf pan and bake for about 55 minutes. Remove from the oven and allow to cool for 2 hours.

4. To serve, slice and serve plain or with ice cream.

THE LAST WORD

If you don't regularly use buttermilk, don't buy a whole quart just for 3 tablespoons. Instead, combine 3 tablespoons whole milk with ½ teaspoon vinegar and leave the mixture at room temperature for 1 hour.

White Chocolate Banana Sesame Loaf

◆

Makes 1 loaf cake

More bananas for New Orleans. It seems we can't get enough. This cake was a Mr. Lou inspiration. It's unique and light and wonderful for breakfast or brunch.

5 tablespoons unsalted butter, melted, in all
2 tablespoons fine white bread crumbs (page 17)
¾ cup sugar
2 teaspoons brandy
1 teaspoon pure vanilla extract
2 ripe bananas, mashed
¾ cup all-purpose flour

1 teaspoon baking soda
1 large egg
3 ounces (1½ cups) shredded coconut
3 ounces white chocolate, chopped
½ cup chopped pecans
2 tablespoons sesame seeds
Confectioners' sugar

1. Preheat the oven to 350°F. Grease a standard loaf pan (4 × 4 × 3 inches deep) with 1 tablespoon of the melted butter. Sprinkle the bottom and sides of the pan with the bread crumbs and tap out any excess.

3. In a large bowl combine the sugar, brandy, vanilla, bananas, and the remaining 4 tablespoons melted butter, and mix well. Add the flour, baking soda, egg, coconut, and white chocolate, and stir until all of the ingredients are thoroughly incorporated.

4. Pour the batter into the loaf pan. Spread the pecans on top and press down gently into the batter with a spatula. Sprinkle the top with the sesame seeds and bake for 1 hour. Remove from the oven and allow to cool on a rack before unmolding.

5. To serve, unmold the cake, sprinkle with confectioners' sugar, slice, and serve. Serve immediately or store, refrigerated, wrapped in plastic wrap, for 2 days.

Cinnamon Rum Raisin Ice Cream
with Fried Plantains and Spun Sugar

Makes about 1 gallon

Many people don't make ice cream at home because purchasing and learning to use an ice cream maker seems too daunting—not worth the trouble. But this new ice cream, made without benefit of cranking, without pounds of salt, is creamy and delicious. If you really believe the ice cream you buy in the store is just as good as any you might make at home, try this and see how quickly you can change your mind.

1 cup raisins
1 cup white rum
4 cups heavy cream
1½ cups milk
1¼ cups sugar
1 teaspoon ground cinnamon
¼ teaspoon ground nutmeg

1 vanilla bean, split and scraped
　(page 14), pod reserved
10 egg yolks (see Note)
1 large bowl ice water
Fried Plantains (recipe follows)
Spun Sugar (recipe follows)

1. Place two ½-gallon bowls or containers in the freezer.

2. In a large pot macerate the raisins in the rum for 5 minutes. Place the pot over high heat, bring the rum to a boil, and cook out the alcohol, for about 4 minutes. Add the cream, milk, sugar, cinnamon, nutmeg, and the vanilla bean paste and pod to the pot. Reduce the heat to medium and bring just to the *start* of a boil (bubbles forming around the edges), whisking. Turn off the heat. Discard the vanilla pod, or rinse it off and bury in sugar.

3. In a large bowl whisk the egg yolks. Temper the yolks by adding 1 tablespoon, then another of the hot mixture to the yolks to prevent them from scrambling. Whisk a bit more of the hot mixture into the bowl, and continue slowly until all of the hot cream mixture has been incorporated into the egg yolks. Place this bowl over the bowl of ice water, and continue to whisk gently until the mixture is thick, creamy, and thoroughly blended.

4. Remove the containers from the freezer and fill them with the ice cream mixture, distributing the raisins evenly; stir well. Place the containers in the freezer, and stir the ice cream every half hour or so for 3 hours. Cover and freeze until solid, for about 4 hours.

5. Just before serving, prepare the Fried Plantains and the Spun Sugar.

6. To serve 4, scoop some ice cream into 4 shallow bowls, arrange 3 or 4 slices of Fried Plantains around the ice cream, and pull the Spun Sugar over the top. Keeps about 1 month.

Note: Keep the egg yolks covered to prevent a skin from forming on them.

FRIED PLANTAINS

◆

Makes 4 servings to top ice cream

2 ripe plantains	**1 tablespoon sugar**
6 cups vegetable oil	**1 teaspoon cinnamon**

1. Peel the plantains and slice them diagonally into ½-inch slices.

2. Heat the oil in a large pot until very hot (about 375°F). Fry the plantains in 2 batches until brown and crisp, for about 3 to 4 minutes. Drain them on paper towels.

3. In a small bowl combine the sugar with the cinnamon, and blend thoroughly. Roll the fried plantain slices in the mixture and serve immediately with ice cream.

SPUN SUGAR

◆

Makes enough for 4 servings of ice cream

This is fun and easy to make, and turns a dish of ice cream into a magical gossamer web. Serve it and watch everyone's eyes widen.

½ cup sugar   1 shallow bowl ice water
2 tablespoons water

1. In a small saucepan over medium-high heat, combine the sugar with the 2 tablespoons water. Bring to a boil and cook, stirring occasionally, until the mixture is syrupy and brown and has reached a temperature of 290°F on a candy thermometer, for about 3 minutes. (Watch this closely and remove from the heat before it scorches.)

2. Quickly dip the pot into the ice water to bring down the temperature of the caramel. Remove from the ice water and immediately dip a whisk into the mixture and pull threads of the caramel over ice cream. You must work quickly, or the mixture will harden in the saucepan. If it does, reheat it over medium heat, taking care not to let it scorch, and repeat the process. The candy will harden when it hits the ice cream.

THE LAST WORD

For an easy cleanup, add some water to the pot, place over medium-high heat, and bring to a boil. Stick a whisk in the pot and twirl it. The hardened caramel should come out in 1 piece. To clean the plates, run cold water over them—the pieces of candy will crack off.

PICTURE PEOPLE

INDEX